LLEWELLYN'S 2019

DAILY PLANETARY GUIDE

Copyright 2018 Llewellyn Worldwide Ltd. All rights reserved.
Typography property of Llewellyn Worldwide Ltd.
Llewellyn is a registered trademark of Llewellyn Worldwide Ltd.

ISBN: 978-0-7387-4607-4. Astrological calculations compiled and programmed
by Rique Pottenger based on the earlier work of Neil F. Michelsen.

Astrological proofreading by Phoebe Aina Allen
Cover design by Shira Atakpu
Editing by Andrea Neff

Llewellyn Publications
A Division of Llewellyn Worldwide Ltd.
2143 Wooddale Drive
Woodbury, MN 55125-2989
www.llewellyn.com

Printed in China

2018

SEPTEMBER	OCTOBER	NOVEMBER	DECEMBER

SEPTEMBER

S	M	T	W	T	F	S
						1
2	3	4	5	6	7	8
9	10	11	12	13	14	15
16	17	18	19	20	21	22
23	24	25	26	27	28	29
30						

OCTOBER

S	M	T	W	T	F	S
	1	2	3	4	5	6
7	8	9	10	11	12	13
14	15	16	17	18	19	20
21	22	23	24	25	26	27
28	29	30	31			

NOVEMBER

S	M	T	W	T	F	S
				1	2	3
4	5	6	7	8	9	10
11	12	13	14	15	16	17
18	19	20	21	22	23	24
25	26	27	28	29	30	

DECEMBER

S	M	T	W	T	F	S
						1
2	3	4	5	6	7	8
9	10	11	12	13	14	15
16	17	18	19	20	21	22
23	24	25	26	27	28	29
30	31					

2019

JANUARY

S	M	T	W	T	F	S
		1	2	3	4	5
6	7	8	9	10	11	12
13	14	15	16	17	18	19
20	21	22	23	24	25	26
27	28	29	30	31		

FEBRUARY

S	M	T	W	T	F	S
					1	2
3	4	5	6	7	8	9
10	11	12	13	14	15	16
17	18	19	20	21	22	23
24	25	26	27	28		

MARCH

S	M	T	W	T	F	S
					1	2
3	4	5	6	7	8	9
10	11	12	13	14	15	16
17	18	19	20	21	22	23
24	25	26	27	28	29	30
31						

APRIL

S	M	T	W	T	F	S
	1	2	3	4	5	6
7	8	9	10	11	12	13
14	15	16	17	18	19	20
21	22	23	24	25	26	27
28	29	30				

MAY

S	M	T	W	T	F	S
			1	2	3	4
5	6	7	8	9	10	11
12	13	14	15	16	17	18
19	20	21	22	23	24	25
26	27	28	29	30	31	

JUNE

S	M	T	W	T	F	S
						1
2	3	4	5	6	7	8
9	10	11	12	13	14	15
16	17	18	19	20	21	22
23	24	25	26	27	28	29
30						

JULY

S	M	T	W	T	F	S
	1	2	3	4	5	6
7	8	9	10	11	12	13
14	15	16	17	18	19	20
21	22	23	24	25	26	27
28	29	30	31			

AUGUST

S	M	T	W	T	F	S
				1	2	3
4	5	6	7	8	9	10
11	12	13	14	15	16	17
18	19	20	21	22	23	24
25	26	27	28	29	30	31

SEPTEMBER

S	M	T	W	T	F	S
1	2	3	4	5	6	7
8	9	10	11	12	13	14
15	16	17	18	19	20	21
22	23	24	25	26	27	28
29	30					

OCTOBER

S	M	T	W	T	F	S
		1	2	3	4	5
6	7	8	9	10	11	12
13	14	15	16	17	18	19
20	21	22	23	24	25	26
27	28	29	30	31		

NOVEMBER

S	M	T	W	T	F	S
					1	2
3	4	5	6	7	8	9
10	11	12	13	14	15	16
17	18	19	20	21	22	23
24	25	26	27	28	29	30

DECEMBER

S	M	T	W	T	F	S
1	2	3	4	5	6	7
8	9	10	11	12	13	14
15	16	17	18	19	20	21
22	23	24	25	26	27	28
29	30	31				

2020

JANUARY

S	M	T	W	T	F	S
			1	2	3	4
5	6	7	8	9	10	11
12	13	14	15	16	17	18
19	20	21	22	23	24	25
26	27	28	29	30	31	

FEBRUARY

S	M	T	W	T	F	S
						1
2	3	4	5	6	7	8
9	10	11	12	13	14	15
16	17	18	19	20	21	22
23	24	25	26	27	28	29

MARCH

S	M	T	W	T	F	S
1	2	3	4	5	6	7
8	9	10	11	12	13	14
15	16	17	18	19	20	21
22	23	24	25	26	27	28
29	30	31				

APRIL

S	M	T	W	T	F	S
			1	2	3	4
5	6	7	8	9	10	11
12	13	14	15	16	17	18
19	20	21	22	23	24	25
26	27	28	29	30		

MAY

S	M	T	W	T	F	S
					1	2
3	4	5	6	7	8	9
10	11	12	13	14	15	16
17	18	19	20	21	22	23
24	25	26	27	28	29	30
31						

JUNE

S	M	T	W	T	F	S
	1	2	3	4	5	6
7	8	9	10	11	12	13
14	15	16	17	18	19	20
21	22	23	24	25	26	27
28	29	30				

JULY

S	M	T	W	T	F	S
			1	2	3	4
5	6	7	8	9	10	11
12	13	14	15	16	17	18
19	20	21	22	23	24	25
26	27	28	29	30	31	

AUGUST

S	M	T	W	T	F	S
						1
2	3	4	5	6	7	8
9	10	11	12	13	14	15
16	17	18	19	20	21	22
23	24	25	26	27	28	29
30	31					

Contents

Introduction to Astrology

by Kim Rogers-Gallagher

Your horoscope is calculated using the date and time you were born from the perspective of your birth location. From this information, a clock-like diagram emerges that shows where every planet was located at the moment you made your debut. Each chart is composed of the same elements, rearranged, so everyone has one of everything, but none are exactly alike. I think of planets, signs, houses, and aspects as the four astrological building blocks. Each block represents a different level of human existence.

The eight planets along with the Sun and Moon are actual physical bodies. They represent urges or needs we all have. Chiron also falls into this category. The twelve signs of the zodiac are sections of the sky, and each is 30 degrees. The signs describe the behavior a planet or house will use to express itself. The twelve houses in a chart tell us where our planets come to life. Each house represents different life concerns—values, communication, creativity, and so on—that we must live through as life and time progress.

Basically, aspects are angles. Some of the planets will be positioned an exact number of degrees apart, forming angles to one another. For example, 180 degrees is a circle divided by two and is called an opposition. A square is 90 degrees and divides the circle by four. A trine is 120 degrees and divides the circle by three, and so forth. Aspects show which planets will engage in constant dialogue with one another. The particular aspect that joins them describes the nature of their "conversation." Not all planets will aspect all other planets in the houses.

Planets: The First Building Block

Each planet acts like the director of a department in a corporation, and the corporation is, of course, you. For example, Mercury directs your Communications Department and Jupiter oversees your Abundance and Growth Department. When you have the need to communicate, you call on your Mercury; when it's time to take a risk or grow, you use your Jupiter. Let's meet each of the planets individually and take a look at which job duties fall under each planet's jurisdiction.

The Sun

Every corporation needs an executive director who makes the final decisions. The Sun is your Executive Director. The Sun in your chart is your core, your true self. Although each of the planets in your chart is important in its own right, they all "take their orders," figuratively speaking, from the Sun.

Everyone's Sun has the same inner goal: to shine. The house your Sun is in shows where you really want to do good, where you want to be appreciated and loved. Your Sun is your inner supply of pride and confidence, your identity. The Sun is you at your creative best, enjoying life to the fullest.

The Sun shows the focus of the moment, where the world's attention will be directed on that particular day. In fact, in horary and electional astrology, the two branches that pertain most to timing and prediction, the Sun represents the day, the Moon the hour, and the Midheaven the moment. In the physical body, the Sun rules the heart, upper back, and circulatory system.

The Moon

Speaking of the Moon, a good place to meet her and begin to understand her qualities is by the water on a clear night when she's full. Whether you're looking up at her or at that silvery patch she creates that shivers and dances on the water, take a deep breath and allow yourself to be still. She represents the soft interior of each of us that recalls memories, fears, and dreams.

She's a lovely lady who oversees the Department of Feelings; she's the bringer of "moods" (a great Moon word). Her house and placement in your chart reveal how your intuition works, what your emotional needs are, and how you want your needs met. She is the ultimate feminine energy, the part of you that points both to how you were nurtured and to how you will nurture others. In the body, the Moon has jurisdiction over the breasts, ovaries, and womb. She also rules our body fluids, the internal ocean that keeps us alive.

Mercury

☿ Back when gods and goddesses were thought to be in charge of the affairs of humanity, Mercury shuttled messages between the gods and mortals. In today's world, Mercury is the computer, the telephone, and the internet. He's the internal computer that constantly feeds you data about the world. His position and house in your chart show how you think and reason, and how you express yourself to others. You'll recognize him in your speech patterns, in your handwriting, and in the way you walk, because moving through your environment means communicating with it. He operates through your five senses and your brain, and makes you conscious of opposites—light and dark, hot and cold, up and down. He's what you use when you have a conversation, exchange a glance, gesture, or interpret a symbol. Mercury represents the side of you living totally in the present.

If you've ever tried to collect mercury after it escaped from a broken thermometer, you've learned something about Mercury. Just as your Mercury never stops collecting data, those tiny beads you tried so hard to collect brought back a bit of everything they contacted—dog hair, crumbs, and grains of dirt. In the body, Mercury also acts as a messenger. He transmits messages through his function as the central nervous system that lets your eyes and hands collaborate, your eyes blink, and breathing continue.

Venus

♀ Venus spends her energy supplying you with your favorite people, places, and things. If you want chocolate, music, flannel sheets, or the coworker you've got a mad crush on, it's your Venus that tells you how to get it. Venus enjoys beauty and comfort. She shows how to attract what you love, especially people. When you're being charming, whether by using your manners or by adorning yourself, she's in charge of all behavior that is pleasing to others—social chitchat, smiles, hugs, and kisses. Whenever you're pleased, satisfied, or content enough to purr, it's your Venus who made you feel that way. Since money is one of the ways we draw the objects we love to us, she's also in charge of finances. Venus relates to your senses—sight, smell, taste, touch, and sound—the body's receptors.

After all, it's the senses that tell us what feels good and what doesn't. Venus responds to your desire for beautiful surroundings, comfortable clothing, and fine art.

Mars

♂ Mars is in charge of your Self-Defense and Action Department. He's the warrior who fights back when you're attacked—your own personal SWAT team. Your Mars energy makes you brave, courageous, and daring. His placement in your chart describes how you act on your own behalf. He's concerned only with you, and he doesn't consider the size, strength, or abilities of whomever or whatever you're up against. He's the side of you that initiates all activity. He's also in charge of how you assert yourself and how you express anger.

"Hot under the collar," "seeing red," and "all fired up" are Mars phrases. Mars is what you use to be passionate, adventurous, and bold. But he can be violent, accident-prone, and cruel, too. Wherever he is in your chart, you find constant action. Mars pursues. He shows how you "do" things. He charges through situations. This "headstrong" planet corresponds to the head, the blood, and the muscles.

Jupiter

♃ Jupiter is called "the Greater Benefic," and he heads the Department of Abundance and Growth. He's the side of you that's positive, optimistic, and generous. He's where you keep your supply of laughter, enthusiasm, and high spirits. It's Jupiter's expansive, high-spirited energy that motivates you to travel, take classes, and meet new people. Wherever he is in your chart is a place where you'll have an extensive network of friends and associates—folks you can visit, count on, and learn from. Jupiter is the side of you that will probably cause you to experience the "grass is greener" syndrome. Your Jupiter is also what you're using when you find yourself being excessive and wasteful, overdoing, or blowing something out of proportion. Words like "too" and "always" are the property of Jupiter, as are "more" and "better." In general, this planet just loves to make things bigger. In the body, Jupiter corresponds with the liver, the organ that filters what you take in and rids your body of excess. Jupiter also handles physical growth.

Saturn

ħ Saturn represents withholding and resistance to change. He heads the Boundaries and Rules Department. Locate Saturn in your chart to find out where you'll build walls to keep change out, where you may segregate yourself at times, where you'll be most likely to say no. Your Saturn is the authority inside you, the spot where you may inhibit or stall yourself throughout life—most often because you fear failure and would rather not act at all than act inappropriately. This planet teaches you to respect your elders, follow the rules, and do things right the first time. Wherever Saturn is in your chart is a place where you'll feel respectful, serious, and conservative. Your Saturn placement is where you'll know that you should never embellish the facts and never act until you're absolutely sure you're ready. Here is where you won't expect something for nothing. Saturn is also where you're at your most disciplined, where you'll teach yourself the virtues of patience, endurance, and responsibility. Because this planet is so fond of boundaries, it's also the planet in charge of organization, structures, and guidelines. In the physical body, Saturn correlates with the bones and the skin, those structures that hold your body together.

Uranus

♅ There's a spot in everyone's chart where independence is the order of the day, where rules are made specifically to be broken, and where personal freedom is the only way to go, regardless of the consequences. Here's where you'll surprise even yourself at the things you say and do. Meet Uranus, head of the Department of One Never Knows, the place in your chart where shocks, surprises, and sudden reversals are regular fare.

Your Uranus energy is what wakes you up to how confined you feel, breaks you out of the rut you're in, and sets you free. He's a computer wizard and involved in mass communications. Where he's strong in your chart, you will be strong, too. Here is where you'll have genius potential, where you'll be bold enough to ignore the old way to solve a problem and instead find a whole new way. Major scientific and technological breakthroughs like the space program and the internet were inspired by Uranus. In the body, Uranus rules the lower part of the legs, including the calves and ankles, and he co-rules with Mercury the central nervous system.

Neptune

♆ Next time you hear yourself sigh or feel yourself slip into a daydream, think of Neptune. This is the planet in charge of romance, nostalgia, and magic. Although her official title is head of the Department of Avoidance and Fantasy, she's also one of the most creative energies you own. Wherever she is in your chart is where you're psychic. It's also where you're capable of amazing compassion and sensitivity for beings and creatures less fortunate than yourself. It's where you'll be drawn into charity or volunteer work because you realize that we're all part of a bigger plan, that there are no boundaries between you and what's out there.

This combination of sensitivity and harsh reality doesn't always mix well. This may also be a place where you'll try to escape. Sleep, meditation, and prayer are the highest uses of her energies, but alcohol and drugs are also under her jurisdiction. Neptune's place in your chart is where you're equally capable of fooling all of the people all of the time, and of being fooled yourself. In the body, Neptune and the Moon co-rule fluids. Neptune also has a connection with poisons and viruses that invisibly infiltrate our bodies and with the body's immune system, which is how we keep our barriers intact.

Pluto

♇ Pluto is head of the Department of Death, Destruction, and Decay. He's in charge of things that have to happen, and he disposes of situations that have gone past the point of no return, where the only solution is to "let go." He also oversees sex, reincarnation, recycling, regeneration, and rejuvenation. Pluto's spot in your chart is a place where intense, inevitable circumstances will arrive to teach you about agony and ecstasy. Pluto's place in your chart is where you'll be in a state of turmoil or evolution, where there will be ongoing change. This is the side of you that realizes that, like it or not, life goes on after tremendous loss. It is the side of you that will reflect on your losses down the road and try to make sense of them. Most importantly, since Pluto rules life, death, and rebirth, here's where you'll understand the importance of process. You'll be amazingly strong where your Pluto is—he's a well of concentrated, transforming energy. In the body, Pluto is associated with the reproductive organs since here is where the invisible process of life and death begins. He is also in charge of puberty and sexual maturity. He corresponds with plutonium.

Signs: The Second Building Block

Every sign is built of three things: an element, a quality, and a polarity. Understanding each of these primary building blocks gives a head start toward understanding the signs themselves, so let's take a look at them.

The Polarities: Masculine and Feminine

The words "masculine" and "feminine" are often misunderstood or confused in the context of astrology. In astrology, masculine means that an energy is assertive, aggressive, and linear. Feminine means that an energy is receptive, magnetic, and circular. These terms should not be confused with male and female.

The Qualities: Cardinal, Fixed, and Mutable

Qualities show the way a sign's energy flows. The cardinal signs are energies that initiate change. Cardinal signs operate in sudden bursts of energy. The fixed signs are thorough and unstoppable. They're the energies that endure. They take projects to completion, tend to block change at all costs, and will keep at something regardless of whether or not it should be terminated. The mutable signs are versatile, flexible, and changeable. They can be scattered, fickle, and inconstant.

The Elements: Fire, Earth, Air, and Water

The fire signs correspond with the spirit and the spiritual aspects of life. They inspire action, attract attention, and love spontaneity. The earth signs are solid, practical, supportive, and as reliable as the earth under our feet. The earth signs are our physical envoys and are concerned with our tangible needs, such as food, shelter, work, and responsibilities. Air signs are all about the intellectual or mental sides of life. Like air itself, they are light and elusive. They love conversation, communication, and mingling. The water signs correspond to the emotional side of our natures. As changeable, subtle, and able to infiltrate as water itself, water signs gauge the mood in a room when they enter, and operate on what they sense from their environment.

Aries: Masculine, Cardinal, Fire

♈ Aries is ruled by Mars and is cardinal fire—red-hot, impulsive, and ready to go. Aries planets are not known for their patience, and they ignore obstacles, choosing instead to focus on the shortest distance between where they are and where they want to be. Planets in Aries are brave, impetuous, and direct. Aries planets are often very good at initiating projects. They are not, however, as eager to finish, so they will leave projects undone. Aries planets need physical outlets for their considerable Mars-powered energy; otherwise their need for action can turn to stress. Exercise, hard work, and competition are food for Aries energy.

Taurus: Feminine, Fixed, Earth

♉ Taurus, the fixed earth sign, has endless patience that turns your Taurus planet into a solid force to be reckoned with. Taurus folks never, ever quit. Their reputation for stubbornness is earned. They're responsible, reliable, honest as they come, practical, and endowed with a stick-to-it attitude other planets envy. They're not afraid to work hard. Since Taurus is ruled by Venus, it's not surprising to find that these people are sensual and luxury-loving, too. They love to be spoiled with the best—good food, fine wine, or even a Renoir painting. They need peace and quiet like no other, and don't like their schedules to be disrupted. However, they may need a reminder that comfortable habits can become ruts.

Gemini: Masculine, Mutable, Air

♊ This sign is famous for its duality and love of new experiences, as well as for its role as communicator. Gemini is mutable air, which translates into changing your mind, so expect your Gemini planet to be entertaining and versatile. This sign knows a little bit about everything. Gemini planets usually display at least two distinct sides to

11

their personalities, are changeable and even fickle at times, and are wonderfully curious. This sign is ruled by Mercury, so if what you're doing involves talking, writing, gesturing, or working with hand-eye coordination, your Gemini planet will love it. Mercury also rules short trips, so any planet in Gemini is an expert at how to make its way around the neighborhood in record time.

Cancer: Feminine, Cardinal, Water

♋ Cancer is cardinal water, so it's good at beginning things. It's also the most privacy-oriented sign. Cancer types are emotionally vulnerable, sensitive, and easily hurt. They need safe "nests" to return to when the world gets to be too much. Cancer types say "I love you" by tending to your need for food, warmth, or a place to sleep. The problem is that they can become needy, dependent, or unable to function unless they feel someone or something needs them. Cancer rules the home and family. It's also in charge of emotions, so expect a Cancer to operate from his or her gut most of the time.

Leo: Masculine, Fixed, Fire

♌ Leo is fixed fire, and above all else represents pride and ego. Sun-ruled Leo wants to shine and be noticed. Natural performers, people in this sign are into drama and attract attention even when they don't necessarily want it. Occasionally your Leo friends may be touchy and high maintenance. Still, they are generous to a fault. Leo appreciates attention and praise with lavish compliments, lovely gifts, and creative outings designed to amaze and delight. Leo's specialties are having fun, entertaining, and making big entrances and exits.

Virgo: Feminine, Mutable, Earth

♍ Virgo may seem picky and critical, but that may be too simplistic. As a mutable earth sign, your Virgo planet delights in helping, and it's willing to adapt to any task. Having a keen eye for details may be another way to interpret a Virgo planet's automatic fault-finding ability. When Virgo's eye for detail combines with the ability to fix almost anything, you have a troubleshooter extraordinaire. This sign practices discrimination—analyzing, critiquing, and suggesting remedies to potential problems. This sign is also wonderful at making lists, agendas, and schedules. Keep your Virgo planet happy by keeping it busy.

Libra: Masculine, Cardinal, Air

♎ Libra adores balance, harmony, and equal give and take—no easy task. A more charming sign would be difficult to find, though. Libra's cardinal airy nature wants to begin things, and entertaining and socializing are high priorities. These expert people-pleasing Venus-ruled planets specialize in manners, courtesy, and small talk. Alone time may be shunned, and because they're gifted with the ability to pacify, they may sell out their own needs, or the truth, to buy peace and companionship. Seeing both sides of a situation, weighing the options, and keeping their inner balance by remaining honest may be Libra's hardest tasks.

Scorpio: Feminine, Fixed, Water

♏ Planets in this sign are detectives, excelling at the art of strategy. Your Scorpio planets sift through every situation for subtle clues, which they analyze to determine what's really going on. They're also gifted at sending subtle signals back to the environment, and at imperceptibly altering a situation by manipulating it with the right word or movement. Scorpio planets are constantly searching for intimacy. They seek intensity and may be crisis-oriented. They can be relentless, obsessive, and jealous. Remember, this is fixed water. Scorpios feel things deeply and forever. Give your Scorpio planets the opportunity to fire-walk, to experience life-and-death situations.

Sagittarius: Masculine, Mutable, Fire

♐ The enthusiasm of this mutable fire sign, ruled by Jupiter, spreads like a brushfire. These planets tend to never feel satisfied or content, and to always wonder if there's something even more wonderful over the next mountain. Your Sagittarius planets are bored by routine; they're freedom-oriented, generous, and optimistic to a fault. They can be excessive and overindulgent. They adore outdoor activities and foreign places and foreign people. They learn by first having the big picture explained. They're only too happy to preach, advertise, and philosophize. Sagittarius planets can be quite prophetic, and they absolutely believe in the power of laughter, embarrassing themselves at times to make someone laugh.

Capricorn: Feminine, Cardinal, Earth

♑ Your Capricorn planets, ruled by Saturn, have a tendency to build things, such as erecting structures and creating a career for you. Saturn will start up an organization and turn it into the family business. These planets automatically know how to run it no matter what it is. They're authority figures. They exercise caution and discipline, set down rules, and live by them. Capricorn is the sign with the driest wit. Here's where your sense of propriety and tradition will be strong, where doing things the old-fashioned way and paying respect to elders will be the only way to go. They want a return for the time they invest, and don't mind proving how valuable they are.

Aquarius: Masculine, Fixed, Air

♒ Aquarian planets present some unexpected contradictions because they are fixed air and unpredictable. This sign's ruler, Uranus, gets the credit for Aquarius's tumultuous ways. Aquarian energy facilitates invention and humanitarian conquests, to the amazement of the masses, and planets in this sign are into personal freedom like no other. They create their own rules, fight city hall whenever possible, and deliberately break tradition. They adore change. Abrupt reversals are their specialty, so others often perceive them as erratic, unstable, or unreliable. But when Aquarius energy activates, commitment to a cause or an intellectual ideal has a steadfastness like no other sign possesses.

Pisces: Feminine, Mutable, Water

♓ Mutable Pisces can't separate itself emotionally from whatever it's exposed to. While this is the source of Pisces' well-deserved reputation for compassion, it's also the source of a desire to escape reality. Planets in this sign feel everything—for better or worse—so they need time alone to unload and reassemble themselves. Exposure to others, especially in crowds, is exhausting to your Pisces planets. Here is where you may have a tendency to take in stray people and animals and where you'll need to watch for the possibility of being victimized or taken advantage of in some way. Pisces planets see the best in people or situations, and they can be disappointed when reality sets in. These planets are the romantics of the zodiac. Let them dream in healthy ways.

Houses: The Third Building Block

Houses are represented by twelve pie-shaped wedges in a horoscope chart. (See blank chart on page 206.) They're like rooms in a house, and each reflects the circumstances we create and encounter in a specific area of life. One room, the Sixth House, relates to our daily routine and work, while the Eleventh House relates to groups we may be affiliated with, for example. The sign (Aries, Taurus, etc.) on the cusp of each house tells us something about the nature of the room behind the door. Someone with Leo on the Sixth House cusp will create different routines and work habits than a person with Capricorn on that cusp. The sign influences the type of behavior you'll exhibit when those life circumstances turn up. Since the time of day you were born determines the sign on each of the houses, an accurate birth time will result in more accurate information from your chart.

The Twelve Houses

The First House

The First House shows the sign that was ascending over the horizon at the moment you were born. Let's think again of your chart as one big house and of the houses as "rooms." The First House symbolizes your front door. The sign on this house cusp (also known as the Rising Sign or Ascendant) describes the way you dress, move, and adorn yourself, and the overall condition of your body. It relates to the first impression you make on people.

The Second House

This house shows how you handle the possessions you hold dear. That goes for money, objects, and the qualities you value in yourself and in others. This house also holds the side of you that takes care of what you have and what you buy for yourself, and the amount of money you earn. The Second House shows what you're willing to do for money, too, so it's also a description of your self-esteem.

The Third House

This house corresponds to your neighborhood, including the bank, the post office, and the gym where you work out. This is the side of you that performs routine tasks without much conscious thought. The Third House also refers to childhood and grammar school, and it shows your relationships with siblings, your communication style, and your attitude toward short trips.

The Fourth House

This house is the symbolic foundation brought from your childhood home, your family, and the parent who nurtured you. Here is where you'll find the part of you that decorates and maintains your nest. It decides what home in the adult world will be like and how much privacy you'll need. The Fourth House deals with matters of real estate. Most importantly, this house contains the emotional warehouse of memories you operate from subconsciously.

The Fifth House

Here's the side of you that's reserved for play, that only comes out when work is done and it's time to party and be entertained. This is the charming, creative, delightful side of you, where your hobbies, interests, and playmates are found. If it gives you joy, it's described here. Your Fifth House shines when you are creative, and it allows you to see a bit of yourself in those creations—anything from your child's smile to a piece of art. Traditionally this house also refers to speculation and gambling.

The Sixth House

This house is where you keep the side of you that decides how you like things to go along over the course of a day, the side of you that plans a schedule. Since it describes the duties you perform on a daily basis, it also refers to the nature of your work, your work environment, and how you take care of your health. It's how you function. Pets are also traditionally a Sixth House issue, since we tend to them daily and incorporate them into our routine.

The Seventh House

Although it's traditionally known as the house of marriage, partnerships, and open enemies, the Seventh House really holds the side of you that only comes out when you're in the company of just one other person. This is the side of you that handles relating on a one-to-one basis. Whenever you use the word "my" to describe your relationship with another, it's this side of you talking.

The Eighth House

Here's the crisis expert side of you that emerges when it's time to handle extreme circumstances. This is the side of you that deals with agony and ecstasy, with sex, death, and all manner of mergers, financial and otherwise. The Eighth House also holds information on surgeries, psychotherapy, and the way we regenerate and rejuvenate after a loss.

The Ninth House

This house holds the side of you that handles new experiences, foreign places, long-distance travel, and legal matters. Higher education, publishing, advertising, and forming opinions are handled here, as are issues involving the big picture, such as politics, religion, and philosophy.

The Tenth House

This spot in your chart describes what the public knows about you. Your career, reputation, and social status are found here. This is the side of you that takes time to learn and become accomplished. It describes the behavior you'll exhibit when you're in charge, and also the way you'll act in the presence of an authority figure. Most importantly, the Tenth House describes your vocation or life's work—whatever you consider your "calling."

The Eleventh House

Here's the team player in you, the side of you that helps you find your peer groups. The Eleventh House shows the types of organizations you're drawn to join, the kind of folks you consider kindred spirits, and how you'll act in group situations. It also shows the causes and social activities you hold near and dear.

The Twelfth House

This is the side of you that only comes out when you're alone, or in the mood to retreat and regroup. Here's where the secret side of you lives, where secret affairs and dealings take place. Here, too, is where matters like hospital stays are handled. Most importantly, the Twelfth House is the room where you keep all the traits and behaviors that you were taught early on to stifle, avoid, or deny—especially in public. This side of you is very fond of fantasy, illusion, and pretend play.

Aspects and Transits:
The Fourth Building Block

Planets form angles to one another as they move through the heavens. If two planets are 90 degrees apart, they form a square. If they're 180 degrees apart, they're in opposition. Planets in aspect have twenty-four-hour communication going on. The particular angle that separates any two planets describes the nature of their conversation. Astrologers use six angles most often, each of which produces a different type of relationship or "conversation" between the planets they join. Let's go over the meaning of each of the aspects.

Ptolemic Aspects

The Conjunction (0–8 degrees)

When you hear that two things are operating "in conjunction," it means they're operating together. This holds true with planets as well. Two (or more) planets conjoined are a team, but some planets pair up more easily than others. Venus and the Moon work well together because both are feminine and receptive, but the Sun and Mars are both pretty feisty by nature, and may cause conflict. Planets in conjunction are usually sharing a house in your chart.

The Sextile (60 degrees)

The sextile links planets in compatible elements. That is, planets in sextile are either in fire and air signs or earth and water signs. Since these pairs of elements get along well, the sextile encourages an active exchange between the two planets involved, so these two parts of you will be eager to work together.

The Square (90 degrees)

☐ A square aspect puts planets at cross-purposes. Friction develops between them and one will constantly challenge the other. You can see squares operating in someone who's fidgety or constantly restless. Although they're uncomfortable and even aggravating at times, your squares point to places where tremendous growth is possible.

The Trine (120 degrees)

△ Trines are usually formed between planets of the same element, so they understand each other. They show an ease of communication not found in any of the other aspects, and they're traditionally thought of as "favorable." Of course, there is a downside to trines. Planets in this relationship are so comfortable that they can often get lazy and spoiled. (Sometimes they get so comfy they're boring.) Planets in trine show urges or needs that automatically support each other. The catch is that you've got to get them operating.

The Quincunx (150 degrees)

⚻ This aspect joins two signs that don't share a quality, element, or gender, which makes it difficult for them to communicate with each other. It's frustrating. For that reason, this aspect has always been considered to require an adjustment in the way the two planets are used. Planets in quincunx often feel pushed, forced, or obligated to perform. They seem to correspond to health issues.

The Opposition (180 degrees)

☍ When two planets are opposed, they work against each other. For example, you may want to do something, and if you have two opposing planets you may struggle with two very different approaches to getting the job done. If Mars and Neptune are opposing, you may struggle between getting a job done the quick, easy way or daydreaming about all the creative possibilities open to you. It's as if the two are standing across from one another with their arms folded, involved in a debate, neither willing to concede an inch. They can break out of their standoff only by first becoming aware of one another and then compromising. This aspect is the least difficult of the traditionally known "hard" aspects because planets "at odds" with one another can come to some sort of compromise.

Transits

While your horoscope (natal chart) reflects the exact position of planets at the time of your birth, the planets, as you know, move on. They are said to be "transiting." We interpret a transit as a planet in its "today" position making an aspect to a planet in your natal chart. Transiting planets represent incoming influences and events that your natal planets will be asked to handle. The nature of the transiting planet describes the types of situations that will arise, and the nature of your natal planet tells which "piece" of you you're working on at the moment. When a planet transits through a house or aspects a planet in your chart, you will have opportunities for personal growth and change. Every transit you experience adds knowledge to your personality.

Sun Transit

A Sun transit points to the places in your chart where you'll want special attention, pats on the back, and appreciation. Here's where you want to shine. These are often times of public acclaim, when we're recognized, congratulated, or applauded for what we've done. Of course, the ultimate Sun transit is our birthday, the day when we're all secretly sure that we should be treated like royalty.

Moon Transit

When the Moon touches one of the planets in our natal chart, we react from an emotional point of view. A Moon transit often corresponds to the highs and lows we feel that last only a day or two. Our instincts are on high during a Moon transit and we're more liable to sense what's going on around us than to consciously know something.

Mercury Transit

Transiting Mercury creates activity in whatever area of life it visits. The subject is communication of all kinds, so conversation, letters, and quick errands take up our time now. Because of Mercury's love of duality, events will often occur in twos—as if Hermes the trickster were having some fun with us—and we're put in the position of having to do at least two things at once.

Venus Transit

Transiting Venus brings times when the universe gives us a small token of warmth or affection or a well-deserved break. These are often sociable, friendly periods when we do more than our usual share of mingling and are more interested in good food and cushy conditions than anything resembling work. A Venus transit also shows a time when others will give us gifts. Since Venus rules money, this transit can show when we'll receive financial rewards.

Mars Transit

Mars transiting a house can indicate high-energy times. You're stronger and restless, or maybe you're cranky, angry, accident-prone, or violent. When Mars happens along, it's best to work or exercise hard to use up this considerable energy. Make yourself "too tired to be mad." These are ideal times to initiate projects that require a hard push of energy to begin.

Jupiter Transit

Under this transit you're in the mood to travel, take a class, or learn something new about the concerns of any house or planet Jupiter visits. You ponder the big questions. You grow under a Jupiter transit, sometimes even physically. Now is the time to take chances or risk a shot at the title. During a Jupiter transit you're luckier, bolder, and a lot more likely to succeed. This transit provides opportunities. Be sure to take advantage of them.

Saturn Transit

When Saturn comes along, we see things as they truly are. These are not traditionally great times, but they are often times when your greatest rewards appear. When Saturn transits a house or planet, he checks to see if the structure is steady and will hold up. You are then tested, and if you pass, you receive a symbolic certificate of some kind—and sometimes a real one, like a diploma. We will always be tested, but if we fail, life can feel very difficult. Firming up our lives is Saturn's mission. This is a great time to tap into Saturn's willpower and self-discipline to stop doing something. It is not traditionally a good time to begin new ventures, though.

Uranus Transit

The last thing in the world you'd ever expect to happen is exactly what you can expect under a Uranus transit. This is the planet of last-minute plan changes, reversals, and shock effects. So if you're feeling stuck in your present circumstances, when a Uranus transit happens along you won't be stuck for long. "Temporary people" often enter your life at these times, folks whose only purpose is to jolt you out of your present circumstances by appearing to provide exactly what you were sorely missing. That done, they disappear, leaving you with your life in a shambles. When these people arrive, enjoy them and allow them to break you out of your rut—just don't get comfortable.

Neptune Transit

A Neptune transit is a time when the universe asks only that you dream and nothing more. Your sensitivity heightens to the point that harsh sounds can actually make you wince. Compassion deepens, and psychic moments are common. A Neptune transit inspires divine discontent. You sigh, wish, feel nostalgic, and don't see things clearly at all. At the end of the transit, you realize that everything about you is different, that the reality you were living at the beginning of the transit has been gradually eroded or erased right from under your feet, while you stood right there upon it.

Pluto Transit

A Pluto transit is often associated with obsession, regeneration, and inevitable change. Whatever has gone past the point of no return, whatever is broken beyond repair, will pass from your life now. As with a Saturn transit, this time is not known to be wonderful, but when circumstances peel away everything from us and we're forced to see ourselves as we truly are, we do learn just how strong we are. Power struggles often accompany Pluto's visit, but being empowered is the end result of a positive Pluto transit. The secret is to let go, accept the losses or changes, and make plans for the future.

Retrograde Planets

Retrograde literally means "backward." Although none of the planets ever really throw their engines in reverse and move backward, all of them, except the Sun and Moon, appear to do so periodically from our perspective here on Earth. What's happening is that we're moving either faster or slower than the planet that's retrograde, and since we have to look over our shoulder to see it, we refer to it as retrograde.

Mercury Retrograde: A Communication Breakdown

The way retrograde planets seem to affect our affairs varies from planet to planet. In Mercury's case, it means often looking back at Mercury-ruled things—communications, contracts, and so on. Keep in mind that Mercury correlates with Hermes, the original trickster, and you'll understand how cleverly disguised some of these errors can be. Communications become confused or are delayed. Letters are lost or sent to Auckland instead of Oakland, or they end up under the car seat for three weeks. We sign a contract or agreement and find out later that we didn't have all the correct information and what we signed was misleading in some way. We try repeatedly to reach someone on the telephone but can never catch them, or our communications devices themselves break down or garble information in some way. We feel as if our timing is off, so short trips often become more difficult. We leave the directions at home or write them down incorrectly. We're late for appointments due to circumstances beyond our control, or we completely forget about them.

Is there a constructive use for this time period? Yes. Astrologer Erin Sullivan has noted that the ratio of time Mercury spends moving retrograde (backward) and direct (forward) corresponds beautifully with the amount of time we humans spend awake and asleep—about a third of our lives. So this period seems to be a time to take stock of what's happened over the past three months and assimilate our experiences.

A good rule of thumb with Mercury retrograde is to try to confine activities to those that have "re" attached to the beginning of a word: reschedule, repair, return, rewrite, redecorate, restore, replace, renovate, or renew, for example.

Retrogrades of the Other Planets

With Venus retrograde every eighteen months for six weeks, relation-ships and money matters are delayed or muddled.

With Mars retrograde for eleven weeks and then direct for twenty-two months, actions initiated are often rooted in confusion or end up at cross-purposes to our original intentions. Typically under a Mars retrograde, the aggressor or initiator of a battle is defeated.

Jupiter retrogrades for four months and is direct for nine months. Saturn retrogrades for about the same amount of time. Each of the outer planets—Uranus, Neptune, and Pluto—stays retrograde for about six or seven months of every year. In general, remember that actions ruled by a particular planet quite often need to be repeated or done over when that planet is retrograde. Just make sure that what-ever you're planning is something you don't mind doing twice.

Moon Void-of-Course

The Moon orbits Earth in about twenty-eight days, moving through each of the signs in about two days. As she passes through the thirty degrees of each sign, she visits with the planets in order by forming angles, or aspects, with them. Because she moves one degree in just two to two and a half hours, her influence on each planet lasts only a few hours. As she approaches the late degrees of the sign she's passing through, she eventually forms what will be her final aspect to another planet before leaving the sign. From this point until she actually enters the new sign, she is referred to as being "void-of-course" (v/c).

The Moon symbolizes the emotional tone of the day, carrying feelings of the sign she's "wearing" at the moment. She rules in-stincts. After she has contacted each of the planets, she symbolically "rests" before changing her costume, so her instincts are temporarily on hold. It's during this time that many people feel fuzzy, vague, or scattered. Plans or decisions do not pan out. Without the instinctual knowing the Moon provides as she touches each planet, we tend to be unrealistic or exercise poor judgment. The traditional definition of the void-of-course Moon is that "nothing will come of this," and it seems to be true. Actions initiated under a void-of-course Moon are often wasted, irrelevant, or incorrect—usually because information needed to make a sound decision is hidden or missing or has been overlooked.

Now, although it's not a good time to initiate plans when the Moon is void, routine tasks seem to go along just fine. However, this period is really ideal for what the Moon does best: reflection. It's at this time that we can assimilate what has occurred over the past few days. Use this time to meditate, ponder, and imagine. Let your conscious mind rest and allow yourself to feel.

On the lighter side, remember that there are other good uses for the void-of-course Moon. This is the time period when the universe seems to be most open to loopholes. It's a great time to make plans you don't want to fulfill or schedule things you don't want to do. In other words, like the saying goes, "To everything, there is a season." Even void-of-course Moons.

The Moon's Influence

As the Moon goes along her way, she magically appears and disappears, waxing to full from the barest sliver of a crescent just after she's new, then waning back to her invisible new phase again. The four quarters—the New Moon, the second quarter, the Full Moon, and the fourth quarter—correspond to the growth cycle of every living thing.

The Quarters

First Quarter

This phase begins when the Moon and the Sun are conjunct one another in the sky. At the beginning of the phase, the Moon is invisible, hidden by the brightness of the Sun as they travel together. The Moon is often said to be in her "dark phase" when she is just new. The New Moon can't actually be seen until 5½ to 12 hours after its birth. Toward the end of the first-quarter phase, as the Moon pulls farther away from the Sun and begins to wax toward the second quarter stage, a delicate silver crescent appears. This time corresponds to all new beginnings; this is the best time to begin a project.

Second Quarter

The second quarter begins when the Moon has moved 90 degrees away from the Sun. At this point the waxing Moon rises at about noon and sets at about midnight. It's at this time that she can be seen in the western sky during the early evening hours, growing in size from a crescent to her full beauty. This period corresponds to the development and growth of life, and with projects that are coming close to fruition.

Third Quarter

This phase begins with the Full Moon, when the Sun and Moon are opposite each other in the sky. It's now that the Moon can be seen rising in the east at sunset, a bit later each night as this phase progresses. This time corresponds to the culmination of plans and to maturity.

Fourth Quarter

This phase occurs when the Moon has moved 90 degrees past the full phase. She is decreasing in light, rises at midnight, and can be seen now in the eastern sky during the late evening hours. She doesn't reach the highest point in the sky until very early in the morning. This period corresponds to "disintegration"—a symbolic "drawing back" to reflect on what's been accomplished. It's now time to reorganize, clear the boards, and plan for the next New Moon stage.

The Moon Through the Signs

The signs indicate how we'll do things. Since the Moon rules the emotional tone of the day, it's good to know what type of mood she's in at any given moment. Here's a thumbnail sketch to help you navigate every day by cooperating with the Moon no matter what sign she's in.

Aries

The Moon in Aries is bold, impulsive, and energetic. It's a period when we feel feisty and maybe a little argumentative. This is when even the meekest aren't afraid to take a stand to protect personal feelings. Since Aries is the first sign of the zodiac, it's a natural starting point for all kinds of projects, and a wonderful time to channel all that "me first" energy to initiate change and new beginnings. Just watch out for a tendency to be too impulsive and stress-oriented.

Taurus

☽♉ The Moon in Taurus is the Lady at her most solid and sensual, feeling secure and well rooted. There's no need to stress or hurry—and definitely no need to change anything. We tend to resist change when the Moon is in this sign, especially change that's not of our own making. We'd rather sit still, have a wonderful dinner, and listen to good music. Appreciating the beauty of the earth, watching a sunset, viewing some lovely art, or taking care of money and other resources are Taurus Moon activities.

Gemini

☽♊ This mutable air sign moves around so quickly that when the Moon is here we're a bit more restless than usual, and may find that we're suddenly in the mood for conversation, puzzles, riddles, and word games. We want two—at least two—of everything. Now is a great time for letter writing, phone calls, or short trips. It's when you'll find the best shortcuts, and when you'll need to take them, too. Watch for a tendency to become a bit scattered under this fun, fickle Moon.

Cancer

☽♋ The Moon in this cardinal water sign is at her most nurturing. Here the Moon's concerns turn to home, family, children, and mothers, and we respond by becoming more likely to express our emotions and to be sympathetic and understanding toward others. We often find ourselves in the mood to take care of someone, to cook for or cuddle our dear ones. During this time, feelings run high, so it's important to watch out for becoming overly sensitive, dependent, or needy. Now is a great time to putter around the house, have family over, and tend to domestic concerns.

Leo

☽♌ The Leo Moon loves drama with a capital *D*. This theatrical sign has long been known for its big entrances, love of display, and need for attention. When the Moon is in this sign, we're all feeling a need to be recognized, applauded, and appreciated. Now, all that excitement, pride, and emotion can turn into melodrama in the blink of an eye, so it's best to be careful of overreacting or being excessively vain during this period. It's a great time to take in a show (or star in one), be romantic, or express your feelings for someone in regal style.

Virgo

☽♍ The Moon is at her most discriminating and detail-oriented in Virgo, the sign most concerned with fixing and fussing. This Moon sign puts us in the mood to clean, scour, sort, troubleshoot, and help. Virgo, the most helpful of all the signs, is also more health conscious, work-oriented, and duty bound. Use this period to pay attention to your diet, hygiene, and daily schedules.

Libra

☽♎ The Libra Moon is most oriented toward relationships and partnerships. Since Libra's job is to restore balance, however, you may find yourself in situations of emotional imbalance that require a delicate tap of the scales to set them right. In general, this is a social, polite, and friendly time, when others will be cooperative and agree more easily to compromise. A Libra Moon prompts us to make our surroundings beautiful, or to put ourselves in situations where beauty is all around us. This is a great time to decorate, shop for the home, or visit places of elegant beauty.

Scorpio

☽♏ Scorpio is the most intense sign, and when the Moon is here, she feels everything to the nth degree—and needless to say, we do, too. Passion, joy, jealousy, betrayal, love, and desire can take center stage in our lives now, as our emotions deepen to the point of possible obsession. Be careful of a tendency to become secretive or suspicious, or to brood over an offense that was not intended.

Now is a great time to investigate a mystery, do research, "dig"—both figuratively and literally—and allow ourselves to become intimate with someone.

Sagittarius

☽♐ The Moon is at her most optimistic and willing to let go of things in Sagittarius. Jupiter, the planet of long-distance travel and education of the higher mind, makes this a great time to take off for adventure or attend a seminar on a topic you've always been interested in—say, philosophy or religion. This is the sign with the gift of prophecy and wisdom. When the Moon is in this sign, spend time outdoors, be spontaneous, and laugh much too loudly; just watch for a tendency toward excess, waste, and overdoing.

Capricorn

☽♑ The Moon is at her most organized, practical, and business-like in Capricorn. She brings out the dutiful, cautious, and pessimistic side of us. Our goals for the future become all-important. Now is the time to tend to the family business, act responsibly, take charge of something, organize any part of our lives that has become scattered or disrupted, set down rules and guidelines, or patiently listen and learn. Watch for the possibility of acting too businesslike at the expense of others' emotions.

Aquarius

☽♒ The Aquarius Moon brings out the rebel in us. This is a great time to break out of a rut, try something different, and make sure everyone sees us for the unique individuals we are. This sign is ruled by Uranus, so personal freedom and individuality are more important than anything now. Our schedules become topsy-turvy, and our causes become urgent. Watch for a tendency to become fanatical, act deliberately rebellious without a reason, or break tradition just for the sake of breaking it.

Pisces

☽♓ When the Moon slips into this sign, sleep, meditation, prayer, drugs, or alcohol is often what we crave to induce a trancelike state that will allow us to escape from the harshness of reality. Now is when we're most susceptible to emotional assaults of any kind, when we're feeling dreamy, nostalgic, wistful, or impressionable. Now is also when we're at our most spiritual, when our boundaries are at their lowest, when we're compassionate, intuitive, and sensitive to those less fortunate. This is the time to attend a spiritual group or religious gathering.

2019 Eclipse Dates

January 5

Solar Eclipse at 15° ♑ 25'

January 21

Lunar Eclipse at 0° ♌ 52'

July 2

Solar Eclipse at 10° ♋ 38'

July 16

Lunar Eclipse at 24° ♑ 04'

December 26

Solar Eclipse at 4° ♑ 07'

2019 Retrograde Planets

Planet	Begin	Eastern	Pacific	End	Eastern	Pacific
Uranus	8/7/18	12:48 pm	9:48 am	1/6/19	3:27 pm	12:27 pm
Mercury	3/5/19	1:19 pm	10:19 am	3/28/19	9:59 am	6:59 am
Jupiter	4/10/19	1:01 pm	10:01 am	8/11/19	9:37 am	6:37 am
Pluto	4/24/19	2:48 pm	11:48 am	10/2/19		11:39 pm
				10/3/19	2:39 am	
Saturn	4/29/19	8:54 pm	5:54 pm	9/18/19	4:47 am	1:47 am
Neptune	6/21/19	10:36 am	7:36 am	11/27/19	7:32 am	4:32 am
Mercury	7/7/19	7:14 pm	4:14 pm	7/31/19	11:58 pm	8:58 pm
Uranus	8/11/19	10:27 pm	7:27 pm	1/10/20	8:49 pm	5:49 pm
Mercury	10/31/19	11:41 am	8:41 am	11/20/19	2:12 pm	11:12 am

	Dec 2018	Jan 2019	Feb	Mar	Apr	May	Jun	Jul	Aug	Sep	Oct	Nov	Dec 2019	Jan 2020
☿				▓				▓				▓		
♃					▓	▓	▓							
♄						▓	▓	▓	▓					
♅	▓												▓	▓
♆							▓	▓	▓	▓	▓			
♇						▓	▓	▓	▓	▓				

2019 Planetary Phenomena

Information on Uranus and Neptune assumes the use of a telescope. Resource: *Astronomical Phenomena for the Year 2019*, prepared jointly with Her Majesty's Nautical Almanac Office of the United Kingdom Hydrographic Office and the United States Naval Observatory's Nautical Almanac Office. The dates are expressed in Universal Time and must be converted to your Local Mean Time. (See the World Map of Time Zones on page 191.)

Planets Visible in Morning and Evening

Planet	Morning	Evening
Mercury	Jan. 1 – Jan. 15 March 22 – May 14 July 30 – Aug. 26 Nov. 18 – Dec. 25	Feb. 11 – March 8 May 29 – July 13 Sept. 15 – Nov. 6
Venus	Jan. 1 – July 8	Sept. 20 – Dec. 31
Mars	Oct. 17 – Dec. 31	Jan. 1 – July 18
Jupiter	Jan. 1 – June 10	June 10 – Dec. 15
Saturn	Jan. 19 – July 9	July 9 – Dec. 27

Mercury

Mercury can only be seen low in the east before sunrise or low in the west after sunset.

Venus

Venus is a brilliant object in the morning sky from the beginning of the year until the second week of July when it becomes too close to the Sun for observation. It reappears in the second half of September in the evening sky, where it stays until the end of the year.

Mars

Mars is visible as a reddish object in the evening sky at the beginning of the year. It becomes too close to the Sun for observation in mid-July. It reappears in the morning sky during the third week of October.

Jupiter

Jupiter is visible in the morning sky at the beginning of the year. From mid-March it can be seen for more than half the night. By early September it can only be seen in the evening sky. From mid-December it becomes too close to the Sun for observation.

Saturn

Saturn is too close to the Sun for observation from the beginning of the year until the third week of January when it rises just before sunrise. In mid-April it becomes visible for more than half the night. From early October until late December it can only be seen in the evening sky and then becomes too close to the Sun for observation for the remainder of the year.

Uranus

Uranus is visible at the beginning of the year and by mid-January can only been seen in the evening sky. In early April it becomes too close to the Sun for observation. It reappears in mid-May in the morning sky. It can be seen for more than half the night for the remainder of the year.

Neptune

Neptune is visible at the beginning of the year in the evening sky. In mid-February it becomes too close to the Sun for observation and reappears in late March in the morning sky. From early December it can only be seen in the evening sky.

DO NOT CONFUSE (1) Venus with Jupiter in late January and late November, with Saturn in mid-February and mid-December, and with Mercury in mid-April, late September, and late October to early November—on all occasions Venus is the brighter object; (2) Mercury with Mars from mid-June to mid-July, when Mercury is the brighter object.

2019 Weekly Forecasts

by Pam Ciampi

Overview of 2019

Have you ever heard of a state of mental clarity called the *overview effect*? It's a cognitive shift in awareness that occurs when an experience causes you to see the big picture. Many astronauts experience an overview effect after viewing Earth from outer space for the first time as a small blue dot, a place where national boundaries don't exist and political conflicts are unimportant. With this new and different perspective, some of these astronauts come back to Earth with a more spiritual outlook and become environmentalists. Hopefully this overview of the most important celestial happenings in 2019 will have the same effect for you of putting this year in a bigger perspective.

After considering and evaluating the aspects, sign changes, eclipses, and retrogrades for 2019, the theme that emerges this year is of an economic revolution. After years of disturbance and turmoil, it seems that we are on the cusp of a major shift that will not only shake things up but also get things moving in a different direction. This new direction will influence the global economy, the weather, and the 2020 election in the United States. The three planets that have starring roles in this year's show are Uranus, Jupiter, and Mercury.

Uranus Makes Breaking News in 2019

Uranus is the big newsmaker this year. Even though this planet shifted temporarily into Taurus for the first time last May (in 2018), it then retrograded later in the year for one last tour in Aries. But this time Uranus's sign shift is for good. When Uranus exchanges Aries for Taurus in March, it will stay firmly planted in Taurus for the next seven years. Because Uranus rules sudden changes and Taurus is earthy and focused on security issues, this shift puts money, banking, the global economy, and weather patterns on the hot seat. Money exchanges may undergo dramatic new changes (no more paper money?), including new ways of banking and money management that will set us on a seven-year course of worldwide economic revolution. Uranus in Taurus also indicates that weather patterns will experience fierce ups and downs and cause sudden changes in the way we live (see March 4–10).

During this year of ups and downs, Uranus is also on tap to make three unholy alliances with Mars. These shake-up points, which will occur in February, July, and November, are times to be extra-careful because they are potentially dangerous and chock full of pent-up, explosive energy that could lead to uprisings and possibly violence. With that in mind, it's also true that every cloud has a silver lining, and this is a year when Uranus gets to engage in a wonderful trine with Jupiter. This aspect is a celestial gift that blesses genius and encourages freedom and independence, and tops it all off with a sense of humor. Some other outcomes of this trine might include new forms of travel (into outer space) and amazing new technologies. The next time these two planets will grace our skies in a trine aspect is in 2028. With Uranus's sign shift, its alignments with Mars, and its trine with Jupiter, it looks like this planet is telling us that this is going to be a year when nothing stays the same.

Jupiter Goes Out of Bounds in 2019

This is a year when Jupiter (the guardian angel planet) in its own sign of Sagittarius makes two happy conjunctions with Venus, two lucky trines with Mars, and one unique trine with Uranus. Together this indicates a good luck year for those with Sagittarius prominent in their natal chart. But Jupiter also makes three squares to Neptune, which constitutes a major warning to everyone not to push the boundaries too far, because with Uranus changing the economic landscape, it won't be a big surprise if the bubble gets so big that it bursts. Take Jupiter's sage advice and make this a year when you live your life inside the lines.

2019 Transit of Mercury

Mercury retrograde in Scorpio makes headlines in November when this planet takes a unique trip across the face of the Sun called the *Transit of Mercury*. Although it lasts for only a few hours, this rare passage is worth seeing because it won't happen again until 2032.

Mercury will retrograde three times this year in emotional water signs, which can either muddy up the mind and communications or make them ultra-creative.

Year of the Earth Pig

In the Chinese zodiac, 2019 is the Year of the Pig. The element associated with this year's Pig is earth, which indicates an abundant year if the earth Pig is not too lazy to get motivated.

2019 Supermoons and Eclipses

This year features three Supermoons and five eclipses, but don't expect anything like the Total Solar Eclipse of 2017 that swept across the United States. The Total Lunar Eclipse in January of 2019 will be visible on the East Coast of the US, but the other eclipse shadows will fall in different parts of the world.

The first three Supermoons (bigger and brighter than usual) of the year are all Full Moons that occur at zero degrees of their respective signs. This unusual occurrence may be a precursor to Uranus's sign shift, the Jupiter-Neptune squares, and the Transit of Mercury because they mark a change toward something new and different this year.

Also Worthy of Mention

This year also features three minor but important sextiles between Saturn and Neptune. Even though the sextile is not a major aspect, these two planets haven't met like this since 1996, and the next time will be in 2031. These Saturn-Neptune sextiles symbolize three important chances to harmonize your material goods and goals with your spiritual beliefs.

—◆—

As always, thank you to all the readers for supporting the weekly forecasts. They are a labor of love and it is my deepest hope that they will help you experience the overview effect. Wishing you clear skies!

Hot Spots in 2019

January 5—Solar Eclipse (in Capricorn)
The eclipse shadow falls over East Asia.

January 13—Jupiter square Neptune
Fantasy watch! With three Jupiter-Neptune squares sprinkled throughout the year, denial is the name of the collective game from January through September.

January 21—Total Lunar Eclipse/Supermoon (in Leo)
This spectacular sight will be visible in Europe, Asia, and North and South America. Because the first three Full Moons of 2019 are also Supermoons that occur at the first degree of their respective signs, 2019 looks like it could be the start of something new.

January 22—Venus-Jupiter conjunction
O happy day!

February 5—Chinese New Year of the Pig

February 13—Mars-Uranus conjunction at the end of Aries
Expect a volatile day.

February 19—Supermoon (in Virgo)

March 7—Uranus enters Taurus
Uranus (the planet of revolution) enters Taurus (the sign of money) and jumpstarts a period of financial revolution that will last through 2025–2026.

March 20—Full Moon/Supermoon (in Libra)

June 16—Jupiter-Neptune square

July 2—Total Solar Eclipse (in Cancer)
The eclipse shadow covers South America.

September 21—Jupiter-Neptune square

November 11—Transit of Mercury across the Sun
Mercury last crossed in front of the Sun in 2016, and the next time will be in 2039. This is a celestial reminder that once in a while something very small can exert an influence over something much larger and more powerful.

November 24—Venus-Jupiter conjunction
O happy day!

December 2—Jupiter enters Capricorn
Jupiter leaves its cozy home sign of Sagittarius and enters Capricorn, an uncomfortable placement for exuberant Jupiter because Capricorn acts with deliberate caution.

December 15—Jupiter-Uranus trine
Surprises galore!

December 26—Partial Solar Eclipse (in Capricorn)
The eclipse shadow falls over East Asia and the upper part of North America.

January 1–6

The central theme of the astrological calendar is light and darkness, and the forecast is for cloudy skies during the first week of this new year. The energy of the Sun will be shadowed in two ways this week, once at its annual meeting with Saturn and the other by a powerful Solar Eclipse. A conjunction of the Sun with Saturn (the law enforcer of the zodiac) on Wednesday, January 2, carries the somber news that the party's over and it's clean-up time, a time to face the consequences and assume personal responsibility for past actions. Just in case you weren't paying attention, the same theme is repeated on Saturday, January 5, with a Total Solar Eclipse riding on the back of the Capricorn New Moon. Although the monthly New Moon is a dark and quiet time when seeds of new beginnings are best planted, the intensity of the Solar Eclipse in close connection to Saturn and Pluto turns this New Moon into a four-way stop sign that's good for reflecting on the past but not for charging into the future. Although the light this week is not bright enough to start something new, it provides a convenient excuse to wait a while before you start on your New Year's resolutions. Uranus makes a promise to shake things up when it ends its retrograde period on Sunday, January 6. Because this planet is at the last degree of Aries when it wakes up, this change of direction means Uranus is primed to make its first sign shift in seven years. This will happen when it exchanges Aries for Taurus later in March.

Because Uranus traditionally signals abrupt changes and earthy Taurus rules security and money, this shift is a sneak preview of some of the surprises that lie ahead for technology, weather patterns, and the world economy (see March 4–10).

January 7–13

A sign change for Venus, an intense meetup for the Sun, and a fantasy alert for Jupiter and Neptune promise to make this week an up-and-down ride. Be sure to keep your love and money options open on Monday, January 7, because that's when Venus leaves Scorpio and enters fiery and flexible Sagittarius. Venus in Sagittarius can be a flashpoint for exciting new possibilities, but these are likely to burn out quickly like a comet unless you have some additional way to ground them. Because this type of Venus energy will trend for the next month, this is a great time for trying out exciting new adventures that require minimal investment. Friday, January 11, presents a unique opportunity to get to know your self better by looking deep inside, because that's when the Capricorn Sun has its once-a-year meeting with Pluto, the planet that rules the unconscious world. If you've already been working at this level, this would be a good day for a major transformation. The week ends on Sunday, January 13, with the first of three Jupiter-Neptune squares that are on tap this year. Because this square combination is famous for its misplaced optimism and Pollyanna attitude of seeing only the good in everything, it's dangerous. This is a warning that you may be tempted to take on something that's not realistic.

January 14–20

Love, drama, and romance are lighting up this week's sky with a very special Full Moon and a fiery trine between Venus and Mars. Venus and Mars start things off when they fall in love on Friday, January 18, and give you a green light to start a new relationship or find ways to spice up an old one. On Sunday, January 20, the Sun moves from grounded Capricorn into no-holds-barred Aquarius, where surprises and restlessness abound and perspectives swing from genius to alien to outlier. Because this Sun shift occurs on the same day as a dramatic Full Moon Lunar Eclipse in Leo, the message is that it's time to use your unconscious to bring personal projects and events to a conclusion with a big bang. This Leo Full Moon Lunar Eclipse is also a Supermoon that occurs at zero degrees of Leo. A Supermoon is bigger and brighter than a regular Full Moon. As mentioned previously, this year is unique because the first three Full Moons of 2019 (in January, February, and March) are Supermoons at zero degrees of their respective signs of the zodiac—an unusual coincidence that indicates something new is coming our way. The places directly affected by the shadow of this Full Moon Lunar Eclipse are North and South America, Europe, and Asia.

January 21–27

With a difficult square and two happy Jupiter aspects this week, it looks like conflicts will come to a head early but by the weekend it will be smooth sailing. Things start to heat up on Monday, January 21, when Mars makes a frustrating square to Saturn. This Mars-Saturn square is a stop-and-go aspect because although Mars always wants to go, Saturn is the rule maker and order giver and needs to proceed cautiously and slowly. One of the best ways to counter the influence of this square is by doing something physical, like taking a long run or a martial arts class. The good news is that Mars goes to a much happier place on Friday, January 25, when it makes a trine to optimistic Jupiter and gives you a shot of confidence that helps you find a way out. Venus chimes in on a similar note on Tuesday, January 22, as it joins with joyous Jupiter in Sagittarius, which pushes the lever on love and finances to high. Fast-moving Mercury is also on the go on Thursday, January 24, when it enters Aquarius. While Mercury is in Aquarius over the next three weeks, negotiations will be more difficult than usual because Aquarius is a rigid type of energy, which makes it harder to change someone's mind. On the other hand, it's also a time when information can be transmitted intuitively if you're tuned to the right channel.

January 28–February 3

A promising sextile, a difficult square, an exciting trine, and a sign change make this an energetic week. On Thursday, January 31, a sextile between Saturn and Neptune unites the material world with the spiritual world. This sextile is unique because the last time it came around was in 1996, and it will repeat three times this year. On Friday, February 1, a problematic square between Mars and Pluto promises difficulties. Because this hotheaded square comes with confrontations and power struggles ignited by anger issues, the key to handling it is to stay cool. If you take a breath, resist the urge to inflict revenge on the perpetrator of your misery, and let the karma police do their job, you will be able to stay focused on your own objectives. And if you don't succeed this time, there will be a second chance in November when these two heavyweights meet up again. Things lighten up on Saturday, February 2, and you can look forward to some excitement involving love or money because that's when Venus makes a fiery trine with Uranus. Although Venus and Uranus are on schedule to combine in this fortunate way three times this year, this is the most creative and social opportunity of the three meetings, which makes it a great weekend for networking or new friendships. And speaking of getting together with friends, Super Bowl LIII is on Sunday, February 3, which coincides with Venus entering responsible and organized Capricorn. Don't hold me to this, but it could mean that the Patriots will win the Super Bowl *again*, because Coach Belichick has built their team on the Capricorn virtues of keeping your nose to the grindstone and doing your job. Seriously, while Venus is visiting Capricorn for the next month, it's time to get down to brass tacks with your relationships, your finances, and whatever else you value. Achievement through structure and tradition is the key to Capricorn's success. Although Venus is not very warm or fuzzy in Capricorn, this placement does promise tenacity, strong ethics, dedication, and commitment—the same values that make it possible for the little Capricorn Goat to reach the mountaintop.

February 4–10

With a New Moon on the agenda this week, this looks like a time to throw out the old and ring in the new. The Aquarius New Moon on Monday, February 4, is a dark and quiet time that favors planting the seeds of new beginnings. Because Aquarius brings some surprises or reversals and it's also an energy that loves groups and favors innovation, this New Moon is the perfect time to seek out new friends or generate different types of networking possibilities. Because Chinese New Year is based on a lunar calendar, it happens on the day after the New Moon that occurs between January 21 and February 20. This year Chinese New Year is celebrated on the heels of the Aquarius New Moon on Tuesday, February 5. In the Chinese zodiac, 2019 is the Year of the Pig, a symbol of wealth and luxury. The element associated with this year's Pig is earth, which indicates a stable year ahead if the earth Pig can avoid being lethargic and lazy. According to legend, the Pig was the last animal to arrive when the Jade Emperor called for the great meeting, so Pig year marks the end of the twelve-year Chinese zodiac cycle. Mercury makes a shift on Sunday, February 10, when it changes signs and enters Pisces. This switch bears watching because when Mercury combines with Pisces, it can cause an extended period of mind fog, a time when our methods of thinking tend to skip over details and facts in favor of intuition. Although this can be a gift when working in the creative arts, in the everyday world it can lead to distorted communications and scrambled information: "I know you didn't say that, but I thought that's what you meant"—eek! Mercury will be in Pisces much longer than usual this year because of a routine retrograde in March that slows this planet down and turns it backward. With this extended tour on hand, it looks like the devil is in the details for the next two months. This is a time to use your intuition, but don't let it use you.

February 11–17

Surprise! Even though Valentine's Day is Thursday, February 14, it's not Venus, the planet of love, that's making headlines this week; it's Mars, the planet of war. It's interesting that Valentine's Day started out with associations to Mars through the martyr saint Valentinus, and that its connection to a more Venusian type of romantic love and gift giving didn't come about until fourteenth-century England. It all starts on Wednesday, February 13, when Mars takes a major meeting with Uranus in the last degree of fiery Aries. Although this is the only conjunction Uranus and Mars have on tap this year, it is a very dangerous one because it is chock full of explosive, aggressive, hot-blooded energy with little regard for future consequences and could lead to uprisings and violence. The situation improves on Valentine's Day, when Mars has a change of mind and exchanges Aries for the loving sign of Taurus for the next six weeks. Although this sea change means that love and finances will be more stable and long-lasting during this time, if you're thinking of proposing or accepting a proposal this Valentine's Day, make absolutely sure it's the right choice for you. The volatility of the Mars-Uranus conjunction earlier in the week may have encouraged you to throw caution to the wind and forge ahead regardless of the reality of your situation, and the one thing you definitely don't want is to marry in haste and repent in leisure.

February 18—24

A special Full Moon and a Sun sign shift could bring some significant changes to your life this week. On Monday, February 18, the Sun leaves quirky Aquarius for the watery and emotional landscape of Pisces. With the Sun in Pisces, your intuition is on high and your emotions will be running the show for the next thirty days. The emotional and creative sides of life are also accentuated by a big, bright Supermoon at zero degrees of Virgo on Tuesday, February 19. This is the second Super Full Moon at zero degrees of a sign this year and is a reminder of things that have come full circle and are starting over again. This is a week to stay alert and be aware, because the Virgo Full Moon carries a mysterious earthy energy fraught with deep, unconscious undercurrents that can derail your life if you forget that this is a time of endings and bringing things to their natural completion. Communications will be tuned to a very intuitive channel this week, with a conjunction from Mercury to Neptune and a sextile from Mercury to Saturn that could produce imaginative and productive ideas. Power struggles over love and money might get pretty intense on Friday, February 22, when Venus joins together with Pluto. Since this is only a temporary condition that lasts for a few days, take a deep breath and try to stay out of the deep end.

February 25—March 3

This is a relatively quiet week, with an energetic but minor aspect between the Sun and Mars and a conflict and sign change for Venus. On Wednesday, February 27, when the Sun makes a sextile to Mars, it's time to take advantage of this slight energy bump by making things happen at work or at play. Love and finances take a hit on Friday, March 1, when Venus squares Uranus from the last degree of Capricorn. This is the first of three Venus-Uranus scuffles this year, so get ready for repeated conflicts between the desire for security versus the desire for change and autonomy. Later that same day, Venus shifts into freedom-seeking Aquarius, and the attitude toward love and money changes from a focus on the material Capricorn world to being detached, noncommittal, and much more innovative. For the next four weeks while Venus is in Aquarius, you might feel that you need to make your relationship or finances better by discarding the old and getting a new POV. But don't be too hasty, as Aquarius has a tendency to shock and awe and there's always the danger that in getting rid of the old you'll throw the baby out with the bathwater.

March 4—10

Change is the watchword for this week. There's a major sign change on the books for Uranus that will affect you for the next seven years and a change in clock time that will be in effect for the next six months. But before those changes kick in, the first thing you need to do is shift into reverse and proceed with caution, because there's a Mercury retrograde ahead. The first of the three Mercury retrogrades this year will be in effect from March 5 to March 28. Mercury retrograde is one of the things almost everyone has heard of, even if they don't know anything else about astrology. Unfortunately, Mercury retrograde has gotten a bad rap as the source of miscommunications and annoying digital and transportation gremlins. And while it's true that this is not a good time to sign contracts or start something new, it also has an upside. Mercury retrograde is a valuable time-out period that gives you a chance to go backward and reevaluate the last few months, figure out what went wrong, and make it better. It's also a time when lost objects may suddenly reappear and old friends may find you again. Mercury is in Pisces during this retrograde, which means the focus is on spiritual and artistic projects, good works, and forgiveness. The biggest celestial event of the year is up next on Tuesday, March 6, with a major sign shift for Uranus. That's the day when Uranus, the planet that represents revolution, enters Taurus, the sign of security and money. This shift signals an economic and financial revolution that will influence global markets for the next seven years. The last time Uranus was in Taurus was during the 1930s, which resulted in a period of economic disaster that proceeded World War II. Hopefully, this time the sign shift will bring positive new changes in currency (no more paper currency?) and ways of banking as well as amazing new technologies that will revolutionize the world of digital devices and transportation. This sign shift gets some additional juice from the Pisces New Moon, which falls on that same day. This Pisces New Moon echoes the seeds planted by Uranus's new beginnings while reminding us to follow the Golden Rule: Do unto others as you would have them do unto you. This incredible week ends with the beginning of Daylight Saving Time on Sunday, March 10, at 2:00 a.m. local time. It's time to "spring ahead," so set your clocks forward one hour before you go to bed on Saturday night.

March 11–17

A trine and forward shift for Saturn and a couple of nice aspects for Mercury make this a week when you can get a lot accomplished. Saturn is extremely well paired in its home sign of Capricorn (2018–2020) and brings a welcome note of stability to these turbulent times. On Thursday, March 14, this "good cop" version of Saturn aligns in a harmonious trine with Mars for the first of two times this year. Because both Mars and Saturn are in productive earth signs, this makes it an especially good week for working on your physical health, financial objectives, and career goals. Although Mercury is still retrograde, it makes three minor alignments this week that have positive effects on communications. On Friday, March 15, there's a tendency to see only the bright side of things, because that's when Mercury makes a square to happy-go-lucky Jupiter. Mercury makes a sextile with Pluto on Saturday, March 16, and in that case, thought processes will become deeper, with a greater curiosity about what lies beneath the surface. Communications speed up and become more energetic when Mercury sextiles Mars on Sunday, March 17. With all this help from Saturn and Pluto, this Mercury retrograde might turn out to be a whole lot easier than expected.

March 18—24

A Super Full Moon and the spring equinox lead the planetary action this week. Other planets in the headlines include Mars in a trine to Pluto and a square to Venus, the Sun taking its once-a-year meeting with Chiron, and Mercury conjunct Neptune. Kickoff is on Wednesday, March 20, when the Sun enters Aries on the same day as the Libra Full Supermoon. A Supermoon is bigger and brighter than the usual Full Moon, and this one marks the end of the series of three Super Full Moons at zero degrees. Because this Full Moon is in Libra, it's a good time to contact your unconscious to help bring business or relationship issues to a good conclusion. The Sun in Aries carries a bundle of energy and excitement into the next month as it marks the first season change of the year, also called the spring equinox. Because the spring equinox is one of two days a year when light and darkness are in balance, Wednesday is a celestial reminder to check in on your own life (Aries) to see if you are in or out of balance (Libra). It's time to get those creative fires burning that same day when Mars moves into a harmonious alignment with Pluto, making this spring equinox a day of positive star power when mountains can be moved. There's a minor glitch the next day, Thursday, March 21, when Venus squares Mars, because this square brings up anger, temper tantrums, and love-hate situations. However, a speedy recovery is possible on Friday, March 22, when the Sun makes its once-a-year conjunction with Chiron, the comet that represents our deepest wounds and the possibilities for healing them. Get ready for miscommunications to get out of hand on Sunday, March 24, when Mercury retrograde conjoins Neptune.

March 25–31

With Venus and Mars entering new signs and Mercury ending its retrograde period, this is a week when relationships, finances, and communications can all start moving in a new direction. It begins on Tuesday, March 26, when Venus says goodbye to rational and detached Aquarius and hello to Pisces, where emotions, fantasies, and dreams rule. This Venusian trend toward the creative, spiritual, and non-material world will last for the next month. Venus is considered to be "dignified" in Pisces, which is another way of saying that Venus's virtues (compassion, forgiveness, productivity, etc.) are more in play than its vices (possessiveness, laziness, lust, etc.). Like Venus, Mercury is also in Pisces, but the important news of the week is that Mercury ends its retrograde period on Thursday, March 27. This movement means that miscommunications will start to clear up, the gremlins in your digital devices will temporarily fade back into the ethernet, and informational networks will be back to normal. This is a good time to sign contracts. The third shift of this week starts when Mars leaves Taurus and enters Gemini on Sunday, March 31. This movement triggers a flow of fresh, new experiences and ideas that will last until the middle of May. Things may get a bit scattered during this time because with Mars in Gemini, everything moves faster and new options pop up daily. The best way to deal with this information overload is to take a deep breath, pick the best option, and stay focused.

April 1–7

The Aries New Moon dominates a week that also includes some healing energy from Mercury and Mars. Mercury is still in Pisces, but it's faster now that it's in forward gear and makes two connections that affect the mind in different ways this week. There's an illusive conjunction between Mercury and Neptune on Tuesday, April 2, that could be tricky because Neptune obscures and confuses. But help is on the way when Mercury makes a minor sextile to Saturn on Sunday, April 7, and brings your thoughts back to earth. More healing energy is on tap when Mars makes a minor but positive sextile with Chiron on Wednesday, April 3, echoing the Sun's healing meeting with Chiron last week. Then on Friday, April 5, the Aries New Moon—the star of the week—brings all the fiery energy and inspiration you need to plant the seeds of a new beginning in any area of your life. Because both the Sun and the Moon are in Aries and Aries is a sign that focuses on the self, this is your chance to start something that will challenge and excite you. The Aries New Moon is the absolute best New Moon of the year to launch a product, open a shop, start a new job or relationship, or jumpstart that blog that's been in your head forever. It's all about timing, and this is the best time of the year to do it. Harness the fiery energy of Aries and make it work.

April 8–14

Your personal willpower will be hard at work this week while the Sun makes alignments to three major players. Two of these connections will create some difficult challenges, but the third one is a gift. On Wednesday, April 10, when the Sun moves into a tough square with Saturn, the law enforcer, you can count on learning an important lesson. This is a time to be patient instead of getting frustrated because things aren't going the way you expected. There's another slowdown that same day when Jupiter turns retrograde. This retrograde begins a four-month time-out period that's an opportunity to reconnect with the virtues of faith, hope, and charity. It's also a time to make any philosophical adjustments so you'll be in the right place at the right time to be lucky when Jupiter turns direct in August. Things could get out of hand on Thursday, April 11, when a short-lived square from Mercury to Jupiter exaggerates your perceptions and makes things seem better than they really are. The forecast is still looking cloudy on Saturday, April 13, when the Sun squares off with Pluto. This conflict can set off difficult power struggles that can't be ignored and can't be won. But just when it looks like all is lost, a celestial gift arrives on Sunday, April 14, in the form of a bright light from the Sun in trine aspect to optimistic Jupiter. With this lucky combination bringing good fortune your way, solutions to any problem can appear out of the blue.

April 15–21

This is a busy Easter week because in addition to another Libra Full Moon and a sign shift for the Sun, Mercury and Venus are also scheduled to change signs. Mercury starts things off when it enters Aries on Wednesday, April 17, and communications shift into a fast-paced, aggressive space for the next four weeks. Because this Mercury-in-Aries combo flies on winged feet, this is a time to be careful with your words and not say everything you think. The Libra Full Moon on Friday, April 19, is special because it's the second Libra Full Moon of the year. This offers an unusual second chance to bring your outstanding financial and relationship issues to a proper conclusion (again). On Saturday, April 20, Venus follows Mercury's lead and moves into Aries for the next four weeks. Unfortunately, this is a negative shift for the planet of love because Aries is the sign of war. Saturday is also the day when the Sun exchanges fiery Aries for earthy Taurus. The Sun will be in Taurus for the next month, so use this productive energy to manifest your visions in the physical world. This year you might overhear someone saying that Easter is late, and they are right. Easter is celebrated on different dates every year, because it's calculated to occur on the first Sunday after the first Full Moon (this year on Friday, April 19) after the spring equinox (this year on March 20). The earliest date on which Easter can fall is March 21 and the latest is April 25. This year Easter falls on Sunday, April 21.

April 22–28

There are three important alignments to consider when making your plans for this week because they involve the heavy-hitters of the zodiac: Uranus, Pluto, Neptune, and Mars. The first may bring unexpected changes when the Taurus Sun joins with Uranus on Monday, April 22. Although the unstable nature of Uranus makes it difficult to predict whether this conjunction will be positive or negative, Taurus is an earth sign, which suggests that either the economy or weather conditions will be a major part of the forecast. Next on the agenda is Pluto, which adds to the intrigue on Wednesday, April 24, when it goes retrograde for the next five months. Pluto retrogrades are times when it's possible for major constructive work to take place on underlying power struggles. Because Pluto is in Capricorn, this retrograde is expected to have the greatest effect on the areas of government, banking, law enforcement, and the construction industry. The last big alignment of the week is on Saturday, April 27. This is definitely one to watch because Mars and Neptune only get into a conflict once a year. Even though this square lasts for two to three days, its effects can be debilitating. Its signatures are confusion, low energy, and feelings of discouragement, with hints of scandal, lies, and deceit. Between the Sun-Uranus conjunction, Pluto's reversal, and the Mars-Neptune square, this is a week to keep your head down and wear a virtual suit of armor.

April 29–May 5

The high points this week are the Taurus New Moon, a change of direction for Saturn, and a lucky face-off between Mars and Jupiter. Things get off to a sluggish start when Saturn turns retrograde on Monday, April 29. But on the other hand, this shift into reverse for Saturn marks the best time of the year to review your career situation, reevaluate your life direction, and consolidate your resources. Because Saturn always means "less is more," this four-and-a-half-month retrograde period is a useful time to go back over the seeds of the past and weed out what you don't need. A pragmatic and organized Taurus New Moon on Saturday, May 4, adds grounding and support to the Saturn retrograde. Because Taurus is a "greenie" type of sign (like Virgo and Capricorn), this New Moon marks a dark and quiet time that is perfect for planting the seeds of new beginnings in down-to-earth matters like better time management, healthy eating, doing work you love, and making sound financial decisions. Any new beginnings initiated during the two-week period of the Taurus New Moon will get a boost on Sunday, May 5, when Mars opposes Jupiter. This face-off between the planet of dynamic energy and the planet of good fortune increases personal confidence and fosters a craving for adventure and risk taking. The downside is a tendency to overreach and rely more on luck than on effort. Although this year luck is on your side, because Jupiter is in its own sign of Sagittarius, with this square on the books, if you're planning to set out on a new path or launch a new project, keep a discerning eye on the past and a steady hand on the tiller of this energy that knows no bounds.

May 6–12

Buyer beware! This is a difficult week for Mercury and Venus, and there's a chance you might jump to the wrong conclusion or get your feelings hurt. It all begins on Monday, May 6, when Mercury triggers a communications slowdown by leaving fiery Aries and moving into practical Taurus for the next month. Even though this sign shift means that the information network might not be as fast-paced and stimulating as it was over the last three weeks, it's certain to be more stable and down-to-earth. On Wednesday, May 8, Mercury hits a bump during its once-a-year joining with Uranus. Because this Mercury-Uranus conjunction scores high on intuition and flashes of insight but low on methodical analysis, it makes this a week when it will be super-easy to jump to the wrong conclusion. And with Mercury in stubborn Taurus, once you make a choice, it will be almost impossible to change it. One of the saddest times of the year comes on Tuesday, May 7, when Venus squares a retrograde Saturn. This is the first of two Venus-Saturn conflicts this year that correspond to feelings of isolation, loneliness, or rejection. Although this is not a happy prospect, the best way out is to try not to take matters personally (easy to say, hard to do), work on self-love and acceptance, and keep reminding yourself that it will all turn out okay in the end. Venus has another challenge on Thursday, May 9, which makes this look like a tough week for relationships. But right before that happens, there's a brief but happy trine from Venus to Jupiter that brings hope to the direst of circumstances. The problem is that it's followed later that same day by power struggles coming from an intense and difficult square between Venus and Pluto. Hang in there, because there's a chance for things to calm down and stabilize before Mother's Day when the Sun makes a harmonious trine with Saturn on Saturday, May 11.

May 13–19

The Scorpio Full Moon and a trine from the Sun to Pluto dominate this week, which also includes a sign change for Mars and a chance for Mercury to come to the rescue. The powerful trine from the Sun to Pluto on Monday, May 13, is handy if you want to exert your influence on a situation or if you feel the need to create a path to a deep-seated desire. The forecast shifts on Wednesday, May 15, with two different energy shifts that are coming our way. The first is a plus, because it's when Venus exits Aries and moves into Taurus, its best placement in the zodiac. Venus will be in Taurus for the next four weeks, which means that if you don't get greedy, you can anticipate a month of harmony in love and finances. The second shift later that same day is the polar opposite and should put you on guard! That's when Mars, the planet that likes to slash and burn, goes "underwater" in Cancer, the sign that cares and nurtures. So if you feel a little more crabby than usual from now until the beginning of July, it's because this type of fire-water combination is sensitive and has a tendency to be defensive. The communications highway looks like a smooth ride this week, because Mercury makes a trine to Saturn on Thursday, May 16, and another trine to Pluto on Saturday, May 18. The Sun-Pluto power theme is repeated again at the Full Moon in Scorpio on Saturday, but in a positive way. This Full Moon has the necessary juice to transform something negative into something positive. It's a time to illuminate repressed feelings, dirty secrets, and other skeletons that have been rattling around in your inner closet. It's the best time of the year to push the "I'm finally going to let that go" button and make it stick.

May 20–26

If you're tired of a slow and deliberate pace and itching to move into the fast lane, this could be your week. All the action takes place on Tuesday, May 21, when both the Sun and Mercury leave Taurus and move into Gemini, where things are moving at a much faster rate and your personal solar power lightens up. Because Gemini lives to communicate, the next month when the Sun is in Gemini is a great time for learning new skills, socializing, and buying new digital devices. Gemini's mantra that variety is the spice of life can also bring an exciting smorgasbord of new people and perspectives. Mercury in Gemini has home-field advantage because this is where it can be doubly rational and triply curious. Because the tendency is to move fast from topic to topic during this brief Mercury transit, it is not a time to engage in in-depth discussions but rather is a chance to brainstorm, network, and consider your options.

May 27–June 2

This week features two tricky planetary situations that could prove to be important turning points. Mercury newly minted in Gemini starts things off when it runs into traffic at midweek by getting into a scuffle with Neptune and a face-off with Jupiter. Because Jupiter and Neptune are also in a square to each other, this configuration is called a *T-square*, with Neptune and Jupiter at the short arms of the "T" and Mercury holding down the long end. With Neptune's penchant for the unconscious in conflict with an overly optimistic Jupiter and both fighting with the planet of communication, this can be a week when it's easy to fall off the beaten path and not even know it! Communications will be fraught with confusion, because Jupiter ignores the bad and exaggerates the good and Neptune denies the bad and fantasizes about the good. This T-square is a celestial warning that this is a week to do a reality check before you say or do anything. But help is on the way on Sunday, June 2, in the form of a passionate and earthy trine between Venus and Pluto that helps center and ground you during these tricky times. Take care if you begin an important relationship within three days on either side of this trine, because there may be something about it that causes a deep and long-term impact, even if the relationship itself doesn't last.

June 3–9

The celestial forecast indicates that things will be on the move this week, with a Gemini New Moon and two planets changing signs. The energy level rises on Monday, June 3, as the restless Gemini New Moon brings impatience to plant the seeds of something new. Because both the Sun and the Moon are in Gemini, the focus of the new beginnings is on communications, learning something new, planning a short trip, or getting in touch with siblings or close friends. A square from the New Moon to Neptune makes this a week when it's going to be harder to discern what is real and true and what just looks good. Later in the week both Mercury and Venus leave the safety of their respective home signs to take up residence in different energy fields. When Mercury leaves Gemini and enters Cancer on Tuesday, June 4, communications move to a much more sensitive and emotional level for the next three weeks. With this planet-sign combination there is a tendency to take things more personally, so you may feel more crabby and defensive than usual. Then on Saturday, June 8, Venus leaves the safety and beauty of Taurus for a phase in flighty Gemini. This switch from the earth element to air lightens attitudes toward love and money for the next month but also makes us more unfocused. Gemini always brings up a lot of opportunities, so your job for the next month is to figure out which possibility is the best choice for you and then stick to it. The week ends when the Sun makes a once-a-year square to Neptune on Sunday, June 9. Since this aspect brings low energy, temporary fogginess, and a desire to escape, this is a good day to get some extra sleep and enjoy your dreams.

June 10–16

There's a cake recipe called Death by Chocolate that is like this week's lineup featuring Jupiter and Neptune, two planets that love to go over the top and out of this world. The week begins on Monday, June 10, with Jupiter involved in a face-off with the Sun for the only time this year. If you're in line for any kind of reward for previous good deeds, this opposition is usually the time when you'll get it, because it increases the chances for happiness and success. The only caveat is to stay within the limits of reality. Another Neptune note is struck late on Thursday, May 13, with the first Mars-Neptune trine of the year. Although not high-energy or openly aggressive, this combo has a side that attracts a desire to fight for the underdog. It also has a mystique and an ethereal sexiness that can attract a spiritual type of romance into your life. The energy goes downhill on Friday, June 14, and that's when you're going to have to put a lot of effort into getting what you want. The source of all the trouble is a face-off between Mars and Saturn. Although this opposition lasts for only a week and is the only time these two planets are in opposition this year, it still isn't going to be easy and you should prepare yourself to hang on for the long run. Jupiter gets into trouble with Neptune again on Father's Day, Sunday, June 16. This is the second of three squares these two planets are scheduled to make this year and is another fantasy alert. With Jupiter expanding all the possibilities and Neptune blurring the line between fact and fiction, it will be easy to get caught up in a situation where the bubble has gotten so big it's ready to burst (shades of the 2008 recession).

June 17–23

This summer solstice week highlights a sensitive Full Moon, a potentially violent encounter between Mars and Pluto, a shift into reverse for Neptune, and an easygoing opposition between Venus and Jupiter. The Sagittarius Full Moon lights up the night on Monday, June 17, and signals a time to finish up whatever has been left undone this month, especially in the areas of teaching, learning, travel, and sports. This is a Full Moon to be careful of, because it's part of an unstable Neptune configuration that increases sensitivity and also heightens a desire for risk taking. There is also a higher risk of infection on the physical level and of getting into dangerous situations in general. A sextile from Saturn to Neptune should help to stabilize the atmosphere on Tuesday, June 18, but there's another roadblock ahead on Wednesday, June 19, when the warrior planet (Mars) faces off with the dark force (Pluto). However, this opposition has a lovely silver lining, because both planets are not operating at their full potential. Mars's fire is weakened because it is visiting watery Cancer, and Pluto is on a retreat because it is retrograde. Another lucky feature is that this is the only time these planets will be in opposition this year. The big news of the week marks the second point in the seasonal cycle. On Friday, June 21, it's time to say goodbye to spring and hello to summer. The summer solstice is celebrated every year on the day when the Sun enters the sign of Cancer, and this passage marks the longest day of the year. Because this is the day when the Sun reaches its highest point in the sky, the month when the Sun is in Cancer is one of the most fertile times of the year and is a great time for growth spurts in any area of your life. That same day, June 21, Neptune is on schedule to reverse direction for the next four months. Neptune retrograde is a time to turn inward and get in touch with your higher self. Even though the influence of a Neptune retrograde is very subtle, it can still be powerful if you focus on creativity or spirituality. A T-square between Venus-Jupiter and Neptune on Sunday, June 23, brings an end to this busy week. Because this trio of planets creates myriad opportunities, it's going to be super-easy to overdo anything, from romance to spending. Enjoy yourself, but don't reach so far out of bounds that you can't get back.

June 24–30

Communications and self-worth are highlighted this week, with Mercury as the starring planet and Venus in a minor supporting role. A Venus-Neptune square on Monday, June 24, can signal some uncomfortable challenges with self-esteem or disappointments in love. If you're feeling like nobody likes you or you're tempted by addictive behaviors, you've probably gone way off base. Luckily, this conflict lasts for only a few days and is merely a temporary blip on the screen. Mercury, always restless, is on the move again on Wednesday, June 26, when it leaves Cancer and enters fiery Leo. This is a special sign switch because it marks a time when Mercury is going nowhere fast. A scheduled retrograde in July makes sure that communications will be complicated this summer, because Mercury will spend most of its time going back and forth between fiery Leo and emotionally defensive Cancer. While Mercury is in passionate and grandiose Leo for the next three and a half weeks, you might choose words and language that are overly dramatic and meant to override any opinion but your own. While Mercury is in the sign of the royals, it might be wise to keep in mind these words from Michel de Montaigne: "On the highest throne in the world, we still sit only on our own bottom."

July 1–7

It's eclipse season again and this week includes a Total New Moon Solar Eclipse, two sign changes, and a Mercury retrograde that will bring most events to a stall. On Monday, July 1, Mars makes the first switch when it exchanges Cancer for Leo, where the life force will be burning bright for the next six weeks. But on Tuesday, July 2, a Cancer New Moon that is also a Total Solar Eclipse has something to say about that. The Total Solar Eclipse cancels out any hope of moving forward this week. This New Moon is similar to the Capricorn New Moon Solar Eclipse last January (see January 1–6) in that it's a signpost to put off planting the seeds of any new beginnings until things calm down next week. There's a temporary reprieve on Wednesday, July 3, when Venus moves into sensitive and caring Cancer and relationships and finances switch into a more sympathetic and softer space that will last for the next four weeks. But it's back to a week of no-go on Sunday, July 7, when Mercury goes retrograde until July 31. This second Mercury retrograde of the year (the third is in November) is a time to proceed with caution, but it also comes with benefits that include finding lost objects and getting your money back on purchases that didn't work out. The downside is confusion with communications and information, bugs in electrical devices, and changes in travel plans. It isn't a favorable time to sign any kind of contract without checking and rechecking the fine print. To make things even more confusing, Mercury will be in two different signs during this retrograde. It will spend the first part of the retrograde in fiery Leo and the remainder in emotional Cancer. This is a good time to go back over the last few months to review and evaluate your successes or failures and make any necessary adjustments. It's also a time when lost objects or old friends may suddenly turn up again.

July 8–14

There's no two ways about it: with the Sun involved in two challenging face-offs plus a dangerous square between Mars and Uranus, this is going to be a tough week. So be super-careful and stay away from anything that smacks of risky business. It starts out with a dark cloud on the horizon on Tuesday, July 9, when the Sun makes a once-a-year opposition to Saturn, the law enforcer of the zodiac. This Sun-Saturn combo points to conflicts (past or present) with authority figures and is one of the lowest energetic points of the year. It is also a time to remember that less is more. Although this alone is a good reason to sit tight and wait this one out, there's even more trouble waiting in the wings with the Sun hurtling toward a face-off with Pluto on Sunday, July 14. You'll definitely want to watch your step, because this aspect can bring out obsessive-compulsive behaviors, jealousy, and a strong desire to seek revenge. A sensitive Sun-Neptune trine late on Wednesday, July 10, provides welcome relief in the form of easy escape routes, but it can also overstimulate your imagination—which, given the dire nature of the Sun-Saturn and Sun-Pluto face-offs, might not be a good thing. Be careful to avoid accidents on Thursday, July 11, because a dangerous Mars-Uranus square that day carries an overload of possibilities for shake-ups and even violence. Because Uranus is in earthy Taurus, this square could have a negative impact on global banking or weather patterns. The good news is that this is the only Mars-Uranus square this year. The bad news is that it happens during this already difficult week.

July 15–21

This could be a complicated week, with a Full Moon Lunar Eclipse, Venus under siege, and confusion from Mercury. The Capricorn Full Moon on Tuesday, July 16, falls on the back of a Partial Lunar Eclipse, making this a day when sitting at home with the blinds drawn looks like your best option. This eclipse will have a strong effect on career, businesses, and corporations, so luckily the shadow of this eclipse will not fall over the United States. Things get more complicated when Venus makes a difficult opposition to Saturn on Wednesday, July 17, and then another opposition to Pluto on Sunday, July 21. These two showdowns suggest that this is a week to avoid taking risks in relationships and with your finances, because Venus-Saturn and Venus-Pluto can bring disappointment, jealousy, and crises. Things begin to shift on Thursday, July 18, when Venus trines Neptune. This sensitive and beautiful trine may introduce you to the perfect lover, or you may become involved in a selfless relationship. But just because something looks good is not a guarantee that it's real. Thinking clearly and making good choices will be even more of a challenge on Friday, July 19, because that's when Mercury retrogrades out of Leo to revisit

Cancer for the second time this year. Mercury will remain in Cancer for another three and a half weeks, and this move adds an emotional and defensive element to a communication style that's already compromised. The Sun adds more energy to this sensitive mix when it conjoins Mercury in Cancer on Sunday, July 21.

July 22–28

All things are bright and beautiful this week, with Leo welcoming two planets into its royal warmth and Mars making a successful trine to Jupiter. It starts on Monday, July 22, when the Sun enters Leo and it's time for you or your creations (children, art, music, writing, etc.) to take center stage. The best time of the year to do what you enjoy, to be your own leader, and to be proud of yourself is under the Leo Sun. If you take the opportunity on Wednesday, July 24, to express your feelings to a loved one when Mercury retrogrades back into a conjunction with Venus, your efforts will be richly rewarded. Make sure you're ready to take advantage of another celestial opportunity when Mars trines Jupiter on Thursday, July 25, because this lucky astrological signature practically guarantees the success of any actions taken at this time. This is the second and last time these planets will form a trine this year (the first was in January). Venus follows the Sun into Leo on Saturday, July 27, and this shift gives you an official celestial pass to invite some drama and excitement into your love life and enjoy the heck out of yourself for the next month.

July 29–August 4

Although there will be a lot of turbulence due to two Uranus conflicts disturbing this week's atmosphere, there's also a lucky Leo New Moon and a change in the right direction for Mercury to help ease the pain. The week starts out on Monday, July 29, with a general feeling of uneasiness and uncertainty that comes from Uranus in a challenging square to the Sun. This same square repeats again when Uranus squares Venus on Friday, August 2, but this time the focus is on relationships and finances. This is the second time this year that Uranus has signaled abrupt changes in the political sphere, the environment, and our personal lives by challenging the Sun and Venus. The best way to deal with Uranus's uncontrolled energy is to keep your head down, try to stay on track, and let the winds of change swirl around you, not through you. The Leo New Moon in the middle of the week on Wednesday, July 31, is accompanied by a fortunate trine to Jupiter, the guardian angel of the zodiac. This trine lessens the severity of some of the Uranian chaos. Because the Leo New Moon is a dark time of the lunar month, it's perfect for planting the seeds of something inspiring and creative. With passionate Leo as your motivating force this month, the more drama and excitement the better. Although Mercury is still in Cancer, it comes to the end of its retrograde period on the same day as the Leo New Moon. Now that Mercury is ready to move forward again, confusing communications, digital problems, and transportation issues start to fade away like a bad memory.

August 5–11

With Jupiter making two trines and then changing direction, this week's spotlight is shining brightly on the giant planet's favorite activities: long-distance travel, sports, and your belief system. Mercury also makes a cameo appearance when it changes signs, and Uranus urges us to move our fears off stage for the next four months. On Wednesday, August 7, the Sun makes an especially harmonious trine to Jupiter that brings a blessed period of good luck, prosperity, and abundance. Venus repeats the same performance on Thursday, August 8, when it also trines Jupiter, but this time it brightens up relationships and finances. The three other events happening on Sunday, August 11, include one step forward and two steps back. The first one is a forward motion, when Jupiter goes direct that day. Now that Jupiter is ready to move forward, it's time to make those sweeping changes in your life that you've been thinking about for the last four months when it was retrograde. And because you're dealing with Jupiter, be sure to do them in a really big way. The next event on that same day is Mercury marching into Leo for the second time this year. This double (six weeks) Mercury in Leo energy is due to Mercury's retrograde earlier this summer, and while it does give you another chance to play with words, it could get tiresome if you insist on grandstanding and forget to share the conversational spotlight over the next three weeks. Later that same day, Uranus does a double take as it begins its retrograde period. Uranus is still a dragon even when it's retrograde, but since it's going to be asleep for the next five months, it's a good time to take a break from any fears about universal chaos.

August 12–18

The Aquarius Full Moon highlights this week of minor aspects and one sign change. It all starts late on Tuesday, August 13, when the Leo Sun personifies love and beauty by joining together with Venus, which leads us to the Aquarius Full Moon on Thursday, August 15. This Full Moon is the beginning of a two-week opportunity to be your own leader and see that social groups or political events reach their natural conclusion. Even with Venus in the picture, this could still be a challenge because the Leo Sun/Aquarius Moon axis is stubborn, and although it wants completion, it prefers that others do most of the work. Friday, August 16, is a day to keep calm and carry on, because when Mercury squares Uranus there is a lot of nervous tension in the air that could bring surprising or upsetting news. Nerves calm down the next day, Saturday, August 17, when energetic Mars enters Virgo in the evening and actions become more service-oriented and less aggressive for the next seven weeks. The downside of this combination is that because you're trying so hard to be perfect, you can get prickly and overly critical.

August 19–25

Virgo is the name of the game this week, with a Venus-Mars conjunction and two planets entering the sign of the Virgin. Virgo is the sixth sign of the zodiac and is devoted to serving others and being practically perfect. Virgo refines anything it touches, but it does so at a cost. Virgo is not a "whatever" type of energy; it specifies exactly how something must be done to achieve the best possible result. Because Venus will be in its detriment when it moves into Virgo on Wednesday, August 21, this is a time when you can get picky and moody if love and finances are not perfectly arranged and clean as a whistle. This trend will continue for the next four weeks. The Sun follows Venus into Virgo on

Friday, August 23, and marks the time of the year to prepare yourself for the coming winter by checking in on your diet, your health, and your job in order to modify any areas that aren't working as well as they could. Besides being the worker bees of the zodiac, those born under the sign of the Virgin are gentle and humble souls whose greatest joy is helping others. This energy is doubled the next day, August 24, because that's when Venus and Mars join forces at their only meet-and-greet of the year in Virgo. This is a signal that it's a good time for making adjustments in love or finances. If you pay strict attention to the fine print, there will be some sweet deals to be had.

August 26–September 1

Three trines to Uranus, a New Moon, and a sign change bring a surprisingly happy conclusion to the summer. It all begins on Monday, August 26, when Venus trines Uranus for the second time this year and opens up a time of experimentation with old and new relationships and freedom-loving friendships. The excitement continues as Mars makes its only trine of the year to Uranus on Wednesday, August 28, and although this means it's time to fly your freak flag as high as you want, with this kind of volatile planetary mix it's best not to push your luck by taking unnecessary risks. Communications of all kinds reach a much more practical level when Mercury enters earthy Virgo on Thursday, August 29. For the next three weeks Mercury will be hanging out on its home field, where communications are about the facts and nothing but the facts. You have the ability to solve any problem that comes your way if you can meld Virgo's attention to detail with the Mercury-Uranus trine on Sunday, September 1, which sharpens your intuition. The earthy Virgo New Moon on Friday, August 30, is involved in a harmonious trine with Uranus that can bring happy surprises to your job or to health issues. This Virgo New Moon is a celestial green light that says it's time to plant the seeds of new beginnings in the areas of your work, health, and service to others. This is a week when it will be very easy to make adjustments if you are willing to plan and organize.

September 2–8

Finding your center of gravity might be a challenge this week. There's a lot of celestial noise disturbing the atmosphere, with an unusual number of planets making connections to each other, including four different planets making their last call of the year. Almost every area of life will be under scrutiny because all the planets except Uranus get involved when the Sun, Mercury, and Venus take turns responding to Mars, Jupiter, Saturn, Neptune, and Pluto. It all begins on Monday, September 2 (which is also Labor Day), with Venus in conflict with Jupiter. This square is a warning that if you apply Jupiter's boundless optimism to your personal relationships or the state of your bank account, you could find yourself in big trouble. These same energies are still under siege on Wednesday, September 4, when Venus makes its only opposition of the year to Neptune and triggers confusion between what is real and what is not. Things shift to the positive on Friday, September 6, when Venus makes its last trine of the year to Pluto, offering a clearer and deeper perspective about relationships and the state of your finances. But in spite of this relief, it's still going to be hard to keep your head on straight, because Mercury, the messenger, is busy connecting in three different ways to five different planets! Virgo's compulsion for detail gives way to impulsive Mars when the Sun joins Mercury in Virgo and then they both merge with Mars midweek. The overly spontaneous style of conversation engendered by the Sun-Mercury-Mars trio is a warning not to fall prey to foot-in-the mouth disease. The good part is that this trio is kept in check by trines from Saturn on Thursday and Friday, September 5 and 6. But there are two more potential roadblocks to deal with before the end of the week. The first is a square to Jupiter from Sun-Mercury on Sunday, September 8, which signals a time when it's especially easy to slip up because things look better than they are. The second roadblock is the first and only Mercury-Neptune opposition of the year on Saturday, September 7, which indicates a tendency toward lies, misunderstandings, and confusion. With all these conflicting energies in effect for most of this week, it's best to lay low and avoid making any big decisions. But all's well that end's well, because on Sunday, September 8, Mars trines Saturn for the second and last time this year. If you have somehow managed to keep calm and carry on amid all the chaos, this trine can help make any project or event a huge success.

September 9–15

The agenda this week includes a Pisces Full Moon with a powerful trine, two sign changes, two oppositions, and a square. Idealization is in free flow on Tuesday, September 10, when the Sun opposes Neptune for the first and only time this year. But be aware that this Sun-Neptune showdown has a tendency to erode your self-confidence and you might feel like you have to give everything away. An action-packed square from Mars to Jupiter on Thursday, September 12, is full of forceful energy, but things could get out of control due to that square and the Pisces Full Moon just around the corner on Friday night, September 14. As with the Sun-Neptune opposition, this Pisces Full Moon is filled with smoke and mirrors, which makes it harder to see clearly and finish up projects and end bad habits. But on the positive side, the Pisces Full Moon also features a trine from the Sun to Pluto that provides a path to access your personal power. However, using that power may be a challenge with the opposition from Mars to Neptune on the books later that same day that is accompanied by feelings of weakness and low self-confidence. Things look up on Saturday, September 14, when both Mercury and Venus enter Libra, which is one of the best neighborhoods for Venus. These entries into Libra, which favor diplomacy and fairness, indicate smooth sailing for communications, business partnerships, contracts, and personal relationships and should help to balance out this week's challenges.

September 16–22

A positive change of direction, a powerful trine, and two squares are the headliners this week. Saturn ends its retrograde period and turns direct on Wednesday September 18. This is a signal to take action on the lessons you learned during the retrograde period (starting at the end of last April). Hopefully you've tied up all those loose ends, and now that Saturn is in gear again, it's time to leave the past behind and use Saturn's discipline and constructive energy to move into the future.

A powerful Mars-Pluto trine makes you feel like you can conquer the world on Thursday, September 19. Take good heed of this unique opportunity because this is the only time these two power mongers will be in harmony this year. There are some clouds in the forecast on Saturday, September 21, when an overly optimistic Jupiter squares Neptune for the last time this year. This final fantasy alert brings an end to the cycle of positivity mixed with illusion that has permeated 2019. You may come down with a bad case of the blues on Sunday, September 22, when Mercury squares Saturn. Although this is a signature of depression and a negative outlook, it lasts for only a few days and is the last time these two planets will be in conflict this year.

September 23–29

A change of season and two minor squares top this week's agenda. The Sun enters Libra on Monday, September 23, and marks the first day of fall, or the fall equinox. Libra is the sign of the Scales, and this is one of the two days of balance between light and darkness in the calendar year (the other is the spring equinox). The fall equinox is a celestial reminder to take a moment today and align yourself with the heavens by seeing if all parts of your life are in balance. You can be stingy with love or tight with money on Wednesday, September 25, when Venus makes its last square of the year to Saturn, because this is a kind of Scrooge aspect, where you tend to feel lonely or like you're not getting enough of what you need in terms of love or money. On the other hand, this is a call to buck up and focus on your duties and responsibilities to others. Thursday, September 26, is a good day for getting to the bottom of things because that's when intense Mercury comes into conflict with Pluto. This square marks one last opportunity this year to probe the depths of some deeply hidden secret.

September 30–October 6

This week's agenda includes two sign changes, a change of direction, an opposition, and a square. Venus starts things off late on Monday, September 30, when it squares Pluto for the last time this year. This conflict signals a time when your relationship and your bank account may be challenged by power and control issues, but there are no worries if they are on solid ground. On Wednesday, October 2, Pluto gains strength when it ends its five-month retrograde period. Now that Pluto is back online, it is time to stop reassessing your deepest desires and start acting on them. There are two more significant sign changes the next day, Thursday, October 3, that can have an effect on your actions and your style of communication. The first is when Mercury enters Scorpio, where it will stay not for the usual three weeks but for nine weeks. This extended tour in Scorpio is due to its retrograde in November. During this retrograde in Scorpio, Mercury will also make a rare Transit of the Sun (see November 11). While Mercury is in Scorpio, the style of communication is deeper, edgier, and more intense. Mars enters Libra that same day, but that's a different story because Libra is a place where the assertiveness of Mars is weakened. Libra is so focused on all things being equal that while Mars is visiting the sign of the Scales, it makes it harder to channel your warrior energy and ready yourself to storm the gates. Mars will be making nice instead of war until the middle of November. Thinking processes speed up when Mercury opposes Uranus for the only time late on Sunday, October 6. The only opposition between these two planets this year may cause temporary tensions and anxiety or be an occasion for a bout of genius. Either way, patience and self-discipline will be in short supply.

October 7–13

A virile Aries Full Moon dominates a week where Venus takes a beating from a difficult sign shift and has a tussle with Uranus. When Venus was in Libra last month, relationships were golden, but get ready for things to change on Tuesday, October 8, when Venus enters Scorpio. Traditionally, Scorpio is a tough neighborhood for Venus because Scorpio can be intense, obsessive, jealous, and intent on power struggles and Venus just wants to be nice. Venus is still under the gun on Saturday, October 12, when it opposes Uranus for the only time this year. This face-off between Venus and Uranus can bring excitement to your love life, but it is also very unstable and the final outcome is unpredictable. All in all this is a tough week for relationships and finances. On the other hand, the Aries Full Moon on Sunday, October 13, shines a brave, courageous, and bold light into the darkness. Because the Full Moon is traditionally a time to wind up projects and complete a mission and Aries is all about you, this is the perfect time to reach out and get yourself something you've always wanted. Jupiter's positive connections to both the Sun and the Moon at this lunation adds lucky breaks, blessings, and the promise of success.

October 14–20

A power struggle is the star of this week, with Mercury and Venus standing by with help. A square from the Sun to Pluto on Monday, October 14, brings possibilities for infighting, backbiting, bickering, or hidden manipulations that might involve someone who is your superior. Even though this is the second and last skirmish between these two planets this year, it could still get ugly. Be careful and keep your cool if things don't go your way. Your imagination and creativity will soar when Mercury trines Neptune the next day, Tuesday, October 15, and your sensitivity button is turned on high. If you can manage to keep things in check, a minor sextile from Mercury to Pluto on Saturday, October 19, can help reveal the deeper purpose of an action or reaction, and a grounding sextile from Venus to Saturn on Sunday, October 20, offers a basis to commit to a relationship or your financial situation.

October 21–27

This week starts out on a sweet note with a trine, but things get more challenging as we move toward a difficult New Moon. Love is in the air when Venus trines Neptune on Monday, October 21, so this is the perfect time to relax and focus on romance and creativity. Enjoy this pleasant day because on Wednesday, October 23, you'll be singing a different tune when the Sun enters Scorpio, the sign connected with crises and transformation. This Sun sign shift marks the time of year when the earth prepares for shorter days and colder weather by drawing its life force downward so that trees and plants lose their leaves. On a personal level it's the time to go deep inside and get rid of your physical, emotional, and psychological dead leaves so you will be ready to move forward toward your personal springtime. Crisis is one way to get rid of the waste, and healing treatments or therapy are also options. Whatever method you choose, Scorpio's goal is always transformation. A difficult Scorpio New Moon on Sunday, October 27, continues the same transformational theme. The first challenge is a frustrating square from war-loving Mars to disciplined Saturn that means you have to work harder than ever to get what you want, followed by a Sun-Uranus opposition late that night that can bring anything from separations and nervous tension to exciting encounters and unexpected surprises. The dark quiet of the Scorpio New Moon is the best time of year to use a crisis to transform yourself by clearing out any person, possession, attitude, bad habit, or job that is no longer a viable part of your life in order to make an intention for a new beginning.

October 28–November 3

Two events are moving things backward this week. The first one is the Mercury retrograde and the other is the shift in clock time from Daylight back to Standard Time, when we "gain" an hour. A positive sign shift for Venus and a nice connection with Mercury will ease some of the difficulties. On Wednesday, October 30, Mercury and Venus join together for the last time this year. This connection will have a brief but positive influence on real estate because it favors buying and selling. There might be more tricks than treats on Halloween this year because Mercury begins its last retrograde of the year on Thursday, October 31. Mercury retrograde provides us with a three-week time-out to go back over the last few months to review and evaluate our successes and failures and make any necessary adjustments. It's also a time when lost objects or old friends may suddenly turn up again. The downside is confusion with communications and information, bugs in electrical devices, and changes in travel plans. It isn't a favorable time to sign any kind of contract without checking and rechecking the fine print. This retrograde means that this year Mercury's tour in Scorpio is extended from October 3 to December 9. There's a collective sigh of a relief on All Saints' Day on Friday, November 1, when Venus leaves Scorpio and gallops into Sagittarius. This sign shift brings a note of optimism and confidence to relationships and finances as well as a desire to take risks and push the boundaries for the next month. It's also that time of the year to "fall back," because Daylight Saving Time ends at 2:00 a.m. local time on Sunday, November 3.

November 4–10

Election Day could be tricky this year with a difficult square dominating the skies midweek, but the Sun and Mercury are standing in the wings with offers of help. The polls or the results of the voting could become a battleground on Tuesday November 5 (Election Day in the US) because the day coincides with a Mars-Pluto square that doesn't have much to recommend it except difficult confrontations and power struggles. Watch for breaking news on how this conflict plays out and affects the elections this year. This square is a warning to stay away from trouble spots and avoid all potentially dangerous situations. Imagination and creativity will be running high when the Scorpio Sun trines Neptune on Friday, November 8, but this aspect is tempered by a call for law and order when the Sun makes a sextile to rule-loving Saturn the same day. That's also the day of the last Saturn-Neptune sextile of the year, which has the potential for the material and spiritual worlds to unite. This is a unique opportunity, because the next time these two planets meet like this will be in 2031.

November 11–17

Veterans Day on Monday, November 11, will be remembered as a special day this year because it is also home to a rare Transit of Mercury. This is the day when Mercury can be seen for approximately five hours as a little black dot crossing over the face of the Sun. Although those in North America will be in a favorable position to view this transit, you will need to use a telescope because Mercury is so small. On average, there are thirteen transits of Mercury each century. The next times Mercury will transit the Sun are in 2032 and 2039. Although it may have little or no effect on a natal horoscope, a Transit of Mercury can still reveal important information that may include warnings of large-scale weather disasters and disturbances to travel plans. Things could get complicated because Mercury is retrograde as well as in Scorpio, which is a dangerous mixture of misunderstandings and crises. The

69

Transit of Mercury is a prelude to the Taurus Full Moon on Tuesday, November 12. This Full Moon is a time when the unconscious comes to light and marks the next two weeks as a good time to wind down artistic projects, complete garden plans, consolidate your savings, and structure your portfolio.

November 18–24

This is a week to stay on your toes, because the Sun and Mars change signs, Mercury ends its retrograde, Venus gets hitched to Jupiter, and Uranus poses a threat. Late on Monday, November 18, Mars, always the competitor, gains more firepower and energy when it enters the intense field of Scorpio. This is the neighborhood where Scorpio has home-team advantage, because it's one of Mars's strongest positions (Aries is the other). Although this switch gives the ability to act on your deepest desires, the tricky part is that when Mars is in Scorpio, it is passive-aggressive. With this in play, the way to achieve your goals is by indirect means and avoiding direct confrontation. Mars will be in this position until January 3, 2020. There's a big hurray on Wednesday, November 20, when the last Mercury retrograde of the year comes to an end. Even though Mercury will be in Scorpio until December 9, now that it is in forward motion, communications, commerce, and travel plans will start to return to normal. The Sun exchanges Scorpio's dark intensity for an optimistic view of the world at large when it enters Sagittarius on Friday, November 22. This switch is an indication that it's time to look at the big picture. Because the energy of Sagittarius is as flexible as it is fiery, many different things will catch your fancy during the next month. The trick is to choose one and stick to it. Sagittarius is a hopeful time of the year that calls on us to be joyful and to express our faith in life and show charity to others less fortunate. The week ends with two very different messages. The first is when Venus makes a happy connection with Jupiter in Sagittarius on Sunday, November 24. Although Venus conjunct Jupiter is a traditional signature of good luck and happiness, there's a dangerous storm brewing later that day when Mars opposes Uranus for the only time this year. This connection between a powerful, militaristic Mars and unpredictable Uranus increases the potential for accidents, violence, or disturbances in weather patterns. This opposition is a warning that everything is not okay and that the boundless optimism and devil-may-care attitude of Sagittarius needs a good dose of old-fashioned common sense.

November 25–December 1

A New Moon that moves things forward, a sign change for Venus, a wake-up call for Neptune, and insightful thoughts and words are all on tap for this Thanksgiving week. When Venus enters Capricorn on Monday, November 25, it casts a darker and more serious light on things that relate to love, money, art, and beauty. This sign switch also means that for the next month you're going to have to be super-responsible and put some extra elbow grease into getting what you really want. The darkness and quiet of the Sagittarius New Moon on Tuesday, November 26, reminds us again to look to the bright side of life and share our abundance with those less fortunate. It's also a call to plant the seeds of a new start by expanding our horizons through sports, foreign travel, or new philosophies. The next day, Wednesday, November 27, Neptune shifts into forward gear, as it turns direct for the first time since June. As Neptune starts to wake up from its five-month nap, it's still dreamtime, but it's also a call to work on insights or visions that were revealed while Neptune was at rest. Your intuition will be on high alert on Thanksgiving Day, Thursday, November 28, because that's when Mercury trines sensitive Neptune for the fourth and last time this year. This aspect can inspire eloquence or make you overly sensitive to the opinions of others.

December 2–8

Jupiter dominates the first week of December as it moves into a new sign that has important consequences for the future. There's also the possibility of brain fog when the Sun gets into a dispute with Neptune. Jupiter enters Capricorn on Monday, December 2, and will remain there until December 2020. In classical astrology, Jupiter is considered to be in its "fall" in this cardinal earth sign. Things get awkward when a planet is in its fall, and when Jupiter is in Capricorn, its path to expansion, joy, and good luck is severely restricted by Capricorn's love of conformity and cautious, conservative philosophy. In Hindu astrology, Jupiter is called "guru" or teacher, and even at its worst, Jupiter will still bring some good fortune to those who work for it. The most significant effect of this move is that it means that Jupiter and Saturn will be conjunct in December 2020. Because Jupiter and Saturn only come together every twenty years, they are known as the "rulers of the age." Some food for thought is that the last time Jupiter and Saturn were conjunct was in Taurus in 2000, which was, of course, right before 9/11, which changed the world. Venus and Mars make a mild but pleasant sextile on Tuesday, December 3, that could unite love and sex in a positive way. A square from the Sun to Neptune on Sunday, December 8, could result in a low-energy day of confusion or disappointment. This is a good day to relax, avoid high-stress activities, and focus on your creativity and dream life.

December 9–15

An imaginative Gemini Full Moon dominates a week that includes a sign change for Mercury, two unique trines, and a complicated conjunction for Venus. Mercury is the first planet out of the gate on Monday, December 9, when after nine weeks it finally takes leave of Scorpio and moves into Sagittarius. This sign change shifts communications from dark to light, as the focused and intense style of Scorpio is exchanged for the expansive and sweeping style of Sagittarius. Sagittarius types of communication use the broadest possible stroke without worrying about filling in the details. This trend will continue for the next three weeks. The Gemini Full Moon late on Wednesday, December 11, lights up the darkness with unconscious energy for completing routine tasks and making final decisions about matters that concern siblings, roommates, or neighbors. A square from Neptune adds a touch of martyr/victim to this Full Moon and also a warning that if you get too far away from reality you could fall off the edge of the cliff. Although the Mars-Neptune trine on Friday, December 13, is not a high-energy aspect, it does enhance the nurturing aspect of this Full Moon and could be a gift for teachers and spiritual seekers. This is a "last chance" trine because it's the second and final trine Mars and Neptune will make this year. Later that same day, a charismatic and sexual Venus-Pluto conjunction comes with the short-lived potential for a large dose of jealousy and obsession. But the week ends on a high note on Sunday, December 15, when Jupiter makes a trine to Uranus. This kind of positive alignment gives you better-than-average odds that you will be wildly successful if you break out of your normal routine and try something new. This Jupiter-Uranus trine is a celestial gift that won't come around again until 2028.

December 16–22

The spotlight this week is on the last seasonal change of the year, the winter solstice. The winter solstice marks the return of the light and the days getting longer and is one of the four major turning points in the astrological calendar. The astrological basis for the winter solstice is the entry of the Sun into Capricorn on Saturday, December 21. This passage marks the time in the Northern Hemisphere when the Sun reaches its lowest point in the sky and produces the shortest day and longest night of the year. The good news is that after December 21, the days will begin to get longer. During the month when the Sun will be in Capricorn, your outward focus will be tuned to your career or your standing in the community, with an emphasis on hunkering down and committing. A positive once-a-year sextile between Mars and Saturn on Thursday, December 19, is a shot in the arm to make things happen. Late that same day, Venus makes a sign switch as it exchanges Capricorn for Aquarius. As a fixed air sign, Aquarius is a cool cookie, emotionally detached and focused on personal independence. This is why you might be more attracted to impersonal group interactions than intense personal relationships for the next four weeks while Venus is visiting Aquarius. The same theme is echoed on Sunday, December 22, when Venus makes its last square of the year to Uranus, which also favors personal freedom over intimacy.

December 23–29

A New Moon Solar Eclipse, a trine, and a joyful conjunction grace this Christmas week. The Sun makes a trine to Uranus on Christmas Eve that promises an original and unique holiday this year, and a special Capricorn New Moon that is also a Solar Eclipse falls on Christmas

Day. Because lucky Jupiter joins the eclipse, it looks like prosperity and good fortune are in this year's holiday forecast. Remember that a New Moon that includes a Solar Eclipse is *not* a good time to plant the seeds of a new beginning. This Solar Eclipse is an annular eclipse, which means that the edge of the Sun will remain visible as a ring around the Moon. Mercury ends the year by making its last movement into Capricorn on Saturday, December 28. Because this shift is centered on methodical thinking and structured ideas, this is a good week to have a sit-down with yourself and figure out your goals for next year.

December 30–31

This year ends on an upbeat note with two gentle, nonthreatening pairings. The first is on Monday, December 30, when a trine between Mercury and Uranus opens the mind to exciting ideas that include new technologies and also new groups of friends. The last aspect of the year, a sweet sextile between the Sagittarius Sun and the Libra Moon on New Year's Eve, suggests that as this year comes to an end, one way to find peace with yourself and others is to surrender to the present, let go of the past, and have faith in the future.

About the Astrologer

Pam Ciampi is a Certified Professional Astrologer (ISAR) who has been in private practice since 1975. She is president emeritus of the San Diego Astrological Society and past president of the San Diego chapter of the National Council for Geocosmic Research. Besides writing the weekly forecasts for *Llewellyn's Daily Planetary Guide* since 2007, she is also the author of several astrological almanacs on gardening by the Moon and has contributed articles to national astrology publications. In 2017 she moved back to the East Coast to be closer to her family.

Pam's other interests include art history, cooking, music, and gardening. After 42 years of working with the most amazing clients all over the world, Pam is in semi-retirement and is only available to take on a limited number of personal clients. Contact her at pamciampi@gmail.com or www.pciampi-astrology.com.

Finding Opportunity Periods

by Jim Shawvan

There are times when the most useful things you can do are ordinary tasks such as laundry, cooking, listening to music, reading, learning, or meditating. There are other times when the universe opens the gates of opportunity. Meetings, decisions, or commitments during these "Opportunity Periods" can lead to new and positive developments in your life. Most people are unaware of these subtle changes in the energies, so they wind up doing laundry when they could be signing an important contract, or they go out to try to meet a new sweetheart when the energies for such a thing are totally blocked.

I developed the Opportunity Periods system over more than thirty years, as I tested first one hypothesis and then another in real life. In about 1998, when I studied classical astrology with Lee Lehman, the system got some added zing, including William Lilly's idea that the Moon when void-of-course in the signs of the Moon and Jupiter "performeth somewhat." The signs of the Moon and Jupiter are Taurus, Cancer, Sagittarius, and Pisces. For those who want to understand the details of the system, they are explained here. If you simply want to use the system, all the information you need is on the calendar pages (you don't need to learn the technicalities).

An Opportunity Period (OP) is a period in which the aspects of the transiting Moon to other transiting planets show no interference with the free flow of decision and action.

Opportunity Periods apply to everyone in the world all at once; although, if the astrological influences on your own chart are putting blocks in your path, you may not be able to use every OP to the fullest. Nevertheless, you are always better off taking important actions and making crucial decisions during an Opportunity Period.

Signs of the Moon and Jupiter

Taurus: the Moon's exaltation
Cancer: the Moon's domicile and Jupiter's exaltation
Sagittarius: Jupiter's fiery domicile
Pisces: Jupiter's watery domicile

Steps to Find Your Opportunity Periods

Under Sun's Beams

Step 1: Determine whether the Moon is "under Sun's beams"; that is, less than 17 degrees from the Sun. If it is, go to step 7. If not, continue to step 2.

Moon Void-of-Course

Step 2: Determine when the Moon goes void-of-course (v/c). The Moon is said to be void-of-course from the time it makes the last Ptolemaic aspect (conjunction, sextile, square, trine, or opposition) in a sign until it enters the next sign.

In eight of the twelve signs of the zodiac, Moon-void periods are NOT Opportunity Periods. In the other four signs, however, they are! According to seventeenth-century astrologer William Lilly, the Moon in the signs of the Moon and Jupiter "performeth somewhat." Lee Lehman says that she has taken this to the bank many times—and so have I.

Stressful or Easy Aspect

Step 3: Determine whether the aspect on which the Moon goes void is a stressful or an easy aspect. Every square is stressful, and every trine and every sextile is easy. Conjunctions and oppositions require judgment according to the nature of the planet the Moon is aspecting, and according to your individual ability to cope with the energies of that planet. For example, the Moon applying to a conjunction of Jupiter, Venus, or Mercury is easy, whereas, for most purposes, the Moon applying to a conjunction of Saturn, Mars, Neptune, Pluto, or Uranus is stressful. However, if you are a person for whom Uranus or Pluto is a familiar and more or less comfortable energy, you may find that the period before the Moon's conjunction to that planet is an Opportunity Period for you. (Since this is true for relatively few people, such periods are not marked as OPs in this book.)

Oppositions can work if the Moon is applying to an opposition of Jupiter, Venus, Mercury, or the Sun (just before the Full Moon). The Moon applying to a conjunction with the Sun (New Moon) presents a whole set of issues on its own. See step 7.

Easy Equals Opportunity

Step 4: If the aspect on which the Moon goes void is an easy aspect, there is an Opportunity Period before the void period. If the aspect on which the Moon goes void is a stressful aspect, there is no Opportunity Period preceding the void period in that sign. To determine the beginning of the Opportunity Period, find the last stressful aspect the Moon makes in the sign. The Opportunity Period runs from the last stressful aspect to the last aspect (assuming that the last aspect is an easy one). If the Moon makes no stressful aspects at all while in the sign, then the Opportunity Period begins as soon as the Moon enters the sign, and ends at the last aspect.

When Is an Aspect Over?

Step 5: When is an aspect over? There are three different answers to this question, and I recommend observation to decide. I also recommend caution.

- An aspect is over (in electional astrology) as soon as it is no longer exact. For example, if the Moon's last stressful aspect in a sign is a square to Saturn at 1:51 p.m., the Opportunity Period (if there is one) would be considered to begin immediately. This is the way the Opportunity Periods are shown in this book.

- Lee Lehman says an aspect is effective (for electional purposes) until it is no longer partile. An aspect is said to be partile if the two planets are in the same degree numerically. For example, a planet at 0° Aries 00' 00" is in partile trine to a planet at 0° Leo 59' 59", but it is not in partile conjunction to a planet at 29° Pisces 59' 59", even though the orb of the conjunction is only one second of arc ($\frac{1}{3,600}$) of a degree.

- An aspect is effective until the Moon has separated from the exact aspect by a full degree, which takes about two hours. This is the most cautious viewpoint. If you have doubts about the wisdom of signing a major contract while the Moon is still within one degree of a nasty aspect, then for your own peace of mind you should give it two hours, to get the one-degree separating orb.

Translating Light and Translating Darkness

Step 6: One should avoid starting important matters when the Moon is translating light from a stressful aspect with a malefic planet to an ostensibly easy aspect with another malefic planet—or even a series of such aspects uninterrupted by any aspects to benefic planets. I refer to this as "translating darkness." Translation of light is a concept used primarily in horary astrology, and it is discussed in great detail in books and on websites on that subject. For example, the Moon's last difficult aspect is a square to Saturn, and there is an apparent Opportunity Period because the Moon's next aspect is a trine to Mars, on which the Moon goes void-of-course. The problem is this: the Moon is translating light from one malefic to another, and this vitiates what would otherwise be an Opportunity Period. The same would be true if the sequence were, for example, Moon square Saturn, then Moon trine Mars, then Moon sextile Neptune—an unbroken series of malefics.

For the purpose of this system, we may regard all of the following planets as malefics: Mars, Saturn, Uranus, Neptune, and Pluto. I can almost hear the howls of protest from the folks who believe there is no such thing as a malefic planet or a bad aspect. On the level of spiritual growth, that is doubtless true, but this book is meant to be used to make your everyday life easier. Anyone who urges others to suffer more than absolutely necessary in the name of spirituality is indulging in great spiritual arrogance themselves.

New Moon, Balsamic Phase, and Cazimi Notes

Step 7: Here are some notes on the period around the New Moon: waxing, waning, Balsamic, under beams, combust, and Cazimi.

As it separates from conjunction with the Sun (New Moon) and moves toward opposition (Full Moon), the Moon is said to be waxing, or increasing in light. Traditionally the period of the waxing Moon is considered favorable for electional purposes.

Then after the Full Moon, as the Moon applies to a conjunction with the Sun, the Moon is said to be waning, or decreasing in light. Traditionally this period is regarded as a poor choice for electional purposes, and the closer the Moon gets to the Sun, the worse it is said to be. In practice, I find that problems seem to occur only as the Moon gets very close to the Sun.

When the Moon is applying to a conjunction with the Sun (New Moon) and is less than 45 degrees away from the Sun, the Moon is said to be in its Balsamic phase. This phase is associated with giving things up and is considered especially unfavorable for starting things you wish to increase.

Any planet within 17 degrees of the Sun is said to be under Sun's beams. Traditionally this weakens the planet, particularly for electional and horary purposes.

Any planet within 8 degrees of the Sun is said to be combust. Traditionally this weakens the planet even more, particularly in electional and horary work.

Any planet whose center is within 17 minutes of arc of the center of the Sun in celestial longitude is said to be Cazimi. Oddly, this is considered the highest form of accidental dignity. In other words, a planet is thought to be weak when under Sun's beams, weaker still when combust, but—surprisingly—very powerful and benefic when Cazimi!

The average speed of the Moon is such that it remains Cazimi for about an hour; that is, half an hour before and half an hour after the exact conjunction with the Sun (New Moon). Other things being equal, you can use the Cazimi Moon to start something if you really want it to succeed.

However, please do not attempt to use the Cazimi Moon at the time of a Solar Eclipse, nor if the Moon is moving from the Cazimi into a stressful aspect. Cazimi is powerful, but it cannot override the difficulties shown by a Solar Eclipse, nor those shown by, say, the Moon's application to a square of Saturn.

If you really need to start something around the time of the New Moon, and you cannot use the Cazimi, it is a good idea to wait until the first Opportunity Period after the Moon has begun waxing. Even if the Moon is still under Sun's beams at that time, it is better than starting the new project while the Moon is still waning. However, if you can reasonably do so, it is best to wait for the first Opportunity Period after the Moon is no longer under Sun's beams; that is, after the Moon has separated from the Sun by at least 17 degrees. For the principles to use at that time, see step 2.

About the Astrologers

Jim Shawvan developed the system of Opportunity Periods over a period of three decades, out of his interest in electional astrology— the art of picking times for important actions such as getting married, opening a business, or incorporating a company (or even matters of only medium importance). Jim began the study of astrology in 1969; he teaches classes in predictive astrology and has lectured numerous times to the San Diego Astrological Society and other astrological groups and conferences.

Jim's articles have appeared in the *Mountain Astrologer* and other publications, a number of which are linked at his website, www.jshawvan.homestead.com. He predicted the delay in the results of the US presidential election of 2000; and in early 2001 he predicted that, in response to anti-American terrorism, the US would be at war in Afghanistan in the first two years of George W. Bush's presidency.

Jim studied cultural anthropology and structural linguistics at Cornell University, and later became a computer programmer and systems analyst. From 1989 to 1997 he was the technical astrologer at Neil Michelsen's Astro Communications Services, handling the most difficult questions and orders. He holds the Certified Astrological Professional certificate issued by the International Society for Astrological Research (ISAR).

Jim offers consultations in the areas of electional, horary, karmic, natal, predictive, relationship, relocation, and travel astrology. Consultations are done by phone or in person, and are taped. The client receives both the recording and the charts.

Contact Jim Shawvan and Right Place Consulting at jshawvan@ yahoo.com or www.jshawvan.homestead.com.

Paula Belluomini, CAP, began studying astrology as a teenager while living in Brazil. Growing up, she became fascinated with the movement of the stars and was passionate about learning how their positions affected life on Earth. She immersed herself in all the literature she could find on the subject, and moved to Southern California in the 1990s to continue her studies through independent coursework.

Paula completed the steps required to become a Certified Astrological Professional (CAP) by the International Society for Astrological

Research (ISAR), including the Astrological Consulting Skills Course in Chicago (ISAR 2009), the Competency Test in New Orleans (UAC 2012), and the ethics training course. She was introduced to Jim Shawvan's Opportunity Periods system in Anaheim (ISAR 2003), and has been following his work ever since.

Paula's main areas of expertise and interest include modern astrology with a psychological approach and relationship analysis, as well as electional, mundane, and traditional astrology. More recently, horary astrology has piqued her interest because of its practicality and ability to answer questions in a more objective way.

In addition to providing astrology consulting services, Paula writes daily posts about current astrological events, participates in study groups, and continues educating herself on the stars.

Aside from astrology, Paula has a degree in marketing and is an experienced graphic and web designer who often creates artwork with astrological themes. For more information, please visit her website at ocastrology.com.

Business Guide

Collections

Try to make collections on days when your Sun is well aspected. Avoid days when Mars or Saturn are aspected. If possible, the Moon should be in a cardinal sign: Aries, Cancer, Libra, or Capricorn. It is more difficult to collect when the Moon is in Taurus or Scorpio.

Employment, Promotion

Choose a day when your Sun is favorably aspected or the Moon is in your tenth house. Good aspects of Venus or Jupiter are beneficial.

Loans

Moon in the first and second quarters favors the lender; in the third and fourth it favors the borrower. Good aspects of Jupiter or Venus to the Moon are favorable to both, as is Moon in Leo, Sagittarius, Aquarius, or Pisces.

New Ventures

Things usually get off to a better start during the increase of the Moon. If there is impatience, anxiety, or deadlock, it can often be broken at the Full Moon. Agreements can be reached then.

Partnerships

Agreements and partnerships should be made on a day that is favorable to both parties. Mars, Neptune, Pluto, and Saturn should not be square or opposite the Moon. It is best to make an agreement or partnership when the Moon is in a mutable sign, especially Gemini or Virgo. The other signs are not favorable, with the possible exception of Leo or Capricorn. Begin partnerships when the Moon is increasing in light, as this is a favorable time for starting new ventures.

Public Relations

The Moon rules the public, so this must be well aspected, particularly by the Sun, Mercury, Uranus, or Neptune.

Selling

Selling is favored by good aspects of Venus, Jupiter, or Mercury to the Moon. Avoid aspects to Saturn. Try to get the planetary ruler of your product well aspected by Venus, Jupiter, or the Moon.

Signing Important Papers

Sign contracts or agreements when the Moon is increasing in a fruitful sign. Avoid days when Mars, Saturn, Neptune, or Pluto are afflicting the Moon. Don't sign anything if your Sun is badly afflicted.

Calendar Pages

How to Use Your *Daily Planetary Guide*

Both Eastern and Pacific times are given in the datebook. The Eastern times are listed in the left-hand column. The Pacific times are in the right-hand column in bold typeface. Note that adjustments have been made for Daylight Saving Time. The void-of-course Moon is listed to the right of the daily aspect at the exact time it occurs. It is indicated by "☽ v/c." On days when it occurs for only one time zone and not the other, it is indicated next to the appropriate column and then repeated on the next day for the other time zone. Note that the monthly ephemerides in the back of the book are shown for midnight Greenwich Mean Time (GMT). Opportunity Periods are designated by the letters "OP." See page 75 for a detailed discussion on how to use Opportunity Periods.

Symbol Key

Planets/	☉	Sun	♃	Jupiter
Asteroids	☽	Moon	♄	Saturn
	☿	Mercury	♅	Uranus
	♀	Venus	♆	Neptune
	♂	Mars	♇	Pluto
	⚷	Chiron		

Signs	♈	Aries	♎	Libra
	♉	Taurus	♏	Scorpio
	♊	Gemini	♐	Sagittarius
	♋	Cancer	♑	Capricorn
	♌	Leo	♒	Aquarius
	♍	Virgo	♓	Pisces

Aspects	☌	Conjunction (0°)	△	Trine (120°)
	✶	Sextile (60°)	⚻	Quincunx (150°)
	☐	Square (90°)	☍	Opposition (180°)

Motion	℞	Retrograde	D	Direct

Moon Phase	●	New Moon	◑	2nd Quarter
	○	Full Moon	◐	4th Quarter

31 Mon
4th ♏
New Year's Eve
OP: After Moon enters Scorpio on Sunday until v/c Moon on Tuesday. Pay attention to your intuition.

☽♏ ⚹ ☉♑	2:46 pm	**11:46 am**
☽♏ ⚹ ♄♑	5:09 pm	**2:09 pm**
♂ enters ♈	9:20 pm	**6:20 pm**
☽♏ △ ♆♓	10:10 pm	**7:10 pm**

1 Tue
4th ♏
New Year's Day
Kwanzaa ends

☽♏ ⚹ ♀♑	10:19 am	**7:19 am**
☽♏ ♂ ♀♏	5:26 pm	**2:26 pm** ☽ v/c
☽♏ △ ⚷♓		**9:30 pm**
☉♑ ♂ ♄♑		**9:50 pm**
☽♏ ⊼ ♅♈		**10:20 pm**

2 Wed
4th ♏

☽♏ △ ⚷♓	12:30 am	
☉♑ ♂ ♄♑	12:50 am	
☽♏ ⊼ ♅♈	1:20 am	
☽ enters ♐	3:58 am	**12:58 am**
☽♐ △ ♂♈	5:41 am	**2:41 am**

3 Thu
4th ♐
OP: After Moon squares Neptune today until Moon enters Capricorn on Friday. The Moon in Sagittarius is very positive.

☽♐ ♂ ♃♐	3:23 am	**12:23 am**
☽♐ □ ♆♓	7:00 am	**4:00 am**
☿♐ □ ⚷♓	5:42 pm	**2:42 pm**
☿♐ △ ♅♈		**9:13 pm**

☿♐ △ ♅♈	12:13 am		
☽♐ □ ⚷♓	10:24 am	**7:24 am**	
☽♐ △ ♅♈	11:10 am	**8:10 am**	
☽♐ ☌ ☿♐	12:41 pm	**9:41 am**	☽ v/c
☽ enters ♑	1:55 pm	**10:55 am**	
☉♑ ⚹ ♆♓	2:57 pm	**11:57 am**	
☽♑ □ ♂♈	7:05 pm	**4:05 pm**	
☿ enters ♑	10:40 pm	**7:40 pm**	

Fri 4
4th ♐

♀♏ △ ⚷♓	1:00 pm	**10:00 am**	
☽♑ ☌ ♄♑	1:32 pm	**10:32 am**	
☽♑ ⚹ ♆♓	6:01 pm	**3:01 pm**	
☽♑ ☌ ☉♑	8:28 pm	**5:28 pm**	
♀♏ ⚻ ♅♈	9:28 pm	**6:28 pm**	

Sat 5
4th ♑
Solar Eclipse | ● New Moon 15 ♑ 25

☽♑ ☌ ♇♑	7:12 am	**4:12 am**	
♅D	3:27 pm	**12:27 pm**	
☽♑ ⚹ ⚷♓	10:17 pm	**7:17 pm**	
☽♑ □ ♅♈	10:56 pm	**7:56 pm**	
☽♑ ⚹ ♀♏		**10:20 pm**	☽ v/c
☽ enters ♒		**10:46 pm**	

Sun 6
1st ♑
Uranus direct

Eastern Time plain / **Pacific Time bold**

DECEMBER 2018

S	M	T	W	T	F	S
						1
2	3	4	5	6	7	8
9	10	11	12	13	14	15
16	17	18	19	20	21	22
23	24	25	26	27	28	29
30	31					

JANUARY

S	M	T	W	T	F	S
		1	2	3	4	5
6	7	8	9	10	11	12
13	14	15	16	17	18	19
20	21	22	23	24	25	26
27	28	29	30	31		

FEBRUARY

S	M	T	W	T	F	S
					1	2
3	4	5	6	7	8	9
10	11	12	13	14	15	16
17	18	19	20	21	22	23
24	25	26	27	28		

7 Mon
1st ♑

OP: After Moon sextiles Mars today until v/c Moon on Wednesday. Good for innovative work with the Moon just out from under-the-beams.

☽♑ ⚹ ♀♏	1:20 am		☽ v/c
☽ enters ♒	1:46 am	
♀ enters ♐	6:18 am	**3:18 am**
☽♒ ⚹ ♂♈	10:42 am	**7:42 am**

8 Tue
1st ♒

| ☽♒ ⚹ ♃♐ | 4:44 am | **1:44 am** |
| ☿♑ □ ♂♈ | 5:05 am | **2:05 am** |

9 Wed
1st ♒

☽♒ ⚹ ♅♈	11:53 am	**8:53 am** ☽ v/c
☽ enters ♓	2:44 pm	**11:44 am**
☽♓ □ ♀♐	8:09 pm	**5:09 pm**

10 Thu
1st ♓

☽♓ ⚹ ☿♑	7:16 am	**4:16 am**
☽♓ ⚹ ♄♑	4:13 pm	**1:13 pm**
☽♓ □ ♃♐	6:48 pm	**3:48 pm**
☽♓ ☌ ♆♓	7:47 pm	**4:47 pm**

☉♑ ☌ ♇♑	6:38 am	**3:38 am**	
☽♓ ⚹ ♇♑	9:11 am	**6:11 am**	
☽♓ ⚹ ☉♑	9:25 am	**6:25 am**	☽ v/c
☽♓ ☌ ⚷♓		**9:09 pm**	

FRI 11
1st ♓

OP: After Moon sextiles Pluto today (see "Translating Darkness" on page 78) until Moon enter Aries on Saturday. Best for active contemplation and the arts.

☽♓ ☌ ⚷♓	12:09 am	
☽ enters ♈	3:18 am	**12:18 am**
☽♈ △ ♀♐	2:20 pm	**11:20 am**
☽♈ ☌ ♂♈	7:12 pm	**4:12 pm**

SAT 12
1st ♓

☽♈ □ ☿♑	4:05 am	**1:05 am**
☽♈ □ ♄♑	4:36 am	**1:36 am**
☽♈ △ ♃♐	7:31 am	**4:31 am**
☿♑ ☌ ♄♑	8:31 am	**5:31 am**
♃♐ □ ♆♓	1:58 pm	**10:58 am**
☽♈ □ ♇♑	8:28 pm	**5:28 pm**
☽♈ □ ☉♑		**10:46 pm**

SUN 13
1st ♈
◐ 2nd Quarter 23 ♈ 48 (Pacific)

Eastern Time plain / **Pacific Time bold**

DECEMBER 2018

S	M	T	W	T	F	S
						1
2	3	4	5	6	7	8
9	10	11	12	13	14	15
16	17	18	19	20	21	22
23	24	25	26	27	28	29
30	31					

JANUARY

S	M	T	W	T	F	S
		1	2	3	4	5
6	7	8	9	10	11	12
13	14	15	16	17	18	19
20	21	22	23	24	25	26
27	28	29	30	31		

FEBRUARY

S	M	T	W	T	F	S
					1	2
3	4	5	6	7	8	9
10	11	12	13	14	15	16
17	18	19	20	21	22	23
24	25	26	27	28		

14 MON
1st ♈

◗ 2nd Quarter 23 ♈ 48 (Eastern)

OP: After Moon enters Taurus today until Moon enters Gemini on Wednesday. Long OP to get practical work done, but between two eclipses try not to make any major decisions.

☽♈□☉♑	1:46 am		
☿♑⚹♆♓	8:13 am	**5:13 am**	
☽♈☌♅♈	10:56 am	**7:56 am**	☽ v/c
☽ enters ♉	1:31 pm	**10:31 am**	

15 TUE
2nd ♉

☽♉⚻♀♐	5:05 am	**2:05 am**
☽♉△♄♑	1:50 pm	**10:50 am**
☽♉⚹♆♓	4:15 pm	**1:15 pm**
☽♉⚻♃♐	4:54 pm	**1:54 pm**
☽♉△☿♑	8:30 pm	**5:30 pm**

16 WED
2nd ♉

☽♉△♀♑	4:17 am	**1:17 am**	
☽♉△☉♑	1:34 pm	**10:34 am**	☽ v/c
☽♉⚹⚷♓	5:30 pm	**2:30 pm**	
☽ enters ♊	8:00 pm	**5:00 pm**	

17 THU
2nd ♊

OP: After Moon opposes Jupiter today until v/c Moon on Friday. Fine for any purpose, but same eclipse warning as for last Monday.

☽♊☍♀♐	2:54 pm	**11:54 am**
☽♊⚹♂♈	3:32 pm	**12:32 pm**
☽♊⚻♄♑	7:02 pm	**4:02 pm**
☽♊□♆♓	8:56 pm	**5:56 pm**
☽♊☍♃♐	10:10 pm	**7:10 pm**

☽♊ ⚻ ☿♑	7:19 am	**4:19 am**	
☽♊ ⚻ ♇♑	8:10 am	**5:10 am**	
♀♐ △ ♂♈	11:49 am	**8:49 am**	
☿♑ ☌ ♇♑	3:03 pm	**12:03 pm**	
☉♑ ⚹ ⚷♓	7:57 pm	**4:57 pm**	
☽♊ □ ⚷♓	8:30 pm	**5:30 pm**	
☉♑ □ ♅♈	8:31 pm	**5:31 pm**	
☽♊ ⚹ ♅♈	8:32 pm	**5:32 pm**	☽ v/c
☽♊ ⚻ ☉♑	8:32 pm	**5:32 pm**	
☽ enters ♋	10:44 pm	**7:44 pm**	

FRI 18
2nd ♊

☽♋ □ ♂♈	7:28 pm	**4:28 pm**	
☽♋ ⚻ ♀♐	8:24 pm	**5:24 pm**	
☽♋ ☍ ♄♑	8:48 pm	**5:48 pm**	
☽♋ △ ♆♓	10:19 pm	**7:19 pm**	
☽♋ ⚻ ♃♐		**9:02 pm**	

SAT 19
2nd ♋

☽♋ ⚻ ♃♐	12:02 am		
☉ enters ♒	4:00 am	**1:00 am**	
☽♋ ☍ ♇♑	9:01 am	**6:01 am**	
☽♋ ☍ ☿♑	1:56 pm	**10:56 am**	
☽♋ □ ♅♈	8:50 pm	**5:50 pm**	☽ v/c
☽♋ △ ⚷♓	8:52 pm	**5:52 pm**	
☽ enters ♌	10:54 pm	**7:54 pm**	
♀♐ □ ♆♓	11:15 pm	**8:15 pm**	
☽♌ ☍ ☉♒		**9:16 pm**	

SUN 20
2nd ♋
Lunar Eclipse | ○ Full Moon 0 ♌ 52 (Pacific)
SUN ENTERS AQUARIUS

Eastern Time plain / **Pacific Time bold**

DECEMBER 2018

S	M	T	W	T	F	S
						1
2	3	4	5	6	7	8
9	10	11	12	13	14	15
16	17	18	19	20	21	22
23	24	25	26	27	28	29
30	31					

JANUARY

S	M	T	W	T	F	S
		1	2	3	4	5
6	7	8	9	10	11	12
13	14	15	16	17	18	19
20	21	22	23	24	25	26
27	28	29	30	31		

FEBRUARY

S	M	T	W	T	F	S
					1	2
3	4	5	6	7	8	9
10	11	12	13	14	15	16
17	18	19	20	21	22	23
24	25	26	27	28		

21 Mon
2nd ♌

Lunar Eclipse | ○ Full Moon 0 ♌ 52 (Eastern)

Martin Luther King Jr. Day

OP: After Moon trines Mars today until v/c Moon on Tuesday (see "Translating Darkness" on page 78). Still under the influence of the eclipse, but good for creative and clear thinking.

☽♌ ☍ ☉♒	12:16 am		
♂♈ □ ♄♑	6:48 am	**3:48 am**	
☽♌ ⚻ ♄♑	8:47 pm	**5:47 pm**	
☽♌ △ ♂♈	9:19 pm	**6:19 pm**	
☽♌ ⚻ ♆♓	10:00 pm	**7:00 pm**	
☽♌ △ ♀♐	11:43 pm	**8:43 pm**	
☽♌ △ ♃♐		**9:12 pm**	

22 Tue
3rd ♌

☽♌ △ ♃♐	12:12 am		
♀♐ ☌ ♃♐	7:26 am	**4:26 am**	
☽♌ ⚻ ♇♑	8:36 am	**5:36 am**	
☽♌ ⚻ ☿♑	7:07 pm	**4:07 pm**	
☽♌ △ ♅♈	8:19 pm	**5:19 pm**	☽ v/c
☽♌ ⚻ ⚷♓	8:26 pm	**5:26 pm**	
☽ enters ♍	10:22 pm	**7:22 pm**	

23 Wed
3rd ♍

☽♍ ⚻ ☉♒	3:11 am	**12:11 am**	
☿♑ □ ♅♈	6:13 am	**3:13 am**	
☿♑ ⚹ ⚷♓	7:28 am	**4:28 am**	
☽♍ △ ♄♑	8:56 pm	**5:56 pm**	
☽♍ ☍ ♆♓	9:55 pm	**6:55 pm**	
☽♍ ⚻ ♂♈	11:25 pm	**8:25 pm**	
☽♍ □ ♃♐		**9:41 pm**	
☿ enters ♒		**9:49 pm**	

24 Thu
3rd ♍

OP: After Moon squares Venus until v/c Moon. Productive hours, mostly for night owls.

☽♍ □ ♃♐	12:41 am		
☿ enters ♒	12:49 am		
☽♍ □ ♀♐	3:27 am	**12:27 am**	
☽♍ △ ♇♑	8:50 am	**5:50 am**	☽ v/c
☽♍ ⚻ ♅♈	8:57 pm	**5:57 pm**	
☽♍ ☍ ⚷♓	9:10 pm	**6:10 pm**	
☽ enters ♎	11:02 pm	**8:02 pm**	
☽♎ △ ☿♒		**10:56 pm**	

FRI 25
3rd ♎

☽♎△☿♒ 1:56 am
☽♎△☉♒ 7:48 am **4:48 am**
♂♈△♃♐ 12:53 pm **9:53 am**
☽♎□♄♑ 11:10 pm **8:10 pm**
☽♎⚻♆♓ 11:55 pm **8:55 pm**

SAT 26
3rd ♎

☽♎⚹♃♐ 3:23 am **12:23 am**
☽♎☍♂♈ 3:56 am **12:56 am**
☽♎⚹♀♐ 10:03 am **7:03 am**
☽♎□♇♑ 11:30 am **8:30 am**
☽♎☍♅♈ **9:21 pm** ☽ v/c
☽♎⚻⚷♓ **9:39 pm**
☽ enters ♏ **11:31 pm**

SUN 27
3rd ♎
◑ 4th Quarter 7 ♏ 38

☽♎☍♅♈ 12:21 am ☽ v/c
☽♎⚻⚷♓ 12:39 am
☽ enters ♏ 2:31 am
☽♏□☿♒ 12:59 pm **9:59 am**
☽♏□☉♒ 4:10 pm **1:10 pm**

Eastern Time plain / **Pacific Time bold**

DECEMBER 2018

S	M	T	W	T	F	S
						1
2	3	4	5	6	7	8
9	10	11	12	13	14	15
16	17	18	19	20	21	22
23	24	25	26	27	28	29
30	31					

JANUARY

S	M	T	W	T	F	S
		1	2	3	4	5
6	7	8	9	10	11	12
13	14	15	16	17	18	19
20	21	22	23	24	25	26
27	28	29	30	31		

FEBRUARY

S	M	T	W	T	F	S
					1	2
3	4	5	6	7	8	9
10	11	12	13	14	15	16
17	18	19	20	21	22	23
24	25	26	27	28		

28 MON
4th ♏

☽♏ ✶ ♄♑	4:46 am	**1:46 am**	
☽♏ △ ♆♓	5:14 am	**2:14 am**	
☽♏ ⚻ ♂♈	12:21 pm	**9:21 am**	
☽♏ ✶ ♀♑	5:39 pm	**2:39 pm** ☽ v/c	

29 TUE
4th ♏

☽♏ ⚻ ♅♈	7:19 am	**4:19 am**
☽♏ △ ⚷♓	7:45 am	**4:45 am**
☽ enters ♐	9:33 am	**6:33 am**
☉≈ ♂ ☿≈	9:52 am	**6:52 pm**

30 WED
4th ♐

OP: After Moon squares Neptune today until Moon enters Capricorn on Thursday. Last Quarter Moon tells us it's a good time to finish up projects.

☽♐ ✶ ☉≈	5:04 am	**2:04 am**
☽♐ ✶ ☿≈	5:32 am	**2:32 am**
☽♐ □ ♆♓	2:06 pm	**11:06 am**
☽♐ ♂ ♃♐	7:23 pm	**4:23 pm**
☽♐ △ ♂♈		**9:50 pm**

31 THU
4th ♐

☽♐ △ ♂♈	12:50 am	
♄♑ ✶ ♆♓	9:15 am	**6:15 am**
☽♐ ♂ ♀♐	12:35 pm	**9:35 am**
☽♐ △ ♅♈	5:33 pm	**2:33 pm** ☽ v/c
☽♐ □ ⚷♓	6:06 pm	**3:06 pm**
☽ enters ♑	7:47 pm	**4:47 pm**

FRI 1
4th ♑

♂♈□♇♑	10:20 pm	**7:20 pm**
☽♑⚹♆♓		**10:41 pm**
☽♑☌♄♑		**10:57 pm**

SAT 2
4th ♑
GROUNDHOG DAY
IMBOLC

☽♑⚹♆♓	1:41 am	
☽♑☌♄♑	1:57 am	
☽♑☌♇♑	3:14 pm	**12:14 pm**
☽♑□♂♈	4:12 pm	**1:12 pm**
♀♐△♅♈	6:41 pm	**3:41 pm**
♀♐□⚷♓		**10:51 pm**

SUN 3
4th ♑

♀♐□⚷♓	1:51 am	
☽♑□♅♈	5:53 am	**2:53 am** ☽ v/c
☽♑⚹⚷♓	6:34 am	**3:34 am**
☽ enters ♒	8:03 am	**5:03 am**
☿♒⚹♃♐	4:54 pm	**1:54 pm**
♀ enters ♑	5:29 pm	**2:29 pm**

Eastern Time plain / **Pacific Time bold**

JANUARY

S	M	T	W	T	F	S
		1	2	3	4	5
6	7	8	9	10	11	12
13	14	15	16	17	18	19
20	21	22	23	24	25	26
27	28	29	30	31		

FEBRUARY

S	M	T	W	T	F	S
					1	2
3	4	5	6	7	8	9
10	11	12	13	14	15	16
17	18	19	20	21	22	23
24	25	26	27	28		

MARCH

S	M	T	W	T	F	S
					1	2
3	4	5	6	7	8	9
10	11	12	13	14	15	16
17	18	19	20	21	22	23
24	25	26	27	28	29	30
31						

4 MON
4th ≈
● New Moon 15 ≈ 45

This Cazimi Moon is usable ½ hour before and ½ hour after the Sun-Moon conjunction. If you have something important to start around now, this is a great time to do it.

☽≈ ☌ ☉≈	4:04 pm	**1:04 pm**
☽≈ ⚹ ♃♐	9:35 pm	**6:35 pm**
☽≈ ☌ ☿≈		**11:11 pm**

5 TUE
1st ≈
LUNAR NEW YEAR (PIG)

☽≈ ☌ ☿≈	2:11 am	
☽≈ ⚹ ♂♈	8:49 am	**5:49 am**
☽≈ ⚹ ♅♈	6:59 pm	**3:59 pm** ☽ v/c
☽ enters ♓	9:02 pm	**6:02 pm**
☽♓ ⚹ ♀♑		**11:33 pm**

6 WED
1st ♓

☽♓ ⚹ ♀♑	2:33 am	

7 THU
1st ♓

OP: After Moon squares Jupiter today until Moon enters Aries on Friday. Favorable for artistic pursuits and helping others.

☽♓ ☌ ♆♓	3:43 am	**12:43 am**
☽♓ ⚹ ♄♑	4:44 am	**1:44 am**
☽♓ □ ♃♐	11:16 am	**8:16 am**
☽♓ ⚹ ♀♑	5:14 pm	**2:14 pm** ☽ v/c
☉≈ ⚹ ♃♐	7:32 pm	**4:32 pm**
☿≈ ⚹ ♂♈	8:24 pm	**5:24 pm**

94

FRI 8
1st ♓

☽♓ ☌ ⚷♓ 8:35 am **5:35 am**
☽ enters ♈ 9:34 am **6:34 am**
☽♈ □ ♀♑ 9:21 pm **6:21 pm**

SAT 9
1st ♈

☽♈ □ ♄♑ 5:06 pm **2:06 pm**
☿≈ ⚹ ♅♈ 5:53 pm **2:53 pm**
☽♈ △ ♃♐ 11:42 pm **8:42 pm**

SUN 10
1st ♈

☽♈ ⚹ ☉≈ 3:39 am **12:39 am**
☽♈ □ ♇♑ 4:51 am **1:51 am**
☿ enters ♓ 5:51 am **2:51 am**
☽♈ ☌ ♂♈ 3:48 pm **12:48 pm**
☽♈ ☌ ♅♈ 6:48 pm **3:48 pm** ☽ v/c
☽ enters ♉ 8:28 pm **5:28 pm**
☽♉ ⚹ ☿♓ 10:57 pm **7:57 pm**

Eastern Time plain / **Pacific Time bold**

JANUARY

S	M	T	W	T	F	S
		1	2	3	4	5
6	7	8	9	10	11	12
13	14	15	16	17	18	19
20	21	22	23	24	25	26
27	28	29	30	31		

FEBRUARY

S	M	T	W	T	F	S
					1	2
3	4	5	6	7	8	9
10	11	12	13	14	15	16
17	18	19	20	21	22	23
24	25	26	27	28		

MARCH

S	M	T	W	T	F	S
					1	2
3	4	5	6	7	8	9
10	11	12	13	14	15	16
17	18	19	20	21	22	23
24	25	26	27	28	29	30
31						

11 Mon
1st ♉

☽♉ △ ♀♑	1:39 pm	**10:39 am**
☽♉ ⚹ ♆♓		**10:31 pm**

12 Tue
1st ♉
● 2nd Quarter 23 ♉ 55

☽♉ ⚹ ♆♓	1:31 am	
☽♉ △ ♄♑	3:05 am	**12:05 am**
☽♉ ⚼ ♃♐	9:36 am	**6:36 am**
☽♉ △ ♀♑	1:54 pm	**10:54 am**
☽♉ □ ☉≈	5:26 pm	**2:26 pm** ☽ v/c
♂♈ ☌ ♅♈		**10:21 pm**

13 Wed
2nd ♉

♂♈ ☌ ♅♈	1:21 am	
☽♉ ⚹ ⚷♓	4:04 am	**1:04 am**
☽ enters ♊	4:32 am	**1:32 am**
☽♊ □ ☿♓	3:36 pm	**12:36 pm**
☽♊ ⚼ ♀♑		**10:49 pm**

14 Thu
2nd ♊
Valentine's Day
OP: After Moon opposes Jupiter today until v/c Moon on Friday.
A few usable hours to think clearly.

☽♊ ⚼ ♀♑	1:49 am	
♂ enters ♉	5:51 am	**2:51 am**
☽♊ □ ♆♓	7:56 am	**4:56 am**
☽♊ ⚼ ♄♑	9:40 am	**6:40 am**
☽♊ ☍ ♃♐	3:56 pm	**12:56 pm**
☽♊ ⚼ ♀♑	7:30 pm	**4:30 pm**
☽♊ △ ☉≈		**11:49 pm**

☽Ⅱ △ ☉≈	2:49 am	
☽Ⅱ ✶ ♅♈	7:48 am	**4:48 am** ☽ v/c
☽Ⅱ □ ⚷ ♓	8:48 am	**5:48 am**
☽ enters ♋	9:03 am	**6:03 am**
☽♋ ✶ ♂♉	10:24 am	**7:24 am**
☽♋ △ ☿ ♓		**11:39 pm**

FRI 15
2nd Ⅱ

☽♋ △ ☿ ♓	2:39 am	
☽♋ ☍ ♀♑	9:23 am	**6:23 am**
☽♋ △ ♆♓	10:48 am	**7:48 am**
☽♋ ☍ ♄♑	12:40 pm	**9:40 am**
☽♋ ⚻ ♃♐	6:42 pm	**3:42 pm**
☽♋ ☍ ♀♑	9:39 pm	**6:39 pm**

SAT 16
2nd ♋

♀♑ ✶ ♆♓	3:44 am	**12:44 am**
☽♋ ⚻ ☉≈	8:03 am	**5:03 am**
☽♋ □ ♅♈	9:17 am	**6:17 am** ☽ v/c
☽♋ △ ⚷ ♓	10:17 am	**7:17 am**
☽ enters ♌	10:21 am	**7:21 am**
☽♌ □ ♂♉	1:57 pm	**10:57 am**
☉≈ ✶ ♅♈		**11:55 pm**

SUN 17
2nd ♋

OP: After Moon squares Mars today until v/c Moon on Tuesday. Wait two hours after the square for this good, long OP.

Eastern Time plain / **Pacific Time bold**

JANUARY
S	M	T	W	T	F	S
		1	2	3	4	5
6	7	8	9	10	11	12
13	14	15	16	17	18	19
20	21	22	23	24	25	26
27	28	29	30	31		

FEBRUARY
S	M	T	W	T	F	S
					1	2
3	4	5	6	7	8	9
10	11	12	13	14	15	16
17	18	19	20	21	22	23
24	25	26	27	28		

MARCH
S	M	T	W	T	F	S
					1	2
3	4	5	6	7	8	9
10	11	12	13	14	15	16
17	18	19	20	21	22	23
24	25	26	27	28	29	30
31						

18 Mon
2nd ♌
PRESIDENTS' DAY
SUN ENTERS PISCES

☉⚹♅♈	2:55 am	
☽ enters ♈	4:10 am	**1:10 am**
♀♑♂♄♑	5:52 am	**2:52 am**
☽♌⚻☿♓	9:18 am	**6:18 am**
☽♌⚻♆♓	11:03 am	**8:03 am**
☽♌⚻♄♑	1:01 pm	**10:01 am**
☽♌⚻♀♑	1:34 pm	**10:34 am**
☉ enters ♓	6:04 pm	**3:04 pm**
☽♌△♃♐	7:00 pm	**4:00 pm**
☽♌⚻♀♑	9:30 pm	**6:30 pm**
☿♓♂♆♓		**10:37 pm**

19 Tue
2nd ♌
○ Full Moon 0 ♍ 42

☿♓♂♆♓	1:37 am	
☽♌△♅♈	8:51 am	**5:51 am** ☽ v/c
☽ enters ♍	9:47 am	**6:47 am**
☽♍⚻♅♈	9:53 am	**6:53 am**
☽♍☍☉♓	10:54 am	**7:54 am**
☽♍△♂♉	3:31 pm	**12:31 pm**
☿♓⚹♄♑	9:39 pm	**6:39 pm**

20 Wed
3rd ♍
OP: After Moon squares Jupiter until v/c Moon. About two hours of productive work.

☽♍☍♆♓	10:22 am	**7:22 am**
☽♍△♄♑	12:32 pm	**9:32 am**
☽♍☍☿♓	2:11 pm	**11:11 am**
☽♍△♀♑	4:45 pm	**1:45 pm**
☽♍□♃♐	6:41 pm	**3:41 pm**
☽♍△♀♑	8:52 pm	**5:52 pm** ☽ v/c

21 Thu
3rd ♍

☽♍⚻♅♈	8:27 am	**5:27 am**
☽ enters ♎	9:17 am	**6:17 am**
☽♎☍♅♈	9:34 am	**6:34 am**
☽♎⚻☉♓	1:53 pm	**10:53 am**
☽♎⚻♂♉	5:27 pm	**2:27 pm**

February

☽︎☌♆ ♓ 10:52 am **7:52 am**
☽︎☍ ♄ ♑ 1:20 pm **10:20 am**
☿ ♓ □ ♃ ♐ 3:40 pm **12:40 pm**
☽︎⚹ ♃ ♐ 7:56 pm **4:56 pm**
☽︎☌ ☿ ♓ 8:21 pm **5:21 pm**
☽︎□ ♀ ♑ 9:46 pm **6:46 pm**
☽︎□ ♀ ♑ 9:52 pm **6:52 pm**
♀♑ ☌ ♀♑ 10:53 pm **7:53 pm**

FRI 22
3rd ♎

☽︎☍ ♅ ♈ 10:11 am **7:11 am** ☽︎ v/c
☽︎ enters ♏ 10:56 am **7:56 am**
☽︎♏ ☌ ♈ 11:25 am **8:25 am**
☿ ♓ ⚹ ♀♑ 12:18 pm **9:18 am**
☽︎♏ △ ☉♓ 7:44 pm **4:44 pm**
☽︎♏ ☍ ♂ ♉ 10:12 pm **7:12 pm**

SAT 23
3rd ♎

☽︎♏ △ ♆ ♓ 2:29 pm **11:29 am**
☽︎♏ ⚹ ♄ ♑ 5:21 pm **2:21 pm**
☽︎♏ ⚹ ♀♑ **11:18 pm**

SUN 24
3rd ♏

Eastern Time plain / **Pacific Time bold**

JANUARY / FEBRUARY / MARCH calendars

99

25 Mon

3rd ♏

OP: After Moon trines Mercury until v/c Moon. (See "Translating Darkness" on page 78.) Only one hour for deep thinking.

☽♏ ✶ ♇♑	2:18 am		
☽♏ △ ☿♓	6:14 am	**3:14 am**	
☽♏ ✶ ♀♑	7:14 am	**4:14 am**	☽ v/c
☽♏ ⚻ ♅♈	3:40 pm	**12:40 pm**	
☽ enters ♐	4:19 pm	**1:19 pm**	
☽♐ △ ⚷♈	5:05 pm	**2:05 pm**	

26 Tue

3rd ♐

◑ 4th Quarter 7 ♐ 34

☽♐ □ ☉♓	6:28 am	**3:28 am**	
☽♐ ⚻ ♂♉	7:32 am	**4:32 am**	
☽♐ □ ♆♓	10:15 pm	**7:15 pm**	

27 Wed

4th ♐

OP: After Moon squares Mercury today until Moon enters Capricorn today or Thursday. Lovely time for play, or for work if you need to.

☽♐ ☌ ♃♐	9:33 am	**6:33 am**	
☽♐ □ ☿♓	8:11 pm	**5:11 pm**	
☉♓ ✶ ♂♉	9:33 pm	**6:33 pm**	
☽♐ △ ♅♈		**10:17 pm**	☽ v/c
☽ enters ♑		**10:48 pm**	
☽♑ □ ⚷♈		**11:52 pm**	

28 Thu

4th ♐

☽♐ △ ♅♈	1:17 am		☽ v/c
☽ enters ♑	1:48 am		
☽♑ □ ⚷♈	2:52 am		
☽♑ △ ♂♉	9:26 pm	**6:26 pm**	
☽♑ ✶ ☉♓	10:09 pm	**7:09 pm**	

March

Mercury Note: Mercury enters its Storm (moving less than 40 minutes of arc per day) on Friday, as it slows down before going retrograde. The Storm acts like the retrograde. Don't start any new projects now—just follow through with the items that are already on your plate. Write down new ideas with date and time they occurred.

Fri 1
4th ♑

♀♑ □ ♅♈ 7:32 am **4:32 am**
☽♑ ⚹ ♆♓ 9:39 am **6:39 am**
♀ enters ♒ 11:45 am **8:45 am**
☽♑ ☌ ♄♑ 1:23 pm **10:23 am**
☽♑ ☌ ♇♑ 10:49 pm **7:49 pm**
♀♒ ⚹ ⚷♈ **9:55 pm**

Sat 2
4th ♑

♀♒ ⚹ ⚷♈ 12:55 am
☽♑ ⚹ ☿♓ 11:55 am **8:55 am**
☽♑ □ ♅♈ 1:47 pm **10:47 am** ☽ v/c
☽ enters ♒ 2:06 pm **11:06 am**
☽♒ ⚹ ⚷♈ 3:30 pm **12:30 pm**
☽♒ ☌ ♀♒ 5:03 pm **2:03 pm**

Sun 3
4th ♒

☽♒ □ ♂♉ 1:54 pm **10:54 am**

Eastern Time plain / **Pacific Time bold**

FEBRUARY

S	M	T	W	T	F	S
					1	2
3	4	5	6	7	8	9
10	11	12	13	14	15	16
17	18	19	20	21	22	23
24	25	26	27	28		

MARCH

S	M	T	W	T	F	S
					1	2
3	4	5	6	7	8	9
10	11	12	13	14	15	16
17	18	19	20	21	22	23
24	25	26	27	28	29	30
31						

APRIL

S	M	T	W	T	F	S
	1	2	3	4	5	6
7	8	9	10	11	12	13
14	15	16	17	18	19	20
21	22	23	24	25	26	27
28	29	30				

March

Mercury Note: Mercury goes retrograde on Tuesday and remains so until March 28, after which it will still be in its Storm until April 6. Projects begun during this entire period may not work out as planned. It's best to use this time for reviews, editing, escrows, and so forth.

4 Mon

4th ♒

☽♒ ✶ ♃♐ 11:30 am **8:30 am**

5 Tue

4th ♒

Mardi Gras (Fat Tuesday)

Mercury retrograde

☽♒ ✶ ♅♈ 3:05 am **12:05 am** ☽ v/c

☽ enters ♓ 3:11 am **12:11 am**

☿℞ 1:19 pm **10:19 am**

6 Wed

4th ♓

● New Moon 15 ♓ 47

Ash Wednesday

♅ enters ♉ 3:26 am **12:26 am**

☽♓ ✶ ♂♉ 6:26 am **3:26 am**

☽♓ ☌ ☉♓ 11:04 am **8:04 am**

☽♓ ☌ ♆♓ 11:47 am **8:47 am**

☽♓ ✶ ♄♑ 3:58 pm **12:58 pm**

☉♓ ☌ ♆♓ 8:00 pm **5:00 pm**

☽♓ □ ♃♐ **9:37 pm**

☽♓ ✶ ♇♑ **9:41 pm**

7 Thu

1st ♓

☽♓ □ ♃♐ 12:37 am

☽♓ ✶ ♇♑ 12:41 am

☽♓ ☌ ☿♓ 2:08 pm **11:08 am** ☽ v/c

☽ enters ♈ 3:27 pm **12:27 pm**

☽♈ ☌ ⚷♈ 5:24 pm **2:24 pm**

FRI 8
1st ♈

☽♈ ✶ ♀♒ 7:29 am **4:29 am**
☉♓ ✶ ♄♑ **11:10 pm**

SAT 9
1st ♈

☉♓ ✶ ♄♑ 2:10 am
☽♈ □ ♄♑ 3:44 am **12:44 am**
☽♈ □ ♇♑ 11:56 am **8:56 am**
☽♈ △ ♃♐ 12:14 pm **9:14 am** ☽ v/c
☽ enters ♉ **11:10 pm**
☽♉ ☌ ♅♉ **11:31 pm**

OP: After Moon squares Pluto until v/c Moon. Just a few minutes to do the right thing.

SUN 10
1st ♈

☽ enters ♉ 3:10 am
☽♉ ☌ ♅♉ 3:31 am
♂♉ ✶ ♆♓ 12:20 pm **9:20 am**
☽♉ □ ♀♒ **9:45 pm**

DAYLIGHT SAVING TIME BEGINS AT 2:00 A.M.

Eastern Time plain / **Pacific Time bold**

FEBRUARY

S	M	T	W	T	F	S
					1	2
3	4	5	6	7	8	9
10	11	12	13	14	15	16
17	18	19	20	21	22	23
24	25	26	27	28		

MARCH

S	M	T	W	T	F	S
					1	2
3	4	5	6	7	8	9
10	11	12	13	14	15	16
17	18	19	20	21	22	23
24	25	26	27	28	29	30
31						

APRIL

S	M	T	W	T	F	S
	1	2	3	4	5	6
7	8	9	10	11	12	13
14	15	16	17	18	19	20
21	22	23	24	25	26	27
28	29	30				

March

11 Mon
1st ♉

OP: After Moon trines Saturn today (see "Translating Darkness" on page 78) until Moon enters Gemini on Tuesday. Time for a hands-on approach to your existing projects.

☽♉	□	♀≈	12:45 am	
☽♉	⚹	♆♓	10:18 am	7:18 am
☽♉	♂	♂♉	11:27 am	8:27 am
☽♉	△	♄♑	2:34 pm	11:34 am
☽♉	⚹	☉♓	7:13 pm	4:13 pm
☽♉	△	♀♑	10:13 pm	7:13 pm
☽♉	⚻	♃✗	10:49 pm	7:49 pm

12 Tue
1st ♉

☽♉	⚹	☿♓	5:31 am	2:31 am	☽ v/c
☽ enters ♊			11:48 am	8:48 am	
☽♊	⚹	♇♈	2:07 pm	11:07 am	

13 Wed
1st ♊

☉♓	⚹	♀♑	10:29 am	7:29 am
☽♊	△	♀≈	1:58 pm	10:58 am
☽♊	□	♆♓	5:44 pm	2:44 pm
☉♓	□	♃✗	9:29 pm	6:29 pm
☽♊	⚻	♄♑	9:57 pm	6:57 pm

14 Thu
1st ♊
☽ 2nd Quarter 23 ♊ 33

☽♊	⚻	♀♑	5:00 am	2:00 am	
☽♊	☍	♃✗	5:50 am	2:50 am	
♂♉	△	♄♑	6:02 am	3:02 am	
☽♊	□	☉♓	6:27 am	3:27 am	
☽♊	□	☿♓	8:30 am	5:30 am	☽ v/c
☽ enters ♋			5:49 pm	2:49 pm	
☽♋	⚹	♅♉	6:31 pm	3:31 pm	
☽♋	□	♇♈	8:15 pm	5:15 pm	
☉♓	♂	☿♓	9:48 pm	6:48 pm	

104

☿♓ □ ♃✗ 7:17 pm **4:17 pm**
☽♋ △ ♆♓ 10:18 pm **7:18 pm**
☽♋ ⊼ ♀≈ 11:28 pm **8:28 pm**
☽♋ ☌ ♄♑ **11:24 pm**

FRI 15
2nd ♋

☽♋ ☌ ♄♑ 2:24 am
☽♋ ⚹ ♂♉ 4:22 am **1:22 am**
☽♋ ☌ ♀♑ 8:53 am **5:53 am**
☽♋ △ ☿♓ 8:54 am **5:54 am**
☿♓ ⚹ ♀♑ 9:08 am **6:08 am**
☽♋ ⊼ ♃✗ 9:54 am **6:54 am**
☽♋ △ ☉♓ 2:03 pm **11:03 am** ☽ v/c
☽ enters ♌ 8:57 pm **5:57 pm**
☽♌ □ ♅♉ 9:47 pm **6:47 pm**
☽♌ △ ⚷♈ 11:27 pm **8:27 pm**

SAT 16
2nd ♋

OP: After Moon trines Mercury (see "Translating Darkness" on page 78) until Moon enters Leo. Okay for working on projects already begun before March 1.

☿♓ ⚹ ♂♉ 11:23 pm **8:23 pm**
☽♌ ⊼ ♆♓ **9:07 pm**

SUN 17
2nd ♌
St. Patrick's Day

FEBRUARY								MARCH								APRIL					
S	M	T	W	T	F	S		S	M	T	W	T	F	S		S	M	T	W	T	F	S
					1	2							1	2			1	2	3	4	5	6
3	4	5	6	7	8	9		3	4	5	6	7	8	9		7	8	9	10	11	12	13
10	11	12	13	14	15	16		10	11	12	13	14	15	16		14	15	16	17	18	19	20
17	18	19	20	21	22	23		17	18	19	20	21	22	23		21	22	23	24	25	26	27
24	25	26	27	28				24	25	26	27	28	29	30		28	29	30				
								31														

18 MON

2nd ♌

OP: After Moon squares Mars until v/c Moon. This OP is usable two hours after the square, leaving one hour for good work.

☽♌ ⊼ ♆♓	12:07 am	
☽♌ ⊼ ♄♑	4:08 am	**1:08 am**
☽♌ ☍ ♀≈	5:27 am	**2:27 am**
☽♌ ⊼ ☿♓	7:14 am	**4:14 am**
☽♌ □ ♂♉	8:06 am	**5:06 am**
☽♌ ⊼ ♀♑	10:10 am	**7:10 am**
☽♌ △ ♃♐	11:19 am	**8:19 am** ☽ v/c
☽♌ ⊼ ☉♓	6:33 pm	**3:33 pm**
☽ enters ♍	9:41 pm	**6:41 pm**
☽♍ △ ♅♉	10:40 pm	**7:40 pm**
☽♍ ⊼ ♂♈		**9:18 pm**

19 TUE

2nd ♍

☽♍ ⊼ ♂♈	12:18 am	
☽♍ ☍ ♆♓		**9:13 pm**

20 WED

2nd ♍

○ Full Moon 0 ♎ 09

SPRING EQUINOX

OSTARA

SUN ENTERS ARIES

INTERNATIONAL ASTROLOGY DAY

☽♍ ☍ ♆♓	12:13 am	
☽♍ △ ♄♑	4:15 am	**1:15 am**
☽♍ ☍ ☿♓	4:35 am	**1:35 am**
♂♉ △ ♀♑	7:41 am	**4:41 am**
☽♍ ⊼ ♀≈	9:29 am	**6:29 am**
☽♍ △ ♀♑	10:04 am	**7:04 am**
☽♍ △ ♂♉	10:10 am	**7:10 am**
☿♓ ✶ ♄♑	10:27 am	**7:27 am**
☽♍ □ ♃♐	11:22 am	**8:22 am** ☽ v/c
☉ enters ♈	5:58 pm	**2:58 pm**
☽ enters ♎	9:28 pm	**6:28 pm**

☽♎ ☍ ☉♈	9:43 pm	**6:43 pm**
☽♎ ⊼ ♅♉	10:36 pm	**7:36 pm**
☽♎ ☍ ♂♈		**9:16 pm**

21 THU

3rd ♎

PURIM (BEGINS AT SUNDOWN ON MARCH 20)

☽♎ ☍ ♂♈	12:16 am	
♀≈ □ ♂♉	4:07 am	**1:07 am**
♀≈ ✶ ♃♐	10:17 am	**7:17 am**
♂♉ ⊼ ♃♐	3:43 pm	**12:43 pm**
☽♎ ⊼ ♆♓		**9:26 pm**
☽♎ ⊼ ☿♓		**11:35 pm**

☽ ⚷ ⊼ ♆ ♓	12:26 am		
☽ ⚷ ⊼ ☿ ♓	2:35 am		
☽ ⚷ □ ♄ ♑	4:39 am	**1:39 am**	
☽ ⚷ □ ♀ ♑	10:29 am	**7:29 am**	
☽ ⚷ ⚹ ♃ ♐	11:59 am	**8:59 am**	
☽ ⚷ ⊼ ♂ ♉	12:52 am	**9:52 am**	
☽ ⚷ △ ♀ ♒	2:10 pm	**11:10 am**	☽ v/c
☉ ♈ ♂ ⚷ ♈	2:38 pm	**11:38 am**	
☽ enters ♏	10:16 pm	**7:16 pm**	
☽ ♏ ♂ ♅ ♉	11:38 pm	**8:38 pm**	
☽ ♏ ⊼ ⚷ ♈		**10:24 pm**	
☽ ♏ ⊼ ☉ ♈		**11:09 pm**	

OP: After Moon sextiles Jupiter until v/c Moon. A couple of very good hours; with Mercury still retrograde, okay to review ideas or for reunions with old friends.

☽ ♏ ⊼ ⚷ ♈	1:24 am	
☽ ♏ ⊼ ☉ ♈	2:09 am	
☽ ♏ △ ♆ ♓		**11:50 pm**

☽ ♏ △ ♆ ♓	2:50 am	
☽ ♏ △ ☿ ♓	3:10 am	**12:10 am**
☽ ♏ ⚹ ♄ ♑	7:25 am	**4:25 am**
☿ ♓ ♂ ♆ ♓	1:28 pm	**10:28 am**
☽ ♏ ⚹ ♀ ♑	1:30 pm	**10:30 am**
☽ ♏ ♂ ♂ ♉	6:38 pm	**3:38 pm**
☽ ♏ □ ♀ ♒	10:24 pm	**7:24 pm** ☽ v/c
☽ enters ♐		**11:06 pm**

Eastern Time plain / **Pacific Time bold**

FEBRUARY							MARCH							APRIL						
S	M	T	W	T	F	S	S	M	T	W	T	F	S	S	M	T	W	T	F	S
					1	2						1	2		1	2	3	4	5	6
3	4	5	6	7	8	9	3	4	5	6	7	8	9	7	8	9	10	11	12	13
10	11	12	13	14	15	16	10	11	12	13	14	15	16	14	15	16	17	18	19	20
17	18	19	20	21	22	23	17	18	19	20	21	22	23	21	22	23	24	25	26	27
24	25	26	27	28			24	25	26	27	28	29	30	28	29	30				
							31													

25 MON
3rd ♏

☽ enters ♐	2:06 am	
☽ ⚹ ♅ ♉	3:46 am	**12:46 am**
☽ △ ⚷ ♈	5:42 am	**2:42 am**
☽ △ ☉ ♈	10:30 am	**7:30 am**

26 TUE
3rd ♐

OP: After Moon squares Neptune today until Moon enter Capricorn on Wednesday. Time to have some fun.

☽ □ ☿ ♓	8:01 am	**5:01 am**
☽ □ ♆ ♓	9:07 am	**6:07 am**
♀ enters ♓	3:43 pm	**12:43 pm**
☽ ☌ ♃ ♐	10:37 pm	**7:37 pm** ☽ v/c

27 WED
3rd ♐
◑ 4th Quarter 7 ♑ 12 (Pacific)

☽ ⚹ ♂ ♉	5:10 am	**2:10 am**
☽ enters ♑	10:07 am	**7:07 am**
☽ ♑ ⚹ ♀ ♓	12:06 pm	**9:06 am**
☽ ♑ △ ♅ ♉	12:10 pm	**9:10 am**
♀ ♓ ⚹ ♅ ♉	12:45 pm	**9:45 am**
☽ ♑ □ ⚷ ♈	2:17 pm	**11:17 am**
☽ ♑ □ ☉ ♈		**9:10 pm**

28 THU
3rd ♑
◑ 4th Quarter 7 ♑ 12 (Eastern)
MERCURY DIRECT

☽ ♑ □ ☉ ♈	12:10 am	
☿ D	9:59 am	**6:59 am**
☽ ♑ ⚹ ☿ ♓	5:48 pm	**2:48 pm**
☽ ♑ ⚹ ♆ ♓	7:33 pm	**4:33 pm**
☽ ♑ ☌ ♄ ♑		**10:00 pm**

FRI 29
4th ♑

☽♑ ☌ ♄♑ 1:00 am
☽♑ ☌ ♇♑ 7:35 am **4:35 am**
☽♑ △ ♂♉ 8:05 pm **5:05 pm** ☽ v/c
☽ enters ♒ 9:46 pm **6:46 pm**
☽♒ □ ♅♉ **9:10 pm**
☽♒ ⚹ ⚷♈ **11:24 pm**

SAT 30
4th ♒

☽♒ □ ♅♉ 12:10 am
☽♒ ⚹ ⚷♈ 2:24 am
☽♒ ⚹ ☉♈ 5:53 pm **2:53 pm**
♂ enters ♊ **11:12 pm**

OP: After Moon squares Uranus Friday or today until v/c Moon on Sunday. It's the Last Quarter Moon and we're still in the Mercury Storm until April 6. Good OP to follow through on existing projects.

SUN 31
4th ♒

♂ enters ♊ 2:12 am
☽♒ ⚹ ♃♐ 11:02 pm **8:02 pm** ☽ v/c

Eastern Time plain / **Pacific Time bold**

FEBRUARY

S	M	T	W	T	F	S
					1	2
3	4	5	6	7	8	9
10	11	12	13	14	15	16
17	18	19	20	21	22	23
24	25	26	27	28		

MARCH

S	M	T	W	T	F	S
					1	2
3	4	5	6	7	8	9
10	11	12	13	14	15	16
17	18	19	20	21	22	23
24	25	26	27	28	29	30
31						

APRIL

S	M	T	W	T	F	S
	1	2	3	4	5	6
7	8	9	10	11	12	13
14	15	16	17	18	19	20
21	22	23	24	25	26	27
28	29	30				

April

1 Mon

4th ♒

April Fools' Day

☽ enters ♓	10:48 am	**7:48 am**
☽♓ □ ♂♊	12:44 pm	**9:44 am**
☽♓ ⚹ ♅♉	1:30 pm	**10:30 am**
☽♓ ☌ ♀♓		**11:31 pm**

2 Tue

4th ♓

☽♓ ☌ ♀♓	2:31 am	
☿♓ ☌ ♆♓	5:36 am	**2:36 am**
☽♓ ☌ ♆♓	9:25 pm	**6:25 pm**
☽♓ ☌ ☿♓	9:58 pm	**6:58 pm**
☽♓ ⚹ ♄♑		**11:58 pm**

3 Wed

4th ♓

☽♓ ⚹ ♄♑	2:58 am		
☽♓ ⚹ ♇♑	9:09 am	**6:09 am**	
☽♓ □ ♃♐	11:36 am	**8:36 am**	☽ v/c
☽ enters ♈	10:56 pm	**7:56 pm**	
♂♊ ⚹ ⚷♈	11:39 pm	**8:39 pm**	

4 Thu

4th ♈

☽♈ ☌ ⚷♈	4:02 am	**1:02 am**
☽♈ ⚹ ♂♊	4:16 am	**1:16 am**

Mercury Note: Mercury finally leaves its Storm on Saturday, April 6. Look over your notes on any ideas that occurred to you while Mercury was retrograde and/or slow. How do they look now?

☽♈ ♂ ☉♈	4:50 am	**1:50 am**
☽♈ □ ♄♑	2:02 pm	**11:02 am**
☽♈ □ ♀♑	7:51 pm	**4:51 pm**
☽♈ △ ♃ ♐	10:15 pm	**7:15 pm** ☽ v/c

FRI 5
4th ♈
● New Moon 15 ♈ 17

☽ enters ♉	9:06 am	**6:06 am**
☽♉ ♂ ♅♉	12:09 pm	**9:09 am**

SAT 6
1st ♈

OP: After Moon conjoins Uranus today until Moon enters Gemini on Monday. Awesome OP as the Moon leaves the Sun's beams; good for everything from romance to work.

☿♓ ⚹ ♄♑	5:17 am	**2:17 am**
☽♉ ⚹ ♀♓	12:04 pm	**9:04 am**
☽♉ ⚹ ♆♓	5:46 pm	**2:46 pm**
☽♉ △ ♄♑	10:59 pm	**7:59 pm**
☽♉ ⚹ ☿♓		**9:04 pm**

SUN 7
1st ♉

Eastern Time plain / **Pacific Time bold**

MARCH						
S	M	T	W	T	F	S
					1	2
3	4	5	6	7	8	9
10	11	12	13	14	15	16
17	18	19	20	21	22	23
24	25	26	27	28	29	30
31						

APRIL						
S	M	T	W	T	F	S
	1	2	3	4	5	6
7	8	9	10	11	12	13
14	15	16	17	18	19	20
21	22	23	24	25	26	27
28	29	30				

MAY						
S	M	T	W	T	F	S
			1	2	3	4
5	6	7	8	9	10	11
12	13	14	15	16	17	18
19	20	21	22	23	24	25
26	27	28	29	30	31	

8 Mon
1st ♉

☽♉ ⚹ ☿♓	12:04 am		
☽♉ △ ♇♑	4:29 am	**1:29 am**	☽ v/c
☽♉ ⚻ ♃♐	6:49 am	**3:49 am**	
☽ enters ♊	5:15 pm	**2:15 pm**	
☽♊ ⚹ ⚷♈	10:31 pm	**7:31 pm**	

9 Tue
1st ♊

☽♊ ☌ ♂♊	4:16 am	**1:16 am**	
☽♊ □ ♀♓		**9:51 pm**	
☽♊ □ ♆♓		**9:58 pm**	
♀♓ ☌ ♆♓		**11:13 pm**	

10 Wed
1st ♊

Jupiter retrograde

☽♊ □ ♀♓	12:51 am		
☽♊ □ ♆♓	12:58 am		
♀♓ ☌ ♆♓	2:13 am		
☉♈ □ ♄♑	4:47 am	**1:47 am**	
☽♊ ⚻ ♄♑	6:01 am	**3:01 am**	
☽♊ ⚹ ☉♈	6:06 am	**3:06 am**	
☽♊ □ ☿♓	10:43 am	**7:43 am**	
☽♊ ⚻ ♇♑	11:13 am	**8:13 am**	
♃℞	1:01 pm	**10:01 am**	
☽♊ ☍ ♃♐	1:27 pm	**10:27 am**	☽ v/c
☿♓ ⚹ ♇♑	5:45 pm	**2:45 pm**	
☽ enters ♋	11:31 pm	**8:31 pm**	
☽♋ ⚹ ♅♉		**11:49 pm**	

11 Thu
1st ♋

☽♋ ⚹ ♅♉	2:49 am		
☽♋ □ ⚷♈	4:50 am	**1:50 am**	
☿♓ □ ♃♐		**9:18 pm**	

☿♓ □ ♃♐	12:18 am	
☽♋ △ ♆♓	6:15 am	**3:15 am**
☽♋ △ ♀♓	11:05 am	**8:05 am**
☽♋ ☌ ♄♑	11:05 am	**8:05 am**
♀♓ ✶ ♄♑	11:08 am	**8:08 am**
☽♋ □ ☉♈	3:06 pm	**12:06 pm**
☽♋ ☌ ♀♑	4:01 pm	**1:01 pm**
☽♋ ⚻ ♃♐	6:07 pm	**3:07 pm**
☽♋ △ ☿♓	7:33 pm	**4:33 pm** ☽ v/c

FRI 12
1st ♋

◐ 2nd Quarter 22 ♋ 35

OP: After Moon opposes Pluto today until Moon enters Leo on Saturday. Lovely afternoon and evening for work, a stroll, food, etc.

☽ enters ♌	3:50 am	**12:50 am**
☉♈ □ ♀♑	4:07 am	**1:07 am**
☽♌ □ ♅♉	7:14 am	**4:14 am**
☽♌ △ ♂♈	9:09 am	**6:09 am**
☽♌ ✶ ♂♊	7:13 pm	**4:13 pm**

SAT 13
2nd ♋

OP: After Moon sextiles Mars today (see "Translating Darkness" on page 78) until v/c Moon on Sunday. Good for constructive work.

☽♌ ⚻ ♆♓	9:31 am	**6:31 am**
☉♈ △ ♃♐	9:41 am	**6:41 am**
☽♌ ⚻ ♄♑	2:10 pm	**11:10 am**
☽♌ ⚻ ♀♓	6:45 pm	**3:45 pm**
☽♌ ⚻ ♀♑	6:50 pm	**3:50 pm**
♀♓ ✶ ♀♑	7:52 pm	**4:52 pm**
☽♌ △ ♃♐	8:49 pm	**5:49 pm**
☽♌ △ ☉♈	9:38 pm	**6:38 pm** ☽ v/c
☽♌ ⚻ ☿♓		**11:22 pm**

SUN 14
2nd ♌
PALM SUNDAY

Eastern Time plain / **Pacific Time bold**

MARCH						
S	M	T	W	T	F	S
					1	2
3	4	5	6	7	8	9
10	11	12	13	14	15	16
17	18	19	20	21	22	23
24	25	26	27	28	29	30
31						

APRIL						
S	M	T	W	T	F	S
	1	2	3	4	5	6
7	8	9	10	11	12	13
14	15	16	17	18	19	20
21	22	23	24	25	26	27
28	29	30				

MAY						
S	M	T	W	T	F	S
			1	2	3	4
5	6	7	8	9	10	11
12	13	14	15	16	17	18
19	20	21	22	23	24	25
26	27	28	29	30	31	

15 Mon
2nd ♌

☽ ♌ ⊼ ☿ ♓	2:22 am	
☽ enters ♍	6:14 am	**3:14 am**
☽ ♍ △ ♅ ♉	9:42 am	**6:42 am**
☽ ♍ ⊼ ♅ ♈	11:34 am	**8:34 am**
♀ ♓ □ ♃ ♐	7:15 pm	**4:15 pm**
☽ ♍ □ ♂ ♊	11:28 pm	**8:28 pm**

16 Tue
2nd ♍

☽ ♍ ☍ ♆ ♓	11:09 am	**8:09 am**
☽ ♍ △ ♄ ♑	3:40 pm	**12:40 pm**
☽ ♍ △ ♀ ♑	8:10 pm	**5:10 pm**
☽ ♍ □ ♃ ♐	10:03 pm	**7:03 pm**
☽ ♍ ☍ ♀ ♓		**9:29 pm** ☽ v/c
☿ enters ♈		**11:01 pm**
☽ ♍ ⊼ ☉ ♈		**11:25 pm**

17 Wed
2nd ♍

☽ ♍ ☍ ♀ ♓	12:29 am	☽ v/c
☿ enters ♈	2:01 am	
☽ ♍ ⊼ ☉ ♈	2:25 am	
☽ enters ♎	7:22 am	**4:22 am**
☽ ♎ ☍ ☿ ♈	7:51 am	**4:51 am**
☽ ♎ ⊼ ♅ ♉	11:00 am	**8:00 am**
☽ ♎ ☍ ♅ ♈	12:50 pm	**9:50 am**
☽ ♎ △ ♂ ♊		**11:46 pm**

18 Thu
2nd ♎

OP: After Moon sextiles Jupiter today (see "Translating Darkness" on page 78) until v/c Moon on Friday. Useful hours if you stay up late.

☽ ♎ △ ♂ ♊	2:46 am	
☽ ♎ ⊼ ♆ ♓	12:17 pm	**9:17 am**
☽ ♎ □ ♄ ♑	4:48 pm	**1:48 pm**
☽ ♎ □ ♀ ♑	9:18 pm	**6:18 pm**
☽ ♎ ✱ ♃ ♐	11:07 pm	**8:07 pm**

Fri 19

2nd ♎︎
○ Full Moon 29 ♎︎ 07
Good Friday

☽♎︎ ⚻ ♀ ♓︎	6:09 am	**3:09 am**	
☽♎︎ ☍ ⊙♈︎	7:12 am	**4:12 am**	☽ v/c
☽ enters ♏︎	8:41 am	**5:41 am**	
☽♏︎ ☍ ♅ ♉︎	12:35 pm	**9:35 am**	
☽♏︎ ⚻ ☿ ♈︎	1:56 pm	**10:56 am**	
☽♏︎ ⚻ ⚷ ♈︎	2:27 pm	**11:27 am**	
☿♈︎ ☌ ⚷ ♈︎	7:47 pm	**4:47 pm**	

Sat 20

3rd ♏︎
Passover begins (at sundown on April 19)
Sun enters Taurus

⊙ enters ♉︎	4:55 am	**1:55 am**	
☽♏︎ ⚻ ♂ ♊︎	7:05 am	**4:05 am**	
♀ enters ♈︎	12:11 pm	**9:11 am**	
☽♏︎ △ ♆ ♓︎	2:39 pm	**11:39 am**	
☽♏︎ ⚹ ♄ ♑︎	7:20 pm	**4:20 pm**	
☽♏︎ ⚹ ♇ ♑︎		**9:00 pm**	☽ v/c

Sun 21

3rd ♏︎
Easter

☽♏︎ ⚹ ♇ ♑︎	12:00 am		☽ v/c
☽ enters ♐︎	11:59 am	**8:59 am**	
☽♐︎ △ ♀ ♈︎	2:19 pm	**11:19 am**	
☽♐︎ ⚻ ⊙♉︎	2:23 pm	**11:23 am**	
☽♐︎ ⚻ ♅ ♉︎	4:21 pm	**1:21 pm**	
☽♐︎ △ ⚷ ♈︎	6:19 pm	**3:19 pm**	
☽♐︎ △ ☿ ♈︎	11:18 pm	**8:18 pm**	

Eastern Time plain / **Pacific Time bold**

MARCH
S	M	T	W	T	F	S
					1	2
3	4	5	6	7	8	9
10	11	12	13	14	15	16
17	18	19	20	21	22	23
24	25	26	27	28	29	30
31						

APRIL
S	M	T	W	T	F	S
	1	2	3	4	5	6
7	8	9	10	11	12	13
14	15	16	17	18	19	20
21	22	23	24	25	26	27
28	29	30				

MAY
S	M	T	W	T	F	S
			1	2	3	4
5	6	7	8	9	10	11
12	13	14	15	16	17	18
19	20	21	22	23	24	25
26	27	28	29	30	31	

22 MON
3rd ♐
EARTH DAY

OP: After Moon squares Neptune today until Moon enters Capricorn on Tuesday. Time for work, entertainment, or anything you choose.

☽♐ ☍ ♂Ⅱ	2:35 pm	**11:35 am**	
☉♉ ♂ ♅♉	7:07 pm	**4:07 pm**	
☽♐ □ ♆♓	8:03 pm	**5:03 pm**	

23 TUE
3rd ♐

☽♐ ♂ ♃♐	7:44 am	**4:44 am**	☽ v/c
♀♈ ♂ ♦♈	12:55 pm	**9:55 am**	
☽ enters ♑	6:50 pm	**3:50 pm**	
☽♑ △ ♅♉	11:46 pm	**8:46 pm**	
☽♑ □ ♦♈		**10:52 pm**	
☽♑ △ ☉♉		**11:02 pm**	

24 WED
3rd ♑
PLUTO RETROGRADE

☽♑ □ ♦♈	1:52 am		
☽♑ △ ☉♉	2:02 am		
☽♑ □ ♀♈	3:12 pm	**12:12 am**	
☽♑ □ ☿♈	2:14 pm	**11:14 am**	
♀℞	2:48 pm	**11:48 am**	
☽♑ ⊼ ♂Ⅱ		**11:35 pm**	

25 THU
3rd ♑

☽♑ ⊼ ♂Ⅱ	2:35 am		
☽♑ ⚹ ♆♓	5:22 am	**2:22 am**	
☽♑ ♂ ♄♑	10:33 am	**7:33 am**	
☽♑ ♂ ♀♑	3:48 pm	**12:48 pm**	☽ v/c

☽ enters ♒ 5:27 am **2:27 am**
☽♒ □ ♅ ♉ 10:57 am **7:57 am**
☽♒ ⚹ ♄ ♈ 1:08 pm **10:08 am**
☽♒ □ ☉ ♉ 6:18 pm **3:18 pm**
☽♒ ⚹ ♀ ♈ 8:58 pm **5:58 pm**

Fri 26

3rd ♑

◑ 4th Quarter 6 ♒ 23

ORTHODOX GOOD FRIDAY

OP: After Moon squares Sun today until v/c Moon on Sunday. With the Last Quarter Moon, this OP is good for steady work on items already under way.

♂♊ □ ♆ ♓ 9:03 am **6:03 am**
☽♒ ⚹ ☿ ♈ 10:35 am **7:35 am**
☽♒ △ ♂ ♊ 6:11 pm **3:11 pm**

Sat 27

4th ♒

PASSOVER ENDS

☽♒ ⚹ ♃ ♐ 5:44 am **2:44 am** ☽ v/c
☽ enters ♓ 6:11 pm **3:11 pm**
☽♓ ⚹ ♅ ♉ **9:02 pm**

Sun 28

4th ♒

ORTHODOX EASTER

Eastern Time plain / **Pacific Time bold**

			MARCH			
S	M	T	W	T	F	S
					1	2
3	4	5	6	7	8	9
10	11	12	13	14	15	16
17	18	19	20	21	22	23
24	25	26	27	28	29	30
31						

			APRIL			
S	M	T	W	T	F	S
	1	2	3	4	5	6
7	8	9	10	11	12	13
14	15	16	17	18	19	20
21	22	23	24	25	26	27
28	29	30				

			MAY			
S	M	T	W	T	F	S
			1	2	3	4
5	6	7	8	9	10	11
12	13	14	15	16	17	18
19	20	21	22	23	24	25
26	27	28	29	30	31	

29 Mon
4th ♓
SATURN RETROGRADE

☽♓ ✶ ♅ ♉	12:02 am	
☽♓ ✶ ☉ ♉	12:34 pm	**9:34 am**
♄℞	8:54 pm	**5:54 pm**

30 Tue
4th ♓

OP: After Moon squares Jupiter today until Moon enters Aries on Wednesday. (Pisces is one of the four signs in which the v/c Moon is a good thing. See page 75.) Use this OP for sorting through emotions, endings, and closures.

☽♓ ♂ ♆♓	6:33 am	**3:33 am**
☽♓ □ ♂♊	10:22 am	**7:22 am**
☽♓ ✶ ♄♑	11:34 am	**8:34 am**
☽♓ ✶ ♀♑	4:48 pm	**1:48 pm**
☽♓ □ ♃♐	5:57 pm	**2:57 pm** ☽ v/c
☿♈ ✶ ♂♊		**11:37 pm**

1 Wed
4th ♓
BELTANE

☿♈ ✶ ♂♊	2:37 am	
☿♈ □ ♄♑	4:50 am	**1:50 am**
☽ enters ♈	6:24 am	**3:24 am**
♂♊ ⊼ ♄♑	8:17 am	**5:17 am**
☽♈ ♂ ♋♈	2:26 pm	**11:26 am**

2 Thu
4th ♈

☽♈ ♂ ♀♈	10:39 am	**7:39 am**
☿♈ □ ♀♑	5:51 pm	**2:51 pm**
☽♈ □ ♄♑	10:17 pm	**7:17 pm**
☿♈ △ ♃♐	11:59 pm	**8:59 pm**
☽♈ ✶ ♂♊		**9:22 pm**

Fri 3
4th ♈

☽♈ ⚹ ♂♊ 12:22 am
☽♈ □ ♇♑ 3:17 am **12:17 am**
☽♈ △ ♃♐ 4:06 am **1:06 am**
☽♈ ☌ ☿♈ 4:47 am **1:47 am** ☽ v/c
☽ enters ♉ 4:18 pm **1:18 pm**
☽♉ ☌ ♅♉ 10:15 pm **7:15 pm**

Sat 4
4th ♉
● New Moon 14♉11

☽♉ ☌ ☉♉ 6:45 pm **3:45 pm**
☽♉ ⚹ ♆♓ **11:02 pm**

This Cazimi Moon is usable ½ hour before and ½ hour after the Sun-Moon conjunction. If you have something important to start around now, this is a great time to do it.

Sun 5
1st ♉
Cinco de Mayo

☽♉ ⚹ ♆♓ 2:02 am
☽♉ △ ♄♑ 6:22 am **3:22 am**
♂♊ ⚻ ♇♑ 8:29 am **5:29 am**
☽♉ △ ♇♑ 11:10 am **8:10 am** ☽ v/c
☽♉ ⚻ ♃♐ 11:41 am **8:41 am**
♂♊ ☍ ♃♐ 5:57 pm **2:57 pm**
☽ enters ♊ 11:40 pm **8:40 pm**

Eastern Time plain / **Pacific Time bold**

APRIL

S	M	T	W	T	F	S
	1	2	3	4	5	6
7	8	9	10	11	12	13
14	15	16	17	18	19	20
21	22	23	24	25	26	27
28	29	30				

MAY

S	M	T	W	T	F	S
			1	2	3	4
5	6	7	8	9	10	11
12	13	14	15	16	17	18
19	20	21	22	23	24	25
26	27	28	29	30	31	

JUNE

S	M	T	W	T	F	S
						1
2	3	4	5	6	7	8
9	10	11	12	13	14	15
16	17	18	19	20	21	22
23	24	25	26	27	28	29
30						

6 MON
1st ♊
RAMADAN BEGINS

☽♊ ⚹ ♅♈	7:27 am	**4:27 am**	
☿ enters ♉	2:25 pm	**11:25 am**	

7 TUE
1st ♊

☽♊ □ ♆♓	8:15 am	**5:15 am**	
♀♈ □ ♄♑	9:26 am	**6:26 am**	
☽♊ ⃠ ♄♑	12:18 pm	**9:18 am**	
☽♊ ⚹ ♀♈	12:35 pm	**9:35 am**	
☽♊ ⃠ ♀♑	4:58 pm	**1:58 pm**	
☽♊ ☍ ♃♐	5:11 pm	**2:11 pm**	
☽♊ ♂ ♂♊	7:50 pm	**4:50 pm**	☽ v/c

8 WED
1st ♊

☽ enters ♋	5:06 am	**2:06 am**	
☿♉ ♂ ♅♉	10:23 am	**7:23 am**	
☽♋ ⚹ ♅♉	11:07 am	**8:07 am**	
☽♋ ⚹ ☿♉	11:13 am	**8:13 am**	
☽♋ □ ♅♈	12:51 pm	**9:51 am**	
☉♉ ⚹ ♆♓	10:52 pm	**7:52 pm**	

9 THU
1st ♋

☽♋ △ ♆♓	12:55 pm	**9:55 am**	
♀♈ △ ♃♐	12:56 pm	**9:56 am**	
♀♈ □ ♀♑	1:20 pm	**10:20 am**	
☽♋ ⚹ ☉♉	1:57 pm	**10:57 am**	
☽♋ ☍ ♄♑	4:44 pm	**1:44 pm**	
☽♋ ⃠ ♃♐	9:15 pm	**6:15 pm**	
☽♋ ☍ ♀♑	9:20 pm	**6:20 pm**	
☽♋ □ ♀♈	10:06 pm	**7:06 pm**	☽ v/c

☽ enters ♌	9:14 am	**6:14 am**
☽♌ □ ♅ ♉	3:19 pm	**12:19 pm**
☽♌ △ ⚷ ♈	4:59 pm	**1:59 pm**
☽♌ □ ☿ ♉	11:33 pm	**8:33 pm**

FRI **10**
1st ♋

☉♉ △ ♄ ♑	5:19 am	**2:19 am**
☽♌ ⚻ ♆ ♓	4:29 pm	**1:29 pm**
☽♌ ⚻ ♄ ♑	8:06 pm	**5:06 pm**
☽♌ □ ☉ ♉	9:12 pm	**6:12 pm**
☽♌ △ ♃ ♐		**9:16 pm**
☽♌ ⚻ ♀ ♑		**9:38 pm**

SAT **11**
1st ♌
◑ 2nd Quarter 21 ♌ 03
OP: After Moon squares Sun today until v/c Moon on Sunday.
Nice Saturday night good for both play and work.

☽♌ △ ♃ ♐	12:16 am	
☽♌ ⚻ ♀ ♑	12:38 am	
☽♌ △ ♀ ♈	6:14 am	**3:14 am**
☽♌ ✶ ♂ ♊	8:24 am	**5:24 am** ☽ v/c
☽ enters ♍	12:22 pm	**9:22 am**
☽♍ △ ♅ ♉	6:33 pm	**3:33 pm**
☽♍ ⚻ ⚷ ♈	8:09 pm	**5:09 pm**

SUN **12**
2nd ♌
MOTHER'S DAY

Eastern Time plain / **Pacific Time bold**

APRIL								MAY								JUNE						
S	M	T	W	T	F	S		S	M	T	W	T	F	S		S	M	T	W	T	F	S
	1	2	3	4	5	6					1	2	3	4								1
7	8	9	10	11	12	13		5	6	7	8	9	10	11		2	3	4	5	6	7	8
14	15	16	17	18	19	20		12	13	14	15	16	17	18		9	10	11	12	13	14	15
21	22	23	24	25	26	27		19	20	21	22	23	24	25		16	17	18	19	20	21	22
28	29	30						26	27	28	29	30	31			23	24	25	26	27	28	29
																30						

13 MON
2nd ♍

☽♍ △ ☿ ♉	10:48 am	**7:48 am**
☉ ⚻ ♃ ♐	2:27 pm	**11:27 am**
☽♍ ☍ ♆ ♓	7:14 pm	**4:14 pm**
☽♍ △ ♄ ♑	10:39 pm	**7:39 pm**
☉ △ ♀ ♑	11:07 pm	**8:07 pm**
☽♍ □ ♃ ♐		**11:32 pm**

14 TUE
2nd ♍

☽♍ □ ♃ ♐	2:32 am	
☽♍ △ ♀ ♑	3:12 am	**12:12 am**
☽♍ △ ☉ ♉	3:30 am	**12:30 am**
♀ ♈ ⚹ ♂ ♊	9:58 am	**6:58 am**
☽♍ □ ♂ ♊	1:19 pm	**10:19 am** ☽ v/c
☽♍ ⚻ ♀ ♈	1:28 pm	**10:28 am**
☽ enters ♎	2:51 pm	**11:51 am**
☽♎ ⚻ ♅ ♉	9:11 pm	**6:11 pm**
☽♎ ☍ ⚷ ♈	10:44 pm	**7:44 pm**

15 WED
2nd ♎

♀ enters ♉	5:46 am	**2:46 am**
☿ ♉ ⚹ ♆ ♓	9:20 pm	**6:20 pm**
☽♎ ⚻ ♆ ♓	9:44 pm	**6:44 pm**
☽♎ ⚻ ☿ ♉	9:48 pm	**6:48 pm**
♂ enters ♋	11:09 pm	**8:09 pm**
☽♎ □ ♄ ♑		**10:00 pm**

16 THU
2nd ♎

☽♎ □ ♄ ♑	1:00 am	
☽♎ ⚹ ♃ ♐	4:39 am	**1:39 am**
☽♎ □ ♀ ♑	5:37 am	**2:37 am** ☽ v/c
☽♎ ⚻ ☉ ♉	9:39 am	**6:39 am**
☽ enters ♏	5:26 pm	**2:26 pm**
☽♏ △ ♂ ♋	6:18 pm	**3:18 pm**
☿ ♉ △ ♄ ♑	7:09 pm	**4:09 pm**
☽♏ ☍ ♀ ♉	8:47 pm	**5:47 pm**
☽♏ ☍ ♅ ♉		**9:04 pm**
☽♏ ⚻ ⚷ ♈		**10:36 pm**

122

☽♏ ☍ ♅ ♉ 12:04 am	
☽♏ ⊼ ♂ ♈ 1:36 am	
☿♉ ⊼ ♃ ♐ 5:49 pm **2:49 pm**	
☽♏ △ ♆ ♓ **10:02 pm**	
☿♉ △ ♀ ♑ **10:48 pm**	

FRI 17
2nd ♏

☽♏ △ ♆ ♓ 1:02 am	
☿♉ △ ♀ ♑ 1:48 am	
☽♏ ✶ ♄ ♑ 4:15 am **1:15 am**	
☽♏ ✶ ♀ ♑ 9:04 am **6:04 am**	
☽♏ ☍ ☿ ♉ 10:26 am **7:26 am**	
♀♉ ♂ ♅ ♉ 12:17 pm **9:17 am**	
☽♏ ☍ ☉ ♉ 5:11 pm **2:11 pm** ☽ v/c	
☽ enters ♐ 9:21 pm **6:21 pm**	
☽♐ ⊼ ♂ ♋ **9:52 pm**	

SAT 18
2nd ♏
○ Full Moon 27 ♏ 39

☽♐ ⊼ ♂ ♋ 12:52 am	
☽♐ ⊼ ♅ ♉ 4:28 am **1:28 am**	
☽♐ ⊼ ♀ ♉ 6:00 am **3:00 am**	
☽♐ △ ♂ ♈ 6:01 am **3:01 am**	

SUN 19
3rd ♐

Eastern Time plain / **Pacific Time bold**

	APRIL							MAY							JUNE					
S	M	T	W	T	F	S	S	M	T	W	T	F	S	S	M	T	W	T	F	S
	1	2	3	4	5	6				1	2	3	4							1
7	8	9	10	11	12	13	5	6	7	8	9	10	11	2	3	4	5	6	7	8
14	15	16	17	18	19	20	12	13	14	15	16	17	18	9	10	11	12	13	14	15
21	22	23	24	25	26	27	19	20	21	22	23	24	25	16	17	18	19	20	21	22
28	29	30					26	27	28	29	30	31		23	24	25	26	27	28	29
														30						

20 MON
3rd ♐

VICTORIA DAY (CANADA)

OP: After Moon squares Neptune today until Moon enters Capricorn on Tuesday. Nice Moon in Sagittarius conjunct Jupiter; good for anything that interests you.

☽♐ □ ♆♓	6:32 am	3:32 am	
☽♐ ♂ ♃♐	1:05 pm	10:05 am	☽ v/c

21 TUE
3rd ♐

SUN ENTERS GEMINI

☽♐ ⊼ ☿♉	3:20 am	12:20 am	
☽♐ ⊼ ☉♉	3:56 am	12:56 am	
☽ enters ♑	3:56 am	12:56 am	
☉ enters ♊	3:59 am	12:59 am	
☿ enters ♊	6:52 am	3:52 am	
☉♊ ♂ ☿♊	9:07 am	6:07 am	
☽♑ ☍ ♂♋	10:35 am	7:35 am	
☽♑ △ ♅♉	11:43 am	8:43 am	
☽♑ □ ♆♈	1:18 pm	10:18 am	
☽♑ △ ♀♉	6:58 pm	3:58 pm	

22 WED
3rd ♑

♂♋ ⚹ ♅♉	10:46 am	7:46 am	
☽♑ ⚹ ♆♓	3:14 pm	12:14 pm	
☽♑ ♂ ♄♑	6:23 pm	3:23 pm	
☽♑ ♂ ♇♑	11:58 pm	8:58 pm	☽ v/c

23 THU
3rd ♑

☽ enters ≈	1:49 pm	10:49 am	
☿♊ ⚹ ♆♈	2:04 pm	11:04 am	
☽≈ △ ☉♊	6:49 pm	3:49 pm	
♂♋ □ ♆♈	7:11 pm	4:11 pm	
☽≈ □ ♅♉	10:17 pm	7:17 pm	
☽≈ ⚹ ♆♈	11:52 pm	8:52 pm	
☽≈ ⊼ ♂♋		9:07 pm	
☽≈ △ ☿♊		11:01 pm	

☽≈ ⊼ ♂♋ 12:07 am
☽≈ △ ☿ ♊ 2:01 am
☽≈ □ ♀ ♉ 12:17 pm **9:17 am**

FRI 24
3rd ≈

OP: After Moon squares Venus today until v/c Moon on Saturday. Another excellent OP with the Moon enclosed by two well-dignified benefics; good for anything you choose.

☽≈ ⚹ ♃ ♐ 8:51 am **5:51 am** ☽ v/c
☽ enters ♓ **11:08 pm**

SAT 25
3rd ≈

☽ enters ♓ 2:08 am
☽♓ ⚹ ♅ ♉ 11:02 am **8:02 am**
☽♓ □ ☉ ♊ 12:34 pm **9:34 am**
☉♊ ⚹ ♄ ♈ 12:37 pm **9:37 am**
☽♓ △ ♂♋ 4:07 pm **1:07 pm**

SUN 26
3rd ≈
◑ 4th Quarter 5 ♓ 09

Eastern Time plain / **Pacific Time bold**

	APRIL								MAY								JUNE				
S	M	T	W	T	F	S		S	M	T	W	T	F	S		S	M	T	W	T	F	S
	1	2	3	4	5	6					1	2	3	4								1
7	8	9	10	11	12	13		5	6	7	8	9	10	11		2	3	4	5	6	7	8
14	15	16	17	18	19	20		12	13	14	15	16	17	18		9	10	11	12	13	14	15
21	22	23	24	25	26	27		19	20	21	22	23	24	25		16	17	18	19	20	21	22
28	29	30						26	27	28	29	30	31			23	24	25	26	27	28	29
																30						

27 Mon

4th ♓

Memorial Day

OP: After Moon squares Jupiter today until Moon enters Aries on Tuesday. Moon in Pisces is perfect for Memorial Day remembrances.

☽♓ □ ☿♊	4:07 am	**1:07 am**	
☽♓ ⚹ ♀♉	7:52 am	**4:52 am**	
☽♓ ☌ ♆♓	3:39 pm	**12:39 pm**	
☽♓ ⚹ ♄♑	6:22 pm	**3:22 pm**	
☽♓ □ ♃♐	8:54 pm	**5:54 pm**	
☽♓ ⚹ ♇♑		**9:21 pm**	☽ v/c

28 Tue

4th ♓

☽♓ ⚹ ♇♑	12:21 am		☽ v/c
☽ enters ♈	2:32 pm	**11:32 am**	
☽♈ ☌ ⚷♈		**9:54 pm**	

29 Wed

4th ♈

☽♈ ☌ ⚷♈	12:54 am		
☽♈ ⚹ ☉♊	5:51 am	**2:51 am**	
☽♈ □ ♂♋	7:30 am	**4:30 am**	
☿♊ □ ♆♓	9:22 pm	**6:22 pm**	

30 Thu

4th ♈

☽♈ ⚹ ☿♊	4:03 am	**1:03 am**	
☽♈ □ ♄♑	5:16 am	**2:16 am**	
☽♈ △ ♃♐	7:21 am	**4:21 am**	
☽♈ □ ♇♑	11:08 am	**8:08 am**	☽ v/c
☿♊ ⚻ ♄♑	11:19 am	**8:19 am**	
♀♉ ⚹ ♆♓	12:50 pm	**9:50 am**	
☿♊ ☍ ♃♐	11:12 pm	**8:12 pm**	
☽ enters ♉		**9:43 pm**	

Fri 31
4th ♈

☽ enters ♉ 12:43 am		
☽♉ ♂ ♅♉	9:26 am	**6:26 am**
♀♉ △ ♄♑	11:26 am	**8:26 am**
☽♉ ✶ ♂♋	7:49 pm	**4:49 pm**
☿♊ ⊼ ♇♑	11:14 pm	**8:14 pm**

Sat 1
4th ♉

♀♉ ⊼ ♃♐	5:20 am	**2:20 am**
☽♉ ✶ ♆♓	11:15 am	**8:15 am**
☽♉ △ ♄♑	1:12 pm	**10:12 am**
☽♉ ⊼ ♃♐	2:52 pm	**11:52 am**
☽♉ ♂ ♀♉	3:55 pm	**12:55 pm**
☽♉ △ ♇♑	6:53 pm	**3:53 pm** ☽ v/c

OP: After Moon conjoins Venus today (see "Translating Darkness" on page 78) until Moon enters Gemini on Sunday. Good Balsamic Moon OP to get rid of unnecessary things.

Sun 2
4th ♉

☽ enters ♊ 7:48 am	**4:48 am**	
☽♊ ✶ ♅♈	5:23 pm	**2:23 pm**
♀♉ △ ♇♑	11:42 pm	**8:42 pm**

Eastern Time plain / **Pacific Time bold**

	MAY							JUNE							JULY					
S	M	T	W	T	F	S	S	M	T	W	T	F	S	S	M	T	W	T	F	S
				1	2	3	4						1			1	2	3	4	5	6
5	6	7	8	9	10	11	2	3	4	5	6	7	8	7	8	9	10	11	12	13
12	13	14	15	16	17	18	9	10	11	12	13	14	15	14	15	16	17	18	19	20
19	20	21	22	23	24	25	16	17	18	19	20	21	22	21	22	23	24	25	26	27
26	27	28	29	30	31		23	24	25	26	27	28	29	28	29	30	31			
							30													

3 MON
4th ♊
● New Moon 12 ♊ 34

☽♊ ♂ ☉♊	6:02 am	**3:02 am**	
☽♊ □ ♆♓	4:39 pm	**1:39 pm**	
☽♊ ⊼ ♄♑	6:17 pm	**3:17 pm**	
☽♊ ☍ ♃♐	7:35 pm	**4:35 pm**	
☽♊ ⊼ ♀♑	11:50 pm	**8:50 pm**	

4 TUE
1st ♊
RAMADAN ENDS

☽♊ ♂ ☿♊	11:42 am	**8:42 am**	☽ v/c
☽ enters ♋	12:17 pm	**9:17 am**	
☿ enters ♋	4:05 pm	**1:05 pm**	
☽♋ ✶ ♅♉	8:36 pm	**5:36 pm**	
☽♋ □ ♪♈	9:37 pm	**6:37 pm**	

5 WED
1st ♋

☽♋ ♂ ♂♋	10:48 am	**7:48 am**
☽♋ △ ♆♓	8:06 pm	**5:06 pm**
☽♋ ☍ ♄♑	9:28 pm	**6:28 pm**
☽♋ ⊼ ♃♐	10:28 pm	**7:28 pm**

6 THU
1st ♋

OP: After Moon sextiles Venus (see "Translating Darkness" on page 78) until Moon enters Leo. Fine for anything; especially good for anything related to beauty and self-care.

☽♋ ☍ ♀♑	3:00 am	**12:00 am**	
☽♋ ✶ ♀♉	10:10 am	**7:10 am**	☽ v/c
☽ enters ♌	3:16 pm	**12:16 pm**	
☽♌ □ ♅♉	11:37 pm	**8:37 pm**	
☽♌ △ ♪♈		**9:33 pm**	

☽♌△♅♈	12:33 am	
☿♋⚹♅♉	10:16 am	**7:16 am**
☿♋□♅♈	5:52 pm	**2:52 pm**
☽♌⚹☉♊	7:47 pm	**4:47 pm**
☽♌☌♆♓	10:42 pm	**7:42 pm**
☽♌☌♄♑	11:50 pm	**8:50 pm**
☽♌△♃♐		**9:35 pm**

FRI 7
1st ♌

☽♌△♃♐	12:35 am	
☽♌☌♀♑	5:28 am	**2:28 am**
☽♌□♀♉	5:23 pm	**2:23 pm** ☽ v/c
☽ enters ♍	5:45 pm	**2:45 pm**
♀ enters ♊	9:37 pm	**6:37 pm**
☽♍△♅♉		**11:16 pm**

SAT 8
1st ♌

☽♍△♅♉	2:16 am	
☽♍☌♂♈	3:07 am	**12:07 am**
☽♍⚹☿♋	7:33 am	**4:33 am**
☉♊□♆♓	3:34 pm	**12:34 pm**
☽♍⚹♂♋	8:45 pm	**5:45 pm**
☽♍☍♆♓		**10:17 pm**
☽♍□☉♊		**10:59 pm**
☽♍△♄♑		**11:12 pm**
☽♍□♃♐		**11:42 pm**

SUN 9
1st ♍
◗ 2nd Quarter 19 ♍ 06 (Pacific)
SHAVUOT (BEGINS AT SUNDOWN ON JUNE 8)
OP: After Moon squares Jupiter today or Monday until v/c Moon on Monday. Productive time mostly for night owls.

Eastern Time plain / **Pacific Time bold**

	MAY								JUNE								JULY				
S	M	T	W	T	F	S		S	M	T	W	T	F	S		S	M	T	W	T	F	S
			1	2	3	4								1			1	2	3	4	5	6
5	6	7	8	9	10	11		2	3	4	5	6	7	8		7	8	9	10	11	12	13
12	13	14	15	16	17	18		9	10	11	12	13	14	15		14	15	16	17	18	19	20
19	20	21	22	23	24	25		16	17	18	19	20	21	22		21	22	23	24	25	26	27
26	27	28	29	30	31			23	24	25	26	27	28	29		28	29	30	31			
								30														

June

10 Mon
1st ♍
◑ 2nd Quarter 19 ♍ 06 (Eastern)

☽♍ ☌ ♆♓	1:17 am	
☽♍ □ ☉Ⅱ	1:59 am	
☽♍ △ ♄♍	2:12 am	
☽♍ □ ♃♐	2:42 am	
☉Ⅱ ⚻ ♄♍	5:04 am	**2:04 am**
☽♍ △ ♀♍	8:01 am	**5:01 am** ☽ v/c
☉Ⅱ ☌ ♃♐	11:28 am	**8:28 am**
☽ enters ♎	8:29 pm	**5:29 pm**
☽♎ △ ♀Ⅱ		**9:55 pm**

11 Tue
2nd ♎

☽♎ △ ♀Ⅱ	12:55 am	
☽♎ ⚻ ♅♉	5:15 am	**2:15 am**
☽♎ ☌ ♅♈	6:03 am	**3:03 am**
☽♎ □ ☿♋	5:03 pm	**2:03 pm**
☽♎ □ ♂♋		**11:19 pm**

12 Wed
2nd ♎

☽♎ □ ♂♋	2:19 am	
☽♎ ⚻ ♆♓	4:29 am	**1:29 am**
☽♎ □ ♄♍	5:11 am	**2:11 am**
☽♎ ✶ ♃♐	5:27 am	**2:27 am**
☽♎ △ ☉Ⅱ	8:57 am	**5:57 am**
☽♎ □ ♀♍	11:15 am	**8:15 am** ☽ v/c
☽ enters ♏		**9:02 pm**

13 Thu
2nd ♎

☽ enters ♏	12:02 am	
☽♏ ☌ ♅♉	9:11 am	**6:11 am**
☽♏ ⚻ ♀Ⅱ	9:36 am	**6:36 am**
☽♏ ⚻ ♅♈	9:55 am	**6:55 am**
♀Ⅱ ✶ ♅♈	1:10 pm	**10:10 am**
☉Ⅱ ⚻ ♀♍	5:45 pm	**2:45 pm**
♂♋ △ ♆♓		**11:11 pm**

130

♂♋△♆♓	2:11 am	
☽♏△☿♋	3:33 am **12:33 am**	
☽♏△♆♓	8:53 am **5:53 am**	
☽♏△♂♋	9:13 am **6:13 am**	
☽♏⚹♄♑	9:21 am **6:21 am**	
♂♋☍♄♑	11:50 am **8:50 am**	
♂♋✶♃♐	11:53 am **8:53 am**	
☽♏⚹♀♑	3:46 pm **12:46 pm** ☽ v/c	
☽♏✶☉♊	5:29 pm **2:29 pm**	

FRI 14
2nd ♏
FLAG DAY

☽ enters ♐	5:03 am **2:03 am**	
☽♐✶♅♉	2:41 pm **11:41 am**	
☽♐△⚷♈	3:22 pm **12:22 pm**	
☽♐☍♀♊	8:23 pm **5:23 pm**	

SAT 15
2nd ♏

☿♋△♆♓	7:43 am **4:43 am**	
☿♋✶♃♐	8:02 am **5:02 am**	
☿♋☍♄♑	10:00 am **7:00 am**	
♃♐□♆♓	11:22 am **8:22 am**	
☽♐☌♃♐	3:09 pm **12:09 pm**	
☽♐□♆♓	3:11 pm **12:11 pm**	
☽♐✶☿♋	4:02 pm **1:02 pm**	
☽♐✶♂♋	6:19 pm **3:19 pm**	

SUN 16
2nd ♐
FATHER'S DAY

Eastern Time plain / **Pacific Time bold**

	MAY								JUNE								JULY				
S	M	T	W	T	F	S		S	M	T	W	T	F	S		S	M	T	W	T	F	S
			1	2	3	4								1			1	2	3	4	5	6
5	6	7	8	9	10	11		2	3	4	5	6	7	8		7	8	9	10	11	12	13
12	13	14	15	16	17	18		9	10	11	12	13	14	15		14	15	16	17	18	19	20
19	20	21	22	23	24	25		16	17	18	19	20	21	22		21	22	23	24	25	26	27
26	27	28	29	30	31			23	24	25	26	27	28	29		28	29	30	31			
								30													

17 Mon
2nd ♐
○ Full Moon 25 ♐ 53

☽♐ ☍ ☉♊	4:31 am	**1:31 am**	☽ v/c
☽ enters ♑	12:13 pm	**9:13 am**	
☽♑ △ ♅♉	10:29 pm	**7:29 pm**	
☽♑ □ ⚷♈	11:06 pm	**8:06 pm**	

18 Tue
3rd ♑

♄♑ ⚹ ♆♓	7:47 am	**4:47 am**
☽♑ ⚻ ♀♊	10:17 am	**7:17 am**
☿♋ ☌ ♂♋	12:04 pm	**9:04 am**
☽♑ ☌ ♄♑	11:53 pm	**8:53 pm**
☽♑ ⚹ ♆♓	11:59 pm	**8:59 pm**

19 Wed
3rd ♑

☽♑ ☍ ♂♋	6:22 am	**3:22 am**	
☿♋ ☍ ♇♑	6:56 am	**3:56 am**	
☽♑ ☌ ♇♑	7:17 am	**4:17 am**	
☽♑ ☍ ☿♋	7:19 am	**4:19 am**	☽ v/c
☽♑ ⚻ ☉♊	6:48 pm	**3:48 pm**	
☽ enters ♒	10:01 pm	**7:01 pm**	
♂♋ ☍ ♇♑	11:26 pm	**8:26 pm**	

20 Thu
3rd ♒

OP: After Moon squares Uranus today until v/c Moon on Friday. The whole day Thursday is an excellent time for any projects you're involved with.

☽♒ □ ♅♉	8:56 am	**5:56 am**
☽♒ ⚹ ⚷♈	9:27 am	**6:27 am**

)≈ △ ♀ Ⅱ   3:42 am **12:42 am**
)≈ ✶ ♃ ♐ 10:02 am **7:02 am**) v/c
Ψ ℞   10:36 am **7:36 am**
☉ enters ♋ 11:54 am **8:54 am**
)≈ ⊼ ♂♋   9:16 pm **6:16 pm**
)≈ ⊼ ☿ ♋   **10:06 pm**

Fri 21
3rd ≈
Summer Solstice
Litha
Neptune retrograde
Sun enters Cancer

)≈ ⊼ ☿ ♋   1:06 am
) enters ♓ 10:01 am **7:01 am**
)♓ △ ☉♋ 11:57 am **8:57 am**
)♓ ✶ ♅ ♉   9:25 pm **6:25 pm**

Sat 22
3rd ≈

♀Ⅱ ☍ ♃ ♐ 12:45 pm **9:45 am**
)♓ □ ♃ ♐ 10:03 pm **7:03 pm**
♀Ⅱ ⊼ ♄ ♑ 10:32 pm **7:32 pm**
)♓ ✶ ♄ ♑ 11:09 pm **8:09 pm**
)♓ □ ♀ Ⅱ 11:14 pm **8:14 pm**
)♓ ♂ Ψ♓ 11:55 pm **8:55 pm**

Sun 23
3rd ♓

Eastern Time plain / **Pacific Time bold**

MAY								JUNE								JULY					
S	M	T	W	T	F	S		S	M	T	W	T	F	S		S	M	T	W	T	F	S
			1	2	3	4								1			1	2	3	4	5	6
5	6	7	8	9	10	11		2	3	4	5	6	7	8		7	8	9	10	11	12	13
12	13	14	15	16	17	18		9	10	11	12	13	14	15		14	15	16	17	18	19	20
19	20	21	22	23	24	25		16	17	18	19	20	21	22		21	22	23	24	25	26	27
26	27	28	29	30	31			23	24	25	26	27	28	29		28	29	30	31			
								30														

24 MON
3rd ♓

OP: After Moon trines Mercury (see "Translating Darkness" on page 78) until Moon enter Aries. A time for worthy insights.

♀Ⅱ □ ♆♓	5:58 am	**2:58 am**
☽♓ ⚹ ♀♍	7:17 am	**4:17 am**
☽♓ △ ♂♋	1:22 pm	**10:22 am**
☽♓ △ ☿♋	7:10 pm	**4:10 pm** ☽ v/c
☽ enters ♈	10:38 pm	**7:38 pm**

25 TUE
3rd ♈
◑ 4th Quarter 3 ♈ 34

☽♈ □ ☉♋	5:46 am	**2:46 am**
☽♈ ☌ ♅♈	10:20 am	**7:20 am**

26 WED
4th ♈

☽♈ △ ♃♐	9:20 am	**6:20 am**
☽♈ □ ♄♑	10:38 am	**7:38 am**
☽♈ ⚹ ♀Ⅱ	5:38 pm	**2:38 pm**
☽♈ □ ♀♑	6:43 pm	**3:43 pm**
☿ enters ♌	8:19 pm	**5:19 pm**

27 THU
4th ♈

OP: After Moon conjoins Uranus today until Moon enters Gemini on Saturday. Long OP to work on practical matters.

☽♈ □ ♂♋	3:51 am	**12:51 am** ☽ v/c
♀Ⅱ ⚻ ♀♑	4:20 am	**1:20 am**
☽ enters ♉	9:32 am	**6:32 am**
☽♉ □ ☿♌	10:23 am	**7:23 am**
☉♋ ⚹ ♅♉	1:45 pm	**10:45 am**
☉♋ □ ♀♈	4:00 pm	**1:00 pm**
☽♉ ☌ ♅♉	8:34 pm	**5:34 pm**
☽♉ ⚹ ☉♋	9:06 pm	**6:06 pm**

Mercury Note: Mercury enters its Storm (moving less than 40 minutes of arc per day) on Friday, as it slows down before going retrograde. The Storm acts like the retrograde. Don't start any new projects now—just follow through with the items that are already on your plate. Write down new ideas with date and time they occurred.

☽ ♉ ⚻ ♃ ♐	5:55 pm	**2:55 pm**	
☽ ♉ △ ♄ ♑	7:20 pm	**4:20 pm**	
☽ ♉ ✶ ♆ ♓	8:38 pm	**5:38 pm**	

FRI 28
4th ♉

☽ ♉ △ ♀ ♑	3:08 am	**12:08 am**	
☽ ♉ ✶ ♂ ♋	2:38 pm	**11:38 am** ☽ v/c	
☽ enters ♊	5:09 pm	**2:09 pm**	
☽ ♊ ✶ ☿ ♌	8:51 pm	**5:51 pm**	

SAT 29
4th ♉

☽ ♊ ✶ ♇ ♈	3:41 am	**12:41 am**	
☽ ♊ ☌ ♃ ♐	11:06 pm	**8:06 pm**	
☽ ♊ ⚻ ♄ ♑		**9:34 pm**	
☽ ♊ □ ♆ ♓		**11:03 pm**	

SUN 30
4th ♊

Eastern Time plain / **Pacific Time bold**

	MAY								JUNE								JULY					
S	M	T	W	T	F	S		S	M	T	W	T	F	S		S	M	T	W	T	F	S
			1	2	3	4								1			1	2	3	4	5	6
5	6	7	8	9	10	11		2	3	4	5	6	7	8		7	8	9	10	11	12	13
12	13	14	15	16	17	18		9	10	11	12	13	14	15		14	15	16	17	18	19	20
19	20	21	22	23	24	25		16	17	18	19	20	21	22		21	22	23	24	25	26	27
26	27	28	29	30	31			23	24	25	26	27	28	29		28	29	30	31			
								30														

1 MON
4th ♊
CANADA DAY

☽♊ ⊼ ♄♑	12:34 am		
☽♊ □ ♆♓	2:03 am		
☽♊ ⊼ ♀♑	8:06 am	**5:06 am**	
☽♊ ☌ ♀♊	5:48 pm	**2:48 pm**	☽ v/c
♂ enters ♌	7:19 pm	**4:19 pm**	
☽ enters ♋	9:24 pm	**6:24 pm**	

2 TUE
4th ♋
Solar Eclipse | ● New Moon 10 ♋ 38

☽♋ □ ⚷♈	7:23 am	**4:23 am**	
☽♋ ✶ ♅♉	7:27 am	**4:27 am**	
☽♋ ☌ ☉♋	3:16 pm	**12:16 pm**	
☽♋ ⊼ ♃♐		**10:29 pm**	

3 WED
1st ♋

☽♋ ⊼ ♃♐	1:29 am		
☽♋ ☍ ♄♑	3:01 am	**12:01 am**	
☽♋ △ ♆♓	4:40 am	**1:40 am**	
☽♋ ☍ ♀♑	10:25 am	**7:25 am**	☽ v/c
♀ enters ♋	11:18 am	**8:18 am**	
☽ enters ♌	11:19 pm	**8:19 pm**	
☽♌ ☌ ♂♌		**10:41 pm**	

4 THU
1st ♌
INDEPENDENCE DAY
OP: After Moon squares Uranus today until v/c Moon today or Friday. Moon in Leo is perfect for Independence Day festivities.

☽♌ ☌ ♂♌	1:41 am		
☽♌ ☌ ☿♌	5:50 am	**2:50 am**	
☽♌ △ ⚷♈	9:03 am	**6:03 am**	
☽♌ □ ♅♉	9:11 am	**6:11 am**	
☽♌ △ ♃♐		**11:24 pm**	☽ v/c

Mercury Note: Mercury goes retrograde on Sunday and remains so until July 31, after which it will still be in its Storm until August 8. Projects begun during this entire period may not work out as planned. It's best to use this time for reviews, editing, escrows, and so forth.

Fri 5
1st ♌

☽♌ △ ♃♐ 2:24 am ☽ v/c
☽♌ ⊼ ♄♑ 4:02 am **1:02 am**
☽♌ ⊼ ♆♓ 5:53 am **2:53 am**
☽♌ ⊼ ♇♑ 11:30 am **8:30 am**
☽ enters ♍ **9:25 pm**

Sat 6
1st ♌

☽ enters ♍ 12:25 am
☽♍ ⚹ ♀♋ 6:00 am **3:00 am**
☽♍ ⊼ ⚷♈ 10:10 am **7:10 am**
☽♍ △ ♅♉ 10:24 am **7:24 am**
☽♍ ⚹ ☉♋ **9:49 pm**

Sun 7
1st ♍
Mercury retrograde

☽♍ ⚹ ☉♋ 12:49 am
☽♍ □ ♃♐ 3:20 am **12:20 am**
☽♍ △ ♄♑ 5:04 am **2:04 am**
☽♍ ☍ ♆♓ 7:11 am **4:11 am**
☽♍ △ ♇♑ 12:50 pm **9:50 am** ☽ v/c
☿℞ 7:14 pm **4:14 pm**
☽ enters ♎ **11:07 pm**

Eastern Time plain / **Pacific Time bold**

JUNE

S	M	T	W	T	F	S
						1
2	3	4	5	6	7	8
9	10	11	12	13	14	15
16	17	18	19	20	21	22
23	24	25	26	27	28	29
30						

JULY

S	M	T	W	T	F	S
	1	2	3	4	5	6
7	8	9	10	11	12	13
14	15	16	17	18	19	20
21	22	23	24	25	26	27
28	29	30	31			

AUGUST

S	M	T	W	T	F	S
				1	2	3
4	5	6	7	8	9	10
11	12	13	14	15	16	17
18	19	20	21	22	23	24
25	26	27	28	29	30	31

8 Mon
1st ♍

☽ enters ♎	2:07 am	
♀☌ □ ♅ ♈	7:42 am	**4:42 am**
☽♎ ✶ ♂♌	9:09 am	**6:09 am**
☽♎ ✶ ☿♌	9:37 am	**6:37 am**
♀☌ ✶ ♅♉	11:32 am	**8:32 am**
☉☌ ⚻ ♃ ✗	11:48 am	**8:48 am**
☽♎ ☍ ♅ ♈	12:08 pm	**9:08 am**
☽♎ ⚻ ♅♉	12:28 pm	**9:28 am**
☽♎ □ ♀☌	12:33 pm	**9:33 am**
☿♌ ☌ ♂♌	6:27 pm	**3:27 pm**
♅ ℞	7:40 pm	**4:40 pm**

9 Tue
1st ♎
◐ 2nd Quarter 16 ♎ 58

☽♎ ✶ ♃ ✗	5:30 am	**2:30 am**
☽♎ □ ☉☌	6:55 am	**3:55 am**
☽♎ □ ♄ ♑	7:22 am	**4:22 am**
☽♎ ⚻ ♆ ♓	9:47 am	**6:47 am**
☉☌ ☍ ♄ ♑	1:07 pm	**10:07 am**
☽♎ □ ♀ ♑	3:36 pm	**12:36 pm** ☽ v/c

10 Wed
2nd ♎

OP: After Moon opposes Uranus today until v/c Moon on Thursday. Wait two hours after the opposition. Good for romance and deep emotions, but we're between two eclipses and Mercury is retrograde, so try not to make any major decisions.

☽ enters ♏	5:29 am	**2:29 am**
☽♏ □ ☿♌	12:48 pm	**9:48 am**
☽♏ □ ♂♌	3:20 pm	**12:20 pm**
☽♏ ⚻ ♃ ♏	3:54 pm	**12:54 pm**
☽♏ ☍ ♅♉	4:21 pm	**1:21 pm**
☽♏ △ ♀☌	9:29 pm	**6:29 pm**
☉☌ △ ♆♓		**9:31 pm**

11 Thu
2nd ♏

☉☌ △ ♆♓	12:31 am	
♂♌ △ ♅♈	3:29 am	**12:29 am**
☽♏ ✶ ♄♑	11:42 am	**8:42 am**
♂♌ □ ♅♉	2:01 pm	**11:01 am**
☽♏ △ ♆♓	2:28 pm	**11:28 am**
☽♏ △ ☉☌	3:33 pm	**12:33 pm**
☽♏ ✶ ♀♑	8:28 pm	**5:28 pm** ☽ v/c

138

☽ enters ♐	11:05 am	**8:05 am**	
☽♐ △ ☿♌	5:33 pm	**2:33 pm**	
☽♐ △ ⚷♈	9:58 pm	**6:58 pm**	
☽♐ 🝬 ♅♉	10:33 pm	**7:33 pm**	
☽♐ △ ♂♌		**9:10 pm**	

Fri 12
2nd ♏

☽♐ △ ♂♌	12:10 am		
☽♐ 🝬 ♀♋	9:30 am	**6:30 am**	
☽♐ ♂ ♃♐	4:11 pm	**1:11 pm**	
☽♐ □ ♆♓	9:30 pm	**6:30 pm** ☽ v/c	

Sat 13
2nd ♐

☽♐ 🝬 ☉♋	3:08 am	**12:08 am**	
☉♋ ☍ ♇♑	10:51 am	**7:51 am**	
☽ enters ♑	7:05 pm	**4:05 pm**	
☽♑ 🝬 ☿♌	11:53 pm	**8:53 pm**	

Sun 14
2nd ♐

Eastern Time plain / **Pacific Time bold**

	JUNE								JULY								AUGUST					
S	M	T	W	T	F	S		S	M	T	W	T	F	S		S	M	T	W	T	F	S
						1			1	2	3	4	5	6						1	2	3
2	3	4	5	6	7	8		7	8	9	10	11	12	13		4	5	6	7	8	9	10
9	10	11	12	13	14	15		14	15	16	17	18	19	20		11	12	13	14	15	16	17
16	17	18	19	20	21	22		21	22	23	24	25	26	27		18	19	20	21	22	23	24
23	24	25	26	27	28	29		28	29	30	31					25	26	27	28	29	30	31
30																					

15 Mon
2nd ♑

☽♑ □ ♂♈	6:24 am	**3:24 am**	
☽♑ △ ♅♉	7:08 am	**4:08 am**	
☽♑ ⊼ ♂♌	11:44 am	**8:44 am**	
☽♑ ☍ ♀♋		**9:42 pm**	

16 Tue
2nd ♑
Lunar Eclipse | ○ Full Moon 24 ♑ 04

☽♑ ☍ ♀♋	12:42 am		
☽♑ ♂ ♄♑	3:18 am	**12:18 am**	
♀♋ ⊼ ♃♐	3:44 am	**12:44 am**	
☽♑ ⚹ ♆♓	6:52 am	**3:52 am**	
☽♑ ♂ ♀♑	1:16 pm	**10:16 am**	
☽♑ ☍ ☉♋	5:38 pm	**2:38 pm**	☽ v/c
♀♋ ☍ ♄♑		**10:34 pm**	

17 Wed
3rd ♑
OP: After Moon opposes Mars today or Thursday until v/c Moon on Thursday. Try to focus on what's important. Same warning as for last Wednesday.

♀♋ ☍ ♄♑	1:34 am		
☽ enters ≈	5:19 am	**2:19 am**	
☽≈ ☍ ☿♌	7:39 am	**4:39 am**	
☽≈ ⚹ ♂♈	5:00 pm	**2:00 pm**	
☽≈ □ ♅♉	5:54 pm	**2:54 pm**	
☽≈ ☍ ♂♌		**10:50 pm**	

18 Thu
3rd ≈

☽≈ ☍ ♂♌	1:50 am		
☽≈ ⚹ ♃♐	11:53 am	**8:53 am**	☽ v/c
♀♋ △ ♆♓	2:03 pm	**11:03 am**	
☽≈ ⊼ ♀♋	6:42 pm	**3:42 pm**	

☿ enters ♋ 3:06 am **12:06 am**
☽≈ ⊼ ☉♋ 10:33 am **7:33 am**
☽≈ ⊼ ☿♋ 4:33 pm **1:33 pm**
☽ enters ♓ 5:19 pm **2:19 pm**

Fri 19
3rd ≈

☽♓ ✶ ♅♉ 6:16 am **3:16 am**
☽♓ ⊼ ♂♌ 5:39 pm **2:39 pm**
☽♓ □ ♃♐ **9:06 pm**
☽♓ ✶ ♄♑ **11:28 pm**

Sat 20
3rd ♓

☽♓ □ ♃♐ 12:06 am
☽♓ ✶ ♄♑ 2:28 am
♀♋ ♂ ♀♑ 4:32 am **1:32 am**
☽♓ ♂ ♆♓ 6:46 am **3:46 am**
☉♋ ♂ ☿♋ 8:34 am **5:34 am**
☽♓ ✶ ♀♑ 1:18 pm **10:18 am**
☽♓ △ ♀♋ 2:20 pm **11:20 am**
☽♓ △ ☿♋ **10:58 pm**

Sun 21
3rd ♓

OP: After Moon conjoins Neptune today until Moon enters Aries on Monday. With Mercury retrograde, use this OP to review ongoing projects.

Eastern Time plain / **Pacific Time bold**

		JUNE							JULY							AUGUST			
S	M	T	W	T	F	S	S	M	T	W	T	F	S	S	M	T	W	T	F	S
						1		1	2	3	4	5	6					1	2	3
2	3	4	5	6	7	8	7	8	9	10	11	12	13	4	5	6	7	8	9	10
9	10	11	12	13	14	15	14	15	16	17	18	19	20	11	12	13	14	15	16	17
16	17	18	19	20	21	22	21	22	23	24	25	26	27	18	19	20	21	22	23	24
23	24	25	26	27	28	29	28	29	30	31				25	26	27	28	29	30	31
30																				

22 Mon
3rd ♓
Sun enters Leo

☽♓ △ ☿♋	1:58 am	
☽♓ △ ☉♋	4:34 am	**1:34 am** ☽ v/c
☽ enters ♈	6:02 am	**3:02 am**
☽♈ ☌ ⚷♈	5:50 pm	**2:50 pm**
☉ enters ♌	10:50 pm	**7:50 pm**

23 Tue
3rd ♈

☽♈ △ ♂♌	9:34 am	**6:34 am**
☽♈ △ ♃♐	12:14 pm	**9:14 am**
☽♈ □ ♄♑	2:31 pm	**11:31 am**
☽♈ □ ♇♑		**10:20 pm**

24 Wed
3rd ♈
◑ 4th Quarter 1 ♉ 51

☽♈ □ ♇♑	1:20 am	
☽♈ □ ♀♋	9:12 am	**6:12 am**
☽♈ □ ☿♋	10:48 am	**7:48 am** ☽ v/c
☽ enters ♉	5:42 pm	**2:42 pm**
☿♋ ☌ ♀♋	8:26 pm	**5:26 pm**
☽♉ □ ☉♌	9:18 pm	**6:18 pm**

25 Thu
4th ♉

☽♉ ☌ ♅♉	6:17 am	**3:17 am**
♂♌ △ ♃♐	8:23 am	**5:23 am**
☽♉ ⚻ ♃♐	10:24 pm	**7:24 pm**
☽♉ □ ♂♌	11:12 pm	**8:12 pm**
☽♉ △ ♄♑		**9:29 pm**

☽♉ △ ♄♑	12:29 am			
☽♉ ⚹ ♆♓	4:59 am	**1:59 am**		
☽♉ △ ♀♑	10:57 am	**7:57 am**		
☽♉ ⚹ ☿♋	5:44 pm	**2:44 pm**		
♂♌ ⚻ ♄♑	10:41 pm	**7:41 pm**		
☽♉ ⚹ ♀♋		**9:28 pm**	☽ v/c	
☽ enters ♊		**11:29 pm**		

Fri 26
4th ♉

OP: After Moon sextiles Mercury today (see "Translating Darkness" on page 78) until Moon enters Gemini today or Saturday. Good for pleasure or work; follow through on matters begun before June 28.

☽♉ ⚹ ♀♋	12:28 am		☽ v/c
☽ enters ♊	2:29 am		
☽♊ ⚹ ☉♌	10:16 am	**7:16 am**	
☽♊ ⚹ ♅♈	1:01 pm	**10:01 am**	
♀ enters ♌	9:54 pm	**6:54 pm**	

Sat 27
4th ♉

☽♊ ☍ ♃♐	5:08 am	**2:08 am**	
☽♊ ⚻ ♄♑	7:00 am	**4:00 am**	
☽♊ ⚹ ♂♌	8:45 am	**5:45 am**	
☽♊ □ ♆♓	11:24 am	**8:24 am**	☽ v/c
☽♊ ⚻ ♀♑	4:57 pm	**1:57 pm**	
☉♌ △ ♅♈	11:43 pm	**8:43 pm**	

Sun 28
4th ♊

Eastern Time plain / **Pacific Time bold**

JUNE						
S	M	T	W	T	F	S
						1
2	3	4	5	6	7	8
9	10	11	12	13	14	15
16	17	18	19	20	21	22
23	24	25	26	27	28	29
30						

JULY						
S	M	T	W	T	F	S
	1	2	3	4	5	6
7	8	9	10	11	12	13
14	15	16	17	18	19	20
21	22	23	24	25	26	27
28	29	30	31			

AUGUST						
S	M	T	W	T	F	S
					1	2	3
4	5	6	7	8	9	10
11	12	13	14	15	16	17
18	19	20	21	22	23	24
25	26	27	28	29	30	31

29 Mon
4th ♊

☽ enters ♋	7:31 am	**4:31 am**
☽♋ □ ♃ ♈	5:17 pm	**2:17 pm**
☽♋ ✳ ♅ ♉	6:37 pm	**3:37 pm**
☉♌ □ ♅ ♉	7:14 pm	**4:14 pm**

30 Tue
4th ♋

☽♋ ⊼ ♃ ♐	8:17 am	**5:17 am**
☽♋ ☍ ♄ ♑	9:57 am	**6:57 am**
☽♋ △ ♆ ♓	2:15 pm	**11:15 am**
♂♌ ⊼ ♆ ♓	4:09 pm	**1:09 pm**
☽♋ ☍ ♀ ♑	7:27 pm	**4:27 pm**
☽♋ ♂ ☿ ♋	11:32 pm	**8:32 pm** ☽ v/c

31 Wed
4th ♋

● New Moon 8 ♌ 37

MERCURY DIRECT

OP: This Cazimi Moon is usable ½ hour before and ½ hour after the Sun-Moon conjunction. If you have something important to start around now, this is a great time to do it. With Mercury just turning direct, what you start now may take longer to succeed, but it will eventually.

☽ enters ♌	9:18 am	**6:18 am**
☽♌ ♂ ♀ ♌	4:51 pm	**1:51 pm**
☽♌ △ ♃ ♈	6:32 pm	**3:32 pm**
☽♌ □ ♅ ♉	7:54 pm	**4:54 pm**
☽♌ ♂ ☉♌	11:12 pm	**8:12 pm**
☿ D	11:58 pm	**8:58 pm**

1 Thu
1st ♌

LAMMAS

☽♌ △ ♃ ♐	8:53 am	**5:53 am**
☽♌ ⊼ ♄ ♑	10:23 am	**7:23 am**
♀♌ △ ♃ ♈	12:58 pm	**9:58 am**
☽♌ ⊼ ♆ ♓	2:41 pm	**11:41 am**
☽♌ ♂ ♂♌	4:48 pm	**1:48 pm** ☽ v/c
☽♌ ⊼ ♀ ♑	7:44 pm	**4:44 pm**

FRI 2
1st ♌

♀♌ □ ♅♉ 6:00 am **3:00 am**
☽ enters ♍ 9:20 am **6:20 am**
☽♍ ⚻ ⚷♈ 6:23 pm **3:23 pm**
☽♍ △ ♅♉ 7:50 pm **4:50 pm**

SAT 3
1st ♍

☽♍ □ ♃♐ 8:39 am **5:39 am**
☽♍ △ ♄♑ 10:03 am **7:03 am**
☽♍ ☍ ♆♓ 2:30 pm **11:30 am**
☽♍ △ ♇♑ 7:35 pm **4:35 pm**

☽♍ ⚹ ☿♋ **9:27 pm** ☽ v/c

OP: After Moon trines Pluto today (see "Translating Darkness" on page 78) until v/c Moon today or Sunday. A few hours to be productive.

SUN 4
1st ♍

☽♍ ⚹ ☿♋ 12:27 am ☽ v/c
☽ enters ♎ 9:30 am **6:30 am**
♂♌ ⚻ ♇♑ 11:59 am **8:59 am**
☽♎ ☍ ⚷♈ 6:42 pm **3:42 pm**
☽♎ ⚻ ♅♉ 8:17 pm **5:17 pm**
☽♎ ⚹ ♀♌ **11:00 pm**

Eastern Time plain / **Pacific Time bold**

JULY

S	M	T	W	T	F	S
	1	2	3	4	5	6
7	8	9	10	11	12	13
14	15	16	17	18	19	20
21	22	23	24	25	26	27
28	29	30	31			

AUGUST

S	M	T	W	T	F	S
				1	2	3
4	5	6	7	8	9	10
11	12	13	14	15	16	17
18	19	20	21	22	23	24
25	26	27	28	29	30	31

SEPTEMBER

S	M	T	W	T	F	S
1	2	3	4	5	6	7
8	9	10	11	12	13	14
15	16	17	18	19	20	21
22	23	24	25	26	27	28
29	30					

AUGUST

Mercury Note: Mercury finally leaves its Storm on Thursday, August 8. Look over your notes on any ideas that occurred to you while Mercury was retrograde and/or slow. How do they look now?

5 MON
1st ♎︎

☽⚹♀♌︎	2:00 am	
☽⚹☉♌︎	6:25 am	**3:25 am**
☽⚹♃♐︎	9:27 am	**6:27 am**
☽□♄♑︎	10:46 am	**7:46 am**
☽⚻♆♓︎	3:33 pm	**12:33 pm**
☽□♀♑︎	8:51 pm	**5:51 pm**
☽⚹♂♌︎	10:26 pm	**7:26 pm**

6 TUE
1st ♎︎

☽□☿♋︎	3:36 am	**12:36 am** ☽ v/c
☽ enters ♏︎	11:31 am	**8:31 am**
☽⚻♅♈︎	9:09 pm	**6:09 pm**
☽☍♅♉︎	10:55 pm	**7:55 pm**

7 WED
1st ♏︎
● 2nd Quarter 14 ♏︎ 56

☉♌︎△♃♐︎	3:31 am	**12:31 am**
☽♏︎□♀♌︎	10:01 am	**7:01 am**
☽♏︎□☉♌︎	1:31 pm	**10:31 am**
☽♏︎⚹♄♑︎	2:02 pm	**11:02 am**
☽♏︎△♆♓︎	7:15 pm	**4:15 pm**
☉♌︎⚻♄♑︎	8:24 pm	**5:24 pm**
☽♏︎⚹♀♑︎		**9:53 pm**

8 THU
2nd ♏︎

OP: After Moon squares Mars until v/c Moon. For any purpose you choose, helped by the trine between Venus and Jupiter.

☽♏︎⚹♀♑︎	12:53 am	
☽♏︎□♂♌︎	5:16 am	**2:16 am**
☽♏︎△☿♋︎	10:58 am	**7:58 am** ☽ v/c
♀♌︎△♃♐︎	4:28 pm	**1:28 pm**
☽ enters ♐︎	4:35 pm	**1:35 pm**
☽♐︎△♅♈︎		**11:43 pm**

☽✗ △ ⚷♈	2:43 am		**FRI**	**9**
♀♌ ⊼ ♄♑	4:24 am	**1:24 am**		2nd ✗
☽✗ ⊼ ♅♉	4:43 am	**1:43 am**		
☽✗ ☌ ♃✗	7:25 pm	**4:25 pm**		
☽✗ △ ♀♌	10:19 pm	**7:19 pm**		
☽✗ △ ☉♌		**9:39 pm**		
☽✗ □ ♆♓		**11:12 pm**		

☽✗ △ ☉♌	12:39 am		**SAT**	**10**
☽✗ □ ♆♓	2:12 am			2nd ✗
☽✗ △ ♂♌	3:50 pm	**12:50 pm** ☽ v/c		
☉♌ ⊼ ♆♓	8:44 pm	**5:44 pm**		
☽✗ ⊼ ☿♋	11:24 pm	**8:24 pm**		
☽ enters ♑		**9:50 pm**		

☽ enters ♑	12:50 am		**SUN**	**11**
♃ D	9:37 am	**6:37 am**		2nd ✗
☽♑ □ ⚷♈	11:23 am	**8:23 am**		JUPITER DIRECT
☽♑ △ ♅♉	1:37 pm	**10:37 am**		URANUS RETROGRADE
♀♌ ⊼ ♆♓	1:43 pm	**10:43 am**		
☿ enters ♌	3:46 pm	**12:46 pm**		
♅ Rx	10:27 pm	**7:27 pm**		

Eastern Time plain / **Pacific Time bold**

JULY							AUGUST							SEPTEMBER						
S	M	T	W	T	F	S	S	M	T	W	T	F	S	S	M	T	W	T	F	S
	1	2	3	4	5	6					1	2	3	1	2	3	4	5	6	7
7	8	9	10	11	12	13	4	5	6	7	8	9	10	8	9	10	11	12	13	14
14	15	16	17	18	19	20	11	12	13	14	15	16	17	15	16	17	18	19	20	21
21	22	23	24	25	26	27	18	19	20	21	22	23	24	22	23	24	25	26	27	28
28	29	30	31				25	26	27	28	29	30	31	29	30					

August

12 Mon
2nd ♑

☽♑ ☌ ♄♑	5:53 am	**2:53 am**	
☽♑ ⚹ ♆♓	11:58 am	**8:58 am**	
☽♑ ⚻ ♀♌	2:31 pm	**11:31 am**	
☽♑ ⚻ ☉♌	3:24 pm	**12:24 pm**	
☽♑ ☌ ♇♑	6:11 pm	**3:11 pm**	☽ v/c

13 Tue
2nd ♑

☽♑ ⚻ ♂♌	5:30 am	**2:30 am**	
☽ enters ≈	11:35 am	**8:35 am**	
☽≈ ☍ ☿♌	4:33 pm	**1:33 pm**	
☽≈ ⚹ ⚷♈	10:21 pm	**7:21 pm**	
☽≈ □ ♅♉		**9:47 pm**	
☉♌ ☌ ♀♌		**11:07 pm**	
♀♌ ⚻ ♇♑		**11:08 pm**	
☉♌ ⚻ ♇♑		**11:08 pm**	

14 Wed
2nd ≈

☽≈ □ ♅♉		**12:47 am**	
☉♌ ☌ ♀♌		**2:07 am**	
♀♌ ⚻ ♇♑		**2:08 am**	
☉♌ ⚻ ♇♑		**2:08 am**	
☽≈ ⚹ ♃♐	4:37 pm	**1:37 pm**	

15 Thu
2nd ≈
○ Full Moon 22 ≈ 24

☽≈ ☍ ☉♌	8:29 am	**5:29 am**	
☽≈ ☍ ♀♌	9:16 am	**6:16 am**	
☿♌ △ ⚷♈	5:15 pm	**2:15 pm**	
☽≈ ☍ ♂♌	9:02 pm	**6:02 pm**	☽ v/c
☽ enters ♓	11:49 pm	**8:49 pm**	

☿♌ □ ♅♉	1:07 pm	**10:07 am**
☽♓ ⚹ ♅♉	1:11 pm	**10:11 am**
☽♓ ⚻ ☿♌	1:12 pm	**10:12 am**

FRI 16
3rd ♓

☽♓ □ ♃♐	5:17 am	**2:17 am**	
☽♓ ⚹ ♄♑	5:36 am	**2:36 am**	
☽♓ ♂ ♆♓	12:08 pm	**9:08 am**	
☽♓ ⚹ ♀♑	6:35 pm	**3:35 pm**	☽ v/c
♂ enters ♍		**10:18 pm**	
☽♓ ⚻ ☉♌		**11:32 pm**	

SAT 17
3rd ♓

OP: After Moon sextiles Pluto today until Moon enters Aries on Sunday. (Pisces is one of the four signs in which the v/c Moon is a good thing. See page 75.) Good for artistic pursuits and group activities.

♂ enters ♍	1:18 am	
☽♓ ⚻ ☉♌	2:32 am	
☽♓ ⚻ ♀♌	5:02 am	**2:02 am**
☽ enters ♈	12:33 pm	**9:33 am**
☽♈ ⚻ ♂♍	1:11 pm	**10:11 am**
☽♈ ♂ ♅♈	11:08 pm	**8:08 pm**

SUN 18
3rd ♓

JULY								AUGUST								SEPTEMBER						
S	M	T	W	T	F	S		S	M	T	W	T	F	S		S	M	T	W	T	F	S
	1	2	3	4	5	6						1	2	3		1	2	3	4	5	6	7
7	8	9	10	11	12	13		4	5	6	7	8	9	10		8	9	10	11	12	13	14
14	15	16	17	18	19	20		11	12	13	14	15	16	17		15	16	17	18	19	20	21
21	22	23	24	25	26	27		18	19	20	21	22	23	24		22	23	24	25	26	27	28
28	29	30	31					25	26	27	28	29	30	31		29	30					

August

19 Mon
3rd ♈

☽♈△ ☿♌	11:41 am	**8:41 am**
☽♈□ ♄♑	5:56 pm	**2:56 pm**
☽♈△ ♃♐	5:58 pm	**2:58 pm**

20 Tue
3rd ♈

OP: After Moon squares Pluto today until v/c Moon today or Wednesday. A whole day when good actions can bring excellent results.

☽♈□ ♇♑	6:53 am	**3:53 am**
☽♈△ ☉♌	8:01 pm	**5:01 pm**
☽♈△ ♀♌		**9:06 pm** ☽ v/c
☽ enters ♉		**9:37 pm**

21 Wed
3rd ♈

☽♈△ ♀♌	12:06 am	☽ v/c
☽ enters ♉	12:37 am	
☿♌⚻ ♄♑	4:26 am	**1:26 am**
☽♉△ ♂♍	4:33 am	**1:33 am**
♀ enters ♍	5:06 am	**2:06 am**
☿♌△ ♃♐	6:05 am	**3:05 am**
☽♉ ♂ ♅♉	1:33 pm	**10:33 am**

22 Thu
3rd ♉

OP: After Moon squares Mercury today until Moon enters Gemini on Friday. Nice OP to work through practical matters.

☽♉△ ♄♑	4:57 am	**1:57 am**
☽♉⚻ ♃♐	5:21 am	**2:21 am**
☽♉□ ☿♌	9:22 am	**6:22 am**
☽♉✶ ♆♓	11:23 am	**8:23 am**
☽♉△ ♀♑	5:33 pm	**2:33 pm** ☽ v/c
☿♌⚻ ♆♓	10:26 pm	**7:26 pm**

☉ enters ♍	6:02 am	**3:02 am**	
☽ enters ♊	10:34 am	**7:34 am**	
☽♊ □ ☉♍	10:56 am	**7:56 am**	
☽♊ □ ♀♍	4:17 pm	**1:17 pm**	
☽♊ □ ♂♍	5:19 pm	**2:19 pm**	
☽♊ ⚹ ⚷♈	8:04 pm	**5:04 pm**	

FRI 23
3rd ♉
◑ 4th Quarter 0 ♊ 12
SUN ENTERS VIRGO

♀♍ ☌ ♂♍	1:05 pm	**10:05 am**	
☽♊ ⚻ ♄♑	1:12 pm	**10:12 am**	
☽♊ ☍ ♃♐	1:53 pm	**10:53 am**	
☿♌ ⚻ ♇♑	2:14 pm	**11:14 am**	
☽♊ □ ♆♓	7:18 pm	**4:18 pm**	
☽♊ ⚻ ♇♑		**10:06 pm**	
☽♊ ⚹ ☿♌		**11:58 pm**	☽ v/c

SAT 24
4th ♊

OP: After Moon squares Neptune today until v/c Moon today or Sunday. Fine for writing, communications, or social events.

☽♊ ⚻ ♇♑	1:06 am		
☽♊ ⚹ ☿♌	2:58 am		☽ v/c
♀♍ ⚻ ⚷♈	6:33 am	**3:33 am**	
☽ enters ♋	5:05 pm	**2:05 pm**	
☽♋ ⚹ ☉♍	9:33 pm	**6:33 pm**	
♂♍ ⚻ ⚷♈	10:13 pm	**7:13 pm**	
☽♋ □ ⚷♈		**10:48 pm**	
☽♋ ⚹ ♂♍		**10:59 pm**	

SUN 25
4th ♊

Eastern Time plain / **Pacific Time bold**

JULY

S	M	T	W	T	F	S
	1	2	3	4	5	6
7	8	9	10	11	12	13
14	15	16	17	18	19	20
21	22	23	24	25	26	27
28	29	30	31			

AUGUST

S	M	T	W	T	F	S
				1	2	3
4	5	6	7	8	9	10
11	12	13	14	15	16	17
18	19	20	21	22	23	24
25	26	27	28	29	30	31

SEPTEMBER

S	M	T	W	T	F	S
1	2	3	4	5	6	7
8	9	10	11	12	13	14
15	16	17	18	19	20	21
22	23	24	25	26	27	28
29	30					

26 Mon
4th ♋

☽ ♋ □ ♂ ♈	1:48 am	
☽ ♋ ⚹ ♂ ♍	1:59 am	
☽ ♋ ⚹ ♀ ♍	3:44 am	**12:44 am**
☽ ♋ ⚹ ♅ ♉	4:27 am	**1:27 am**
♀ ♍ △ ♅ ♉	11:38 am	**8:38 am**
☽ ♋ ☍ ♄ ♑	5:45 pm	**2:45 pm**
☽ ♋ ⊼ ♃ ♐	6:42 pm	**3:42 pm**
☽ ♋ △ ♆ ♓	11:28 pm	**8:28 pm**

27 Tue
4th ♋

☽ ♋ ☍ ♇ ♑	4:55 am	**1:55 am**	☽ v/c
☽ enters ♌	7:53 pm	**4:53 pm**	

28 Wed
4th ♌

OP: After Moon squares Uranus until v/c **Moon.** Good time to wrap up what's already on your plate with the Balsamic Moon.

☽ ♌ △ ♂ ♈	3:55 am	**12:55 am**	
☽ ♌ □ ♅ ♉	6:29 am	**3:29 am**	
♂ ♍ △ ♅ ♉	6:53 am	**3:53 am**	
☉ ♍ ⊼ ♂ ♈	8:17 am	**5:17 am**	
☽ ♌ ⊼ ♄ ♑	6:57 pm	**3:57 pm**	
☽ ♌ △ ♃ ♐	8:07 pm	**5:07 pm**	☽ v/c
☽ ♌ ⊼ ♆ ♓		**9:23 pm**	

29 Thu
4th ♌

☽ ♌ ⊼ ♆ ♓	12:23 am	
☿ enters ♍	3:48 am	**12:48 am**
☽ ♌ ⊼ ♇ ♑	5:35 am	**2:35 am**
☽ enters ♍	7:57 pm	**4:57 pm**
☽ ♍ ☌ ☿ ♍	10:22 pm	**7:22 pm**
☉ ♍ △ ♅ ♉	11:14 pm	**8:14 pm**

FRI 30
4th ♍
● New Moon 6 ♍ 47

☽♍ ⚻ ⚷♈	3:35 am	**12:35 am**
☽♍ △ ♅♉	6:09 am	**3:09 am**
☽♍ ☌ ☉♍	6:37 am	**3:37 am**
☽♍ ☌ ♂♍	8:15 am	**5:15 am**
☽♍ ☌ ♀♍	2:13 pm	**11:13 am**
☽♍ △ ♄♑	6:14 pm	**3:14 pm**
☽♍ □ ♃♐	7:39 pm	**4:39 pm**
☽♍ ☍ ♆♓	11:35 pm	**8:35 pm**

SAT 31
1st ♍
ISLAMIC NEW YEAR

☽♍ △ ♇♑	4:46 am	**1:46 am** ☽ v/c
☿♍ ⚻ ⚷♈	1:57 pm	**10:57 am**
☽ enters ♎	7:08 pm	**4:08 pm**
☽♎ ☍ ⚷♈		**11:42 pm**

SUN 1
1st ♎

☽♎ ☍ ⚷♈	2:42 am	
☽♎ ⚻ ♅♉	5:22 am	**2:22 am**
☿♍ △ ♅♉	10:11 am	**7:11 am**
♀♍ △ ♄♑	2:49 pm	**11:49 am**
☽♎ □ ♄♑	5:40 pm	**2:40 pm**
☽♎ ⚹ ♃♐	7:24 pm	**4:24 pm**
☽♎ ⚻ ♆♓	11:10 pm	**8:10 pm**

Eastern Time plain / **Pacific Time bold**

AUGUST

S	M	T	W	T	F	S
				1	2	3
4	5	6	7	8	9	10
11	12	13	14	15	16	17
18	19	20	21	22	23	24
25	26	27	28	29	30	31

SEPTEMBER

S	M	T	W	T	F	S
1	2	3	4	5	6	7
8	9	10	11	12	13	14
15	16	17	18	19	20	21
22	23	24	25	26	27	28
29	30					

OCTOBER

S	M	T	W	T	F	S
		1	2	3	4	5
6	7	8	9	10	11	12
13	14	15	16	17	18	19
20	21	22	23	24	25	26
27	28	29	30	31		

SEPTEMBER

2 MON
1st ♎︎
LABOR DAY (US)
LABOUR DAY (CANADA)

☽︎♎︎ □ ♀♑︎	4:34 am	**1:34 am** ☽︎ v/c
☉︎♍︎ ☌ ♂︎♍︎	6:42 am	**3:42 am**
♀♍︎ □ ♃ ♐︎	12:26 pm	**9:26 am**
☽︎ enters ♏︎	7:35 pm	**4:35 pm**

3 TUE
1st ♏︎
OP: After Moon sextiles Mercury today (see "Translating Darkness" on page 78) until v/c Moon on Wednesday. Good for any purpose, including romance and relationships.

☽︎♏︎ ⊼ ♅♈︎	3:24 am	**12:24 am**
☽︎♏︎ ☍ ♅♉︎	6:18 am	**3:18 am**
☿♍︎ ☌ ♂︎♍︎	11:40 am	**8:40 am**
☽︎♏︎ ⚹ ♂︎♍︎	1:12 pm	**10:12 am**
☽︎♏︎ ⚹ ☿♍︎	1:21 pm	**10:21 am**
☽︎♏︎ ⚹ ☉︎♍︎	1:58 pm	**10:58 am**
☽︎♏︎ ⚹ ♄♑︎	7:18 pm	**4:18 pm**
☉︎♍︎ ☌ ♀♍︎	9:40 pm	**6:40 pm**
☽︎♏︎ ⚹ ♀♍︎		**9:32 pm**
☽︎♏︎ △ ♆♓︎		**10:09 pm**

4 WED
1st ♏︎

☽︎♏︎ ⚹ ♀♍︎	12:32 am	
☽︎♏︎ △ ♆♓︎	1:09 am	
☽︎♏︎ ⚹ ♀♑︎	6:58 am	**3:58 am** ☽︎ v/c
♀♍︎ ☍ ♆♓︎	7:26 am	**4:26 am**
☽︎ enters ♐︎	11:08 pm	**8:08 pm**

5 THU
1st ♐︎
◐ 2nd Quarter 13 ♐︎ 15

☽︎♐︎ △ ♅♈︎	7:23 am	**4:23 am**
☿♍︎ △ ♄♑︎	8:37 am	**5:37 am**
☽︎♐︎ ⊼ ♅♉︎	10:36 am	**7:36 am**
☽︎♐︎ □ ♂︎♍︎	8:49 pm	**5:49 pm**
☽︎♐︎ □ ☉︎♍︎	11:10 pm	**8:10 pm**

☿♍ □ ♃✗ 3:11 am **12:11 am**
☽✗ ♂ ♃✗ 3:20 am **12:20 am**
☽✗ □ ☿♍ 3:21 am **12:21 am**
☽✗ □ ♆♓ 6:53 am **3:53 am**
☽✗ □ ♀♍ 12:03 pm **9:03 am** ☽ v/c
☉♍ △ ♄♑ 5:56 pm **2:56 pm**
♀♍ △ ♇♑ 11:46 pm **8:46 pm**

Fri 6
2nd ✗

☿♍ ☍ ♆♓ 3:18 am **12:18 am**
☽ enters ♑ 6:37 am **3:37 am**
☽♑ □ ♀♈ 3:16 pm **12:16 pm**
☽♑ △ ♅♉ 6:47 pm **3:47 pm**

Sat 7
2nd ✗

☽♑ △ ♂♍ 8:53 am **5:53 am**
☽♑ ♂ ♄♑ 9:42 am **6:42 am**
☉♍ □ ♃✗ 11:27 am **8:27 am**
☽♑ △ ☉♍ 1:11 pm **10:11 am**
☽♑ ✶ ♆♓ 4:18 pm **1:18 pm**
☽♑ △ ☿♍ 11:02 pm **8:02 pm**
☽♑ ♂ ♀♑ 11:03 pm **8:03 pm**
☿♍ △ ♀♑ 11:09 pm **8:09 pm**
♂♍ △ ♄♑ **9:14 pm**

Sun 8
2nd ♑

OP: After Moon conjoins Pluto today until v/c Moon on Monday. Use for practical matters; only for night owls.

Eastern Time plain / **Pacific Time bold**

AUGUST							SEPTEMBER							OCTOBER						
S	M	T	W	T	F	S	S	M	T	W	T	F	S	S	M	T	W	T	F	S
				1	2	3	1	2	3	4	5	6	7			1	2	3	4	5
4	5	6	7	8	9	10	8	9	10	11	12	13	14	6	7	8	9	10	11	12
11	12	13	14	15	16	17	15	16	17	18	19	20	21	13	14	15	16	17	18	19
18	19	20	21	22	23	24	22	23	24	25	26	27	28	20	21	22	23	24	25	26
25	26	27	28	29	30	31	29	30						27	28	29	30	31		

September

9 Mon
2nd ♑

♂♍△♄♑	12:14 am	
☽♑△♀♍	4:30 am	**1:30 am** ☽ v/c
☽ enters ♒	5:24 pm	**2:24 pm**
☽♒⚹♂♈		**11:12 pm**

10 Tue
2nd ♒
OP: After Moon squares Uranus today until v/c Moon today or Wednesday. A good time to get going with important activities, although we're feeling spaced-out.

☽♒⚹♂♈	2:12 am	
☉♍☍♆♓	3:24 am	**12:24 am**
☽♒□♅♉	5:57 am	**2:57 am**
☽♒☌♂♍		**9:02 pm**
☽♒⚹♃♐		**10:22 pm** ☽ v/c

11 Wed
2nd ♒

☽♒☌♂♍	12:02 am	
☽♒⚹♃♐	1:22 am	☽ v/c
☽♒☌☉♍	6:24 am	**3:24 am**
☽♒☌☿♍	9:58 pm	**6:58 pm**
☽♒☌♀♍	11:47 pm	**8:47 pm**

12 Thu
2nd ♒

♂♍□♃♐	5:06 am	**2:06 am**
☽ enters ♓	5:52 am	**2:52 am**
☽♓⚹♅♉	6:27 pm	**3:27 pm**

156

Fri 13
2nd ♓
○ Full Moon 21 ♓ 05 (Pacific)

☽♓ ⚹ ♄♑	10:04 am	**7:04 am**	
☿♍ ☌ ♀♍	11:11 am	**8:11 am**	
☽♓ □ ♃♐	2:35 pm	**11:35 am**	
☉♍ △ ♇♑	3:42 pm	**12:42 pm**	
☽♓ ☍ ♂♍	4:12 pm	**1:12 pm**	
☽♓ ☌ ♆♓	4:43 pm	**1:43 pm**	
☽♓ ⚹ ♇♑	11:49 pm	**8:49 pm**	
☽♓ ☍ ☉♍		**9:33 pm**	☽ v/c
♂♍ ☍ ♆♓		**10:25 pm**	

Sat 14
2nd ♓
○ Full Moon 21 ♓ 05 (Eastern)

☽♓ ☍ ☉♍	12:33 am		☽ v/c
♂♍ ☍ ♆♓	1:25 am		
☿ enters ♎	3:14 am	**12:14 am**	
♀ enters ♎	9:43 am	**6:43 am**	
☽ enters ♈	6:32 pm	**3:32 pm**	
☽♈ ☍ ♀♎	7:34 pm	**4:34 pm**	
☽♈ ☍ ☿♎	9:08 pm	**6:08 pm**	
☽♈ ☌ ⚷♈		**11:58 pm**	

Sun 15
3rd ♈

☽♈ ☌ ⚷♈	2:58 am	
☽♈ □ ♄♑	10:29 pm	**7:29 pm**

Eastern Time plain / **Pacific Time bold**

AUGUST

S	M	T	W	T	F	S
				1	2	3
4	5	6	7	8	9	10
11	12	13	14	15	16	17
18	19	20	21	22	23	24
25	26	27	28	29	30	31

SEPTEMBER

S	M	T	W	T	F	S
1	2	3	4	5	6	7
8	9	10	11	12	13	14
15	16	17	18	19	20	21
22	23	24	25	26	27	28
29	30					

OCTOBER

S	M	T	W	T	F	S
		1	2	3	4	5
6	7	8	9	10	11	12
13	14	15	16	17	18	19
20	21	22	23	24	25	26
27	28	29	30	31		

SEPTEMBER

16 Mon
3rd ♈

☽♈△♃✗	3:29 am	**12:29 am**
☽♈☌♂♍	7:58 am	**4:58 am**
☽♈□♀♑	12:03 pm	**9:03 am ☽ v/c**
☿♎☍♃♈	12:55 pm	**9:55 am**
☽♈☌☉♍	6:06 pm	**3:06 pm**

17 Tue
3rd ♈

☽ enters ♉	6:31 am	**3:31 am**
☽♉☌♀♎	2:21 pm	**11:21 am**
♀♎☍♃♈	4:21 pm	**1:21 pm**
☿♎☌♅♉	4:57 pm	**1:57 pm**
☽♉☌♅♉	6:31 pm	**3:31 pm**
☽♉☌☿♎	6:46 pm	**3:46 pm**

18 Wed
3rd ♉

SATURN DIRECT

OP: After Moon trines Saturn today (see "Translating Darkness" on page 78) until Moon enters Gemini on Thursday. Okay for pleasure or work, with so many planets in earth signs.

♄D	4:47 am	**1:47 am**
☽♉△♄♑	9:52 am	**6:52 am**
☽♉☌♃✗	3:15 pm	**12:15 pm**
☽♉☌♆♓	4:02 pm	**1:02 pm**
☽♉△♂♍	10:20 pm	**7:20 pm**
☽♉△♀♑	11:02 pm	**8:02 pm**

19 Thu
3rd ♉

♀♎☌♅♉	6:27 am	**3:27 am**
☽♉△☉♍	9:57 am	**6:57 am ☽ v/c**
♂♍△♀♑	11:53 am	**8:53 am**
☽ enters ♊	4:58 pm	**1:58 pm**
☽♊☌♃♈		**9:31 pm**

☽Ⅱ ⚹ ♅♈ 12:31 am
☽Ⅱ △ ♀♎ 6:50 am **3:50 am**
☽Ⅱ △ ☿♎ 1:24 pm **10:24 am**
☽Ⅱ ⊼ ♄♑ 7:16 pm **4:16 pm**
☽Ⅱ ☍ ♃♐ **9:54 pm**
☽Ⅱ □ ♆♓ **10:02 pm**

FRI **20**
3rd Ⅱ

☽Ⅱ ☍ ♃♐ 12:54 am
☽Ⅱ □ ♆♓ 1:02 am
☽Ⅱ ⊼ ♀♑ 7:47 am **4:47 am**
☽Ⅱ □ ♂♍ 10:05 am **7:05 am**
♃♐ □ ♆♓ 12:44 pm **9:44 am**
☽Ⅱ □ ☉♍ 10:41 pm **7:41 pm** ☽ v/c
☽ enters ♋ **9:50 pm**

SAT **21**
3rd Ⅱ
◐ 4th Quarter 28 Ⅱ 49
UN INTERNATIONAL DAY OF PEACE

☽ enters ♋ 12:50 am
☽♋ □ ♅♈ 7:47 am **4:47 am**
☽♋ ⚹ ♅♉ 11:31 am **8:31 am**
☿♎ □ ♄♑ 12:19 pm **9:19 am**
☽♋ □ ♀♎ 7:30 pm **4:30 pm**
☽♋ ☍ ♄♑ **10:39 pm**

SUN **22**
4th Ⅱ

Eastern Time plain / **Pacific Time bold**

AUGUST							SEPTEMBER							OCTOBER					
S	M	T	W	T	F	S	S	M	T	W	T	F	S	S	M	T	W	T	F	S
					1	2	3		1	2	3	4	5	6	7			1	2	3	4	5
4	5	6	7	8	9	10	8	9	10	11	12	13	14	6	7	8	9	10	11	12
11	12	13	14	15	16	17	15	16	17	18	19	20	21	13	14	15	16	17	18	19
18	19	20	21	22	23	24	22	23	24	25	26	27	28	20	21	22	23	24	25	26
25	26	27	28	29	30	31	29	30						27	28	29	30	31		

23 Mon
4th ⊗
Fall Equinox
Mabon
Sun enters Libra

☽⊗ ☌ ♄ ♑	1:39 am	
☽⊗ □ ☿ ♎	3:23 am	**12:23 am**
☉ enters ♎	3:50 am	**12:50 am**
☽⊗ △ ♆ ♓	6:55 am	**3:55 am**
☽⊗ ⚻ ♃ ♐	7:22 am	**4:22 am**
☽⊗ ☌ ♀ ♑	1:21 pm	**10:21 am**
☽⊗ ⚹ ♂ ♍	6:05 pm	**3:05 pm** ☽ v/c

24 Tue
4th ⊗
OP: After Moon squares Uranus today until v/c Moon on Wednesday. Excellent OP during the Last Quarter Moon for finishing up projects already begun.

☽ enters ♌	5:19 am	**2:19 am**
☽♌ ⚹ ☉ ♎	7:12 am	**4:12 am**
☿ ♎ ⚻ ♆ ♓	9:57 am	**6:57 am**
☽♌ △ ♅ ♈	11:40 am	**8:40 am**
☽♌ □ ♅ ♉	3:12 pm	**12:12 pm**
☿ ♎ ⚹ ♃ ♐	5:01 pm	**2:01 pm**

25 Wed
4th ♌

☽♌ ⚹ ♀ ♎	3:35 am	**12:35 am**
☽♌ ⚻ ♄ ♑	4:35 am	**1:35 am**
☽♌ ⚻ ♆ ♓	9:25 am	**6:25 am**
☽♌ △ ♃ ♐	10:21 am	**7:21 am**
☽♌ ⚹ ☿ ♎	12:14 pm	**9:14 am** ☽ v/c
♀ ♎ □ ♄ ♑	3:20 pm	**12:20 pm**
☽♌ ⚻ ♀ ♑	3:32 pm	**12:32 pm**

26 Thu
4th ♌

☽ enters ♍	6:37 am	**3:37 am**
☽♍ ⚻ ♅ ♈	12:29 pm	**9:29 am**
☽♍ △ ♅ ♉	3:53 pm	**12:53 pm**
☿ ♎ □ ♀ ♑	7:52 pm	**4:52 pm**
☉ ♎ ☌ ♅ ♈	9:22 pm	**6:22 pm**

☽♍ △ ♄♑ 4:50 am **1:50 am**
☽♍ ☍ ♆♓ 9:21 am **6:21 am**
☽♍ □ ♃♐ 10:45 am **7:45 am**
☽♍ △ ♀♑ 3:20 pm **12:20 pm**
♀♎ ⚻ ♆♓ 10:50 pm **7:50 pm**
☽♍ ♂ ♂♍ 11:58 pm **8:58 pm** ☽ v/c

FRI 27
4th ♍

☽ enters ♎ 6:03 am **3:03 am**
☽♎ ☍ ♅♈ 11:41 am **8:41 am**
☽♎ ♂ ☉♎ 2:26 pm **11:26 am**
☽♎ ⚻ ♅♉ 3:05 pm **12:05 pm**
♀♎ ✳ ♃♐ 7:41 pm **4:41 pm**
☉♎ ⚻ ♅♉   **9:14 pm**

SAT 28
4th ♍
● New Moon 5 ♎ 20

☉♎ ⚻ ♅♉ 12:14 am
☽♎ □ ♄♑ 4:08 am **1:08 am**
☽♎ ⚻ ♆♓ 8:33 am **5:33 am**
☽♎ ✳ ♃♐ 10:27 am **7:27 am**
☽♎ ♂ ♀♎ 11:38 am **8:38 am**
☽♎ □ ♀♑ 2:40 pm **11:40 am**
☽♎ ♂ ☿♎ 10:06 pm **7:06 pm** ☽ v/c

SUN 29
1st ♎

Eastern Time plain / **Pacific Time bold**

AUGUST							SEPTEMBER							OCTOBER					
S	M	T	W	T	F	S	S	M	T	W	T	F	S	S	M	T	W	T	F	S
					1	2	3	1	2	3	4	5	6	7			1	2	3	4	5
4	5	6	7	8	9	10	8	9	10	11	12	13	14	6	7	8	9	10	11	12
11	12	13	14	15	16	17	15	16	17	18	19	20	21	13	14	15	16	17	18	19
18	19	20	21	22	23	24	22	23	24	25	26	27	28	20	21	22	23	24	25	26
25	26	27	28	29	30	31	29	30						27	28	29	30	31		

30 Mon
1st ♎︎
Rosh Hashanah (begins at sundown on Sept. 29)

☽ enters ♏︎	5:42 am	**2:42 am**
☽♏︎ ⚻ ⚷ ♈︎	11:22 am	**8:22 am**
☽♏︎ ☍ ♅ ♉︎	2:56 pm	**11:56 am**
♀♎︎ □ ♀ ♑︎		**9:18 pm**

1 Tue
1st ♏︎

♀♎︎ □ ♀ ♑︎	12:18 am	
☽♏︎ ⚹ ♄ ♑︎	4:43 am	**1:43 am**
☽♏︎ △ ♆ ♓︎	9:12 am	**6:12 am**
☽♏︎ ⚹ ♀ ♑︎	3:45 pm	**12:45 pm**

2 Wed
1st ♏︎
Pluto direct (Pacific)

☽♏︎ ⚹ ♂ ♍︎	5:46 am	**2:46 am** ☽ v/c
☽ enters ♐︎	7:44 am	**4:44 am**
☽♐︎ △ ⚷ ♈︎	1:38 pm	**10:38 am**
☽♐︎ ⚻ ♅ ♉︎	5:30 pm	**2:30 pm**
☽♐︎ ⚹ ☉♎︎		**9:42 pm**
♀D		**11:39 pm**

3 Thu
1st ♐︎
Pluto direct (Eastern)
OP: After Moon squares Neptune today until Moon enters Capricorn on Friday. Wait two hours after the square for a good sequence of aspects when things can work really well.

☽♐︎ ⚹ ☉♎︎	12:42 am	
♀D	2:39 am	
☿ enters ♏︎	4:14 am	**1:14 am**
☽♐︎ □ ♆ ♓︎	1:14 pm	**10:14 am**
☽♐︎ ☌ ♃ ♐︎	4:40 pm	**1:40 pm**
♂ enters ♎︎		**9:22 pm**

Fri 4
1st ♐

♂ enters ♎ 12:22 am
☽♐ ✶ ♀♎ 3:34 am **12:34 am** ☽ v/c
☽ enters ♑ 1:43 pm **10:43 am**
☽♑ □ ♂♎ 2:26 pm **11:26 am**
☽♑ ✶ ☿♏ 5:52 pm **2:52 pm**
☽♑ □ ⚷♈ 7:55 pm **4:55 pm**
☽♑ △ ♅♉ **9:08 pm**

Sat 5
1st ♑
◐ 2nd Quarter 12 ♑ 09

☽♑ △ ♅♉ 12:08 am
☿♏ ⚻ ⚷♈ 12:05 pm **9:05 am**
☽♑ □ ☉♎ 12:47 pm **9:47 am**
☽♑ ☌ ♄♑ 4:40 pm **1:40 pm**
☽♑ ✶ ♆♓ 9:26 pm **6:26 pm**

Sun 6
2nd ♑

☽♑ ☌ ♇♑ 5:15 am **2:15 am**
☽♑ □ ♀♎ 7:25 pm **4:25 pm** ☽ v/c
☽ enters ♒ 11:42 pm **8:42 pm**
☿♏ ☍ ♅♉ **11:17 pm**

Eastern Time plain / **Pacific Time bold**

SEPTEMBER

S	M	T	W	T	F	S
1	2	3	4	5	6	7
8	9	10	11	12	13	14
15	16	17	18	19	20	21
22	23	24	25	26	27	28
29	30					

OCTOBER

S	M	T	W	T	F	S
		1	2	3	4	5
6	7	8	9	10	11	12
13	14	15	16	17	18	19
20	21	22	23	24	25	26
27	28	29	30	31		

NOVEMBER

S	M	T	W	T	F	S
					1	2
3	4	5	6	7	8	9
10	11	12	13	14	15	16
17	18	19	20	21	22	23
24	25	26	27	28	29	30

7 MON

2nd ≈

OP: After Moon squares Mercury today until v/c Moon on Tuesday. Keep it real and go for it.

☿♏ ♂ ♅ ☿	2:17 am	
☽≈ △ ♂⌒	3:43 am	**12:43 am**
☽≈ ✶ ♆ ♈	6:03 am	**3:03 am**
☽≈ □ ♅ ☿	10:32 am	**7:32 am**
☽≈ □ ☿♏	11:36 am	**8:36 am**
☉⌒□♄\	3:07 pm	**12:07 pm**

8 TUE

2nd ≈

☽≈ △ ☉⌒	5:20 am	**2:20 am**
♀ enters ♏	1:06 pm	**10:06 am**
☽≈ ✶ ♃ ♐	2:27 pm	**11:27 am** ☽ v/c
♂⌒ ♂ ♆ ♈	8:33 pm	**5:33 pm**

9 WED

2nd ≈

YOM KIPPUR (BEGINS AT SUNDOWN ON OCTOBER 8)

☽ enters ♓	12:05 pm	**9:05 am**
☽♓ △ ♀♏	2:47 pm	**11:47 am**
☽♓ ⊼ ♂⌒	7:40 pm	**4:40 pm**
☽♓ ✶ ♅ ☿	10:55 pm	**7:55 pm**
☉⌒⊼♆♓	11:24 pm	**8:24 pm**

10 THU

2nd ♓

☽♓ △ ☿♏	7:49 am	**4:49 am**
☽♓ ✶ ♄\	5:08 pm	**2:08 pm**
☽♓ ♂ ♆♓	9:34 pm	**6:34 pm**
♀♏ ⊼ ♆ ♈	11:31 pm	**8:31 pm**
☽♓ ⊼ ☉⌒	11:37 pm	**8:37 pm**

Fri 11
2nd ♓

☽♓ □ ♃♐ 4:02 am **1:02 am**
☽♓ ✶ ♇♑ 5:55 am **2:55 am** ☽ v/c
☽ enters ♈ **9:46 pm**

OP: After Moon squares Jupiter today until Moon enters Aries today or Saturday. (Pisces is one of the four signs in which the v/c Moon is a good thing. See page 75.) Whole day Friday to take advantage of this OP.

Sat 12
2nd ♓

☽ enters ♈ 12:46 am
♂♎ ⊼ ♅♉ 4:00 am **1:00 am**
☽♈ ☌ ⚷♈ 6:43 am **3:43 am**
☽♈ ⊼ ♀♏ 10:28 am **7:28 am**
☽♈ ☍ ♂♎ 11:43 am **8:43 am**
♀♏ ☍ ♅♉ 6:07 pm **3:07 pm**

Sun 13
2nd ♈
○ Full Moon 20 ♈ 14

☽♈ ⊼ ☿♏ 3:18 am **12:18 am**
☽♈ □ ♄♑ 5:36 am **2:36 am**
☉♎ ✶ ♃♐ 2:02 pm **11:02 am**
☽♈ △ ♃♐ 4:55 pm **1:55 pm**
☽♈ ☍ ☉♎ 5:08 pm **2:08 pm**
☽♈ □ ♇♑ 5:59 pm **2:59 pm** ☽ v/c
☿♏ ✶ ♄♑ **11:56 pm**

Eastern Time plain / **Pacific Time bold**

SEPTEMBER

S	M	T	W	T	F	S
1	2	3	4	5	6	7
8	9	10	11	12	13	14
15	16	17	18	19	20	21
22	23	24	25	26	27	28
29	30					

OCTOBER

S	M	T	W	T	F	S
		1	2	3	4	5
6	7	8	9	10	11	12
13	14	15	16	17	18	19
20	21	22	23	24	25	26
27	28	29	30	31		

NOVEMBER

S	M	T	W	T	F	S
					1	2
3	4	5	6	7	8	9
10	11	12	13	14	15	16
17	18	19	20	21	22	23
24	25	26	27	28	29	30

14 Mon

3rd ♈︎

Columbus Day
Indigenous Peoples' Day
Sukkot begins (at sundown on October 13)
Thanksgiving Day (Canada)

☿♏︎ ✶ ♄♑︎	2:56 am	
☉♎︎ □ ♀♑︎	3:38 am	**12:38 am**
☽ enters ♉︎	12:24 pm	**9:24 am**
☽♉︎ ☌ ♅♉︎	10:29 pm	**7:29 pm**
☽♉︎ ⊼ ♂♎︎		**11:24 pm**

15 Tue

3rd ♉︎

OP: After Moon opposes Mercury today until Moon enters Gemini on Wednesday. Positive for practical work, shopping, pleasure, etc.

☽♉︎ ⊼ ♂♎︎	2:24 am	
☽♉︎ ☍ ♀♏︎	4:33 am	**1:33 am**
☽♉︎ △ ♄♑︎	4:44 pm	**1:44 pm**
☿♏︎ △ ♆♓︎	6:45 pm	**3:45 pm**
☽♉︎ ✶ ♆♓︎	8:23 pm	**5:23 pm**
☽♉︎ ☍ ☿♏︎	8:33 pm	**5:33 pm**

16 Wed

3rd ♉︎

☽♉︎ ⊼ ♃♐︎	4:21 am	**1:21 am**
☽♉︎ △ ♀♑︎	4:37 am	**1:37 am** ☽ v/c
☽♉︎ ⊼ ☉♎︎	8:49 am	**5:49 am**
☽ enters ♊︎	10:30 pm	**7:30 pm**

17 Thu

3rd ♊︎

☽♊︎ ✶ ⚷♈︎	3:46 am	**12:46 am**
☽♊︎ △ ♂♎︎	3:11 pm	**12:11 pm**
☽♊︎ ⊼ ♀♏︎	8:25 pm	**5:25 pm**
☽♊︎ ⊼ ♄♑︎		**11:12 pm**

☽Ⅱ ☌ ♄♑ 2:12 am
☽Ⅱ □ ♆♓ 5:25 am **2:25 am**
☽Ⅱ ☌ ☿♏ 11:02 am **8:02 am**
☽Ⅱ ☌ ♀♑ 1:30 pm **10:30 am**
☽Ⅱ ☍ ♃♐ 1:58 pm **10:58 am**

☽Ⅱ △ ☉♎ 10:14 pm **7:14 pm** ☽ v/c

FRI 18
3rd Ⅱ

OP: After Moon opposes Jupiter until v/c **Moon.** Good for anything; perfect for learning and insights.

☽ enters ♋ 6:43 am **3:43 am**
☽♋ □ ♅♈ 11:36 am **8:36 am**
☽♋ ⚹ ♅♉ 3:47 pm **12:47 pm**
☿♏ ⚹ ♀♑ 6:21 pm **3:21 pm**
☽♋ □ ♂♎ **10:35 pm**

SAT 19
3rd Ⅱ

☽♋ □ ♂♎ 1:35 am
☽♋ △ ♀♏ 9:26 am **6:26 am**
☽♋ ☍ ♄♑ 9:29 am **6:29 am**
♀♏ ⚹ ♄♑ 9:58 am **6:58 am**
☽♋ △ ♆♓ 12:17 pm **9:17 am**
☽♋ ☍ ♀♑ 8:07 pm **5:07 pm**
☽♋ ☌ ♃♐ 9:14 pm **6:14 pm**
☽♋ △ ☿♏ 10:06 pm **7:06 pm**

SUN 20
3rd ♋
SUKKOT ENDS

Eastern Time plain / **Pacific Time bold**

SEPTEMBER						
S	M	T	W	T	F	S
1	2	3	4	5	6	7
8	9	10	11	12	13	14
15	16	17	18	19	20	21
22	23	24	25	26	27	28
29	30					

OCTOBER						
S	M	T	W	T	F	S
		1	2	3	4	5
6	7	8	9	10	11	12
13	14	15	16	17	18	19
20	21	22	23	24	25	26
27	28	29	30	31		

NOVEMBER						
S	M	T	W	T	F	S
					1	2
3	4	5	6	7	8	9
10	11	12	13	14	15	16
17	18	19	20	21	22	23
24	25	26	27	28	29	30

21 Mon
3rd ♋

☽ 4th Quarter 27 ♋ 49

OP: After Moon squares Sun until Moon enters Leo. (Cancer is one of the four signs in which the v/c Moon is a good thing. See page 75.) Short OP during the Last Quarter; time to wrap up existing projects.

☽♋ □ ☉♎	8:39 am	5:39 am	☽ v/c	
☽ enters ♌	12:29 pm	9:29 am		
♀♏ △ ♆♓	3:40 pm	12:40 pm		
☽♌ △ ♅♈	4:58 pm	1:58 pm		
☽♌ □ ♅♉	8:56 pm	5:56 pm		

22 Tue
4th ♌

☽♌ ⚹ ♂♎	8:58 am	5:58 am
☽♌ ⚻ ♄♑	2:05 pm	11:05 am
☽♌ ⚻ ♆♓	4:28 pm	1:28 pm
☽♌ □ ♀♏	6:54 pm	3:54 pm
☽♌ ⚻ ♇♑		9:01 pm
☽♌ △ ♃♐		10:41 pm

23 Wed
4th ♌

SUN ENTERS SCORPIO

☽♌ ⚻ ♇♑	12:01 am		
☽♌ △ ♃♐	1:41 am		
☽♌ □ ☿♏	5:14 am	2:14 am	☽ v/c
☉ enters ♏	1:20 pm	10:20 am	
☽ enters ♍	3:29 pm	12:29 pm	
☽♍ ⚹ ☉♏	3:39 pm	12:39 pm	
☽♍ ⚻ ♅♈	7:37 pm	4:37 pm	
☽♍ △ ♅♉	11:24 pm	8:24 pm	

24 Thu
4th ♍

☽♍ △ ♄♑	4:05 pm	1:05 pm
☽♍ ☍ ♆♓	6:07 pm	3:07 pm
☽♍ ⚹ ♀♏		10:02 pm
☽♍ △ ♇♑		10:26 pm

Mercury Note: Mercury enters its Storm (moving less than 40 minutes of arc per day) on Friday, as it slows down before going retrograde. The Storm acts like the retrograde. Don't start any new projects now—just follow through with the items that are already on your plate. Write down new ideas with date and time they occurred.

☽♍ ✶ ♀♏	1:02 am	
☽♍ △ ♀♑	1:26 am	
☽♍ □ ♃♐	3:37 am **12:37 am**	
♀♏ ✶ ♀♑	5:52 am **2:52 am**	
☽♍ ✶ ☿♏	9:00 am **6:00 am** ☽ v/c	
☽ enters ♎	4:20 pm **1:20 pm**	
☽♎ ☍ ♅♈	8:13 pm **5:13 pm**	
☉♏ ⊼ ♅♈	11:29 pm **8:29 pm**	
☽♎ ⊼ ♅♉	11:52 pm **8:52 pm**	

FRI 25
4th ♍

OP: After Moon squares Jupiter until v/c Moon. A few hours to be productive on items already begun. Mostly for night owls.

☽♎ ♂ ♂♎	3:48 pm **12:48 pm**
☽♎ □ ♄♑	4:32 pm **1:32 pm**
☽♎ ⊼ ♆♓	6:18 pm **3:18 pm**
☽♎ □ ♀♑	**10:38 pm**

SAT 26
4th ♎

☽♎ □ ♀♑	1:38 am	
☽♎ ✶ ♃♐	4:22 am **1:22 am** ☽ v/c	
♂♎ □ ♄♑	10:31 am **7:31 am**	
☽ enters ♏	4:29 pm **1:29 pm**	
☽♏ ⊼ ♅♈	8:17 pm **5:17 pm**	
☽♏ ♂ ☉♏	11:39 pm **8:39 pm**	
☽♏ ☍ ♅♉	11:58 pm **8:58 pm**	

SUN 27
4th ♎

● New Moon 4 ♏ 25

This Cazimi Moon is usable ½ hour before and ½ hour after the Sun-Moon conjunction. The exact Uranus opposition can bring surprises, but the ensuing series of easy aspects indicates success.

Eastern Time plain / **Pacific Time bold**

SEPTEMBER						
S	M	T	W	T	F	S
1	2	3	4	5	6	7
8	9	10	11	12	13	14
15	16	17	18	19	20	21
22	23	24	25	26	27	28
29	30					

OCTOBER						
S	M	T	W	T	F	S
		1	2	3	4	5
6	7	8	9	10	11	12
13	14	15	16	17	18	19
20	21	22	23	24	25	26
27	28	29	30	31		

NOVEMBER						
S	M	T	W	T	F	S
					1	2
3	4	5	6	7	8	9
10	11	12	13	14	15	16
17	18	19	20	21	22	23
24	25	26	27	28	29	30

OCTOBER

Mercury Note: Mercury goes retrograde on Thursday and remains so until November 20, after which it will still be in its Storm until November 25. Projects begun during this entire period may not work out as planned. It's best to use this time for reviews, editing, escrows, and so forth.

28 MON
1st ♏

☉♏ ☌ ♅ ♉	4:15 am	**1:15 am**
☽♏ ⚹ ♄ ♑	5:19 am	**2:19 pm**
☽♏ △ ♆ ♓	6:52 pm	**3:52 pm**
♂♎ ⚻ ♆ ♓	11:57 pm	**8:57 pm**
☽♏ ⚹ ♀ ♑		**11:32 pm**

29 TUE
1st ♏

☽♏ ⚹ ♀ ♑	2:32 am	
☽♏ ☌ ♀ ♏	11:14 am	**8:14 am**
☽♏ ☌ ☿ ♏	1:34 pm	**10:34 am** ☽ v/c
☽ enters ♐	5:58 pm	**2:58 pm**
☽♐ △ ♀ ♈	9:50 pm	**6:50 pm**
☽♐ ⚻ ♅ ♉		**10:41 pm**

30 WED
1st ♐

OP: After Moon sextiles Mars today or Thursday (see "Translating Darkness" on page 78) until Moon enters Capricorn on Thursday. Mercury is stationary, so it's okay to follow through on projects already begun.

☽♐ ⚻ ♅ ♉	1:41 am	
☿♏ ☌ ♀ ♏	6:05 pm	**3:05 pm**
☽♐ □ ♆ ♓	9:49 pm	**6:49 pm**
☽♐ ⚹ ♂♎		**9:10 pm**

31 THU
1st ♐
HALLOWEEN
SAMHAIN
MERCURY RETROGRADE

☽♐ ⚹ ♂♎	12:10 am	
☽♐ ☌ ♃ ♐	10:30 am	**7:30 am** ☽ v/c
☿℞	11:41 am	**8:41 am**
☽ enters ♑	10:38 pm	**7:38 pm**
☽♑ □ ♀ ♈		**11:39 pm**

170

Fri 1
1st ♑
All Saints' Day

☽♑ □ ⚷♈ 2:39 am
☽♑ △ ♅♉ 6:47 am **3:47 am**
☽♑ ⚹ ☉♏ 3:21 pm **12:21 pm**
♀ enters ♐ 4:25 pm **1:25 pm**

Sat 2
1st ♑

☽♑ ☌ ♄♑ 3:29 am **12:29 am**
☽♑ ⚹ ♆♓ 4:35 am **1:35 am**
☽♑ □ ♂♎ 10:11 am **7:11 am**
☽♑ ☌ ♇♑ 1:39 pm **10:39 am**
☽♑ ⚹ ☿♏ **10:46 pm** ☽ v/c

Sun 3
1st ♑
Daylight Saving Time ends at 2:00 a.m.

☽♑ ⚹ ☿♏ 1:46 am ☽ v/c
☽ enters ♒ 6:19 am **3:19 am**
♀♐ △ ⚷♈ 8:20 am **5:20 am**
☽♒ ⚹ ⚷♈ 10:28 am **7:28 am**
☽♒ ⚹ ♀♐ 10:42 am **7:42 am**
☽♒ □ ♅♉ 2:50 pm **11:50 am**

Eastern Time plain / **Pacific Time bold**

OCTOBER

S	M	T	W	T	F	S
		1	2	3	4	5
6	7	8	9	10	11	12
13	14	15	16	17	18	19
20	21	22	23	24	25	26
27	28	29	30	31		

NOVEMBER

S	M	T	W	T	F	S
					1	2
3	4	5	6	7	8	9
10	11	12	13	14	15	16
17	18	19	20	21	22	23
24	25	26	27	28	29	30

DECEMBER

S	M	T	W	T	F	S
1	2	3	4	5	6	7
8	9	10	11	12	13	14
15	16	17	18	19	20	21
22	23	24	25	26	27	28
29	30	31				

NOVEMBER

4 MON
1st ≈
◐ 2nd Quarter 11 ≈ 42

☽≈ □ ☉♏	5:23 am	**2:23 am**
☽≈ △ ♂♎	11:28 pm	**8:28 pm**
♀♐ ⚻ ♅♉		**11:09 pm**

5 TUE
2nd ≈
ELECTION DAY (GENERAL)

♀♐ ⚻ ♅♉	2:09 am	
♂♎ □ ♇♑	5:28 am	**2:28 am**
☽≈ ⚹ ♃♐	6:29 am	**3:29 am**
☽≈ □ ☿♏	9:37 am	**6:37 am** ☽ v/c
☽ enters ♓	6:08 pm	**3:08 pm**
☽♓ ⚹ ♅♉		**11:43 pm**

6 WED
2nd ♓

☽♓ ⚹ ♅♉	2:43 am	
☽♓ □ ♀♐	5:41 am	**2:41 am**
☽♓ △ ☉♏	11:25 pm	**8:25 pm**
☽♓ ⚹ ♄♑		**11:18 pm**
☽♓ ☌ ♆♓		**11:37 pm**

7 THU
2nd ♓

OP: After Moon trines Mercury today (see "Translating Darkness" on page 78) until Moon enters Aries on Friday. (Pisces is one of the four signs in which the v/c Moon is a good thing. See page 75.) Excellent for artistic activity and mind expansion.

☽♓ ⚹ ♄♑	2:18 am	
☽♓ ☌ ♆♓	2:37 am	
☽♓ ⚹ ♇♑	12:33 pm	**9:33 am**
☽♓ ⚻ ♂♎	3:40 pm	**12:40 pm**
☽♓ △ ☿♏	5:52 pm	**2:52 pm**
☽♓ □ ♃♐	8:13 pm	**5:13 pm** ☽ v/c

☽ enters ♈	6:49 am	**3:49 am**	
☽♈ ♂ ♅♈	10:45 am	**7:45 am**	
☉♏ ✶ ♄♑	12:06 pm	**9:06 am**	
☉♏ △ ♆♓	12:56 pm	**9:56 am**	
♄♑ ✶ ♆♓	9:45 pm	**6:45 pm**	
☽♈ △ ♀♐		**10:15 pm**	

FRI 8
2nd ♓

☽♈ △ ♀♐	1:15 am		
☽♈ □ ♄♑	2:55 pm	**11:55 am**	
☽♈ ⊼ ☉♏	5:09 pm	**2:09 pm**	
☿♏ ✶ ♀♑	9:09 pm	**6:09 pm**	
☽♈ ⊼ ☿♏		**9:17 pm**	
☽♈ □ ♀♑		**9:37 pm**	

SAT 9
2nd ♈

☽♈ ⊼ ☿♏	12:17 am		
☽♈ □ ♀♑	12:37 am		
☽♈ ☍ ♂♎	6:58 am	**3:58 am**	
☽♈ △ ♃♐	9:00 am	**6:00 am** ☽ v/c	
☽ enters ♉	6:18 pm	**3:18 pm**	
☽♉ ♂ ♅♉		**11:10 pm**	

SUN 10
2nd ♈

Eastern Time plain / **Pacific Time bold**

OCTOBER

S	M	T	W	T	F	S
		1	2	3	4	5
6	7	8	9	10	11	12
13	14	15	16	17	18	19
20	21	22	23	24	25	26
27	28	29	30	31		

NOVEMBER

S	M	T	W	T	F	S
					1	2
3	4	5	6	7	8	9
10	11	12	13	14	15	16
17	18	19	20	21	22	23
24	25	26	27	28	29	30

DECEMBER

S	M	T	W	T	F	S
1	2	3	4	5	6	7
8	9	10	11	12	13	14
15	16	17	18	19	20	21
22	23	24	25	26	27	28
29	30	31				

11 MON
2nd ♉
VETERANS DAY
REMEMBRANCE DAY (CANADA)

☽♉ ♂ ♅♉	2:10 am	
☉♏ ♂ ☿♏	10:22 am	**7:22 am**
☽♉ ⊼ ♀♐	6:40 pm	**3:40 pm**
☽♉ ⚹ ♆♓		**10:11 pm**
☽♉ △ ♄♑		**10:44 pm**

12 TUE
2nd ♉
○ Full Moon 19 ♉ 52
OP: After Moon opposes Sun today until Moon enters Gemini on Wednesday. Time for a hands-on approach to your existing project.

☽♉ ⚹ ♆♓	1:11 am	
☽♉ △ ♄♑	1:44 am	
☽♉ ♂ ☿♏	4:51 am	**1:51 am**
☽♉ ♂ ☉♏	8:34 am	**5:34 am**
☽♉ △ ♀♑	10:48 am	**7:48 am** ☽ v/c
♂♎ ⚹ ♃♐	1:21 pm	**10:21 am**
☽♉ ⊼ ♃♐	7:45 pm	**4:45 pm**
☽♉ ⊼ ♂♎	7:59 pm	**4:59 pm**

13 WED
3rd ♉

☽ enters ♊	3:46 am	**12:46 am**
☽♊ ⚹ ♅♈	7:12 am	**4:12 am**
☿♏ ⚹ ♄♑	9:35 am	**6:35 am**
☉♏ ⚹ ♀♑	1:00 pm	**10:00 am**
☿♏ △ ♆♓	5:34 pm	**2:34 pm**

14 THU
3rd ♊

☽♊ ⊼ ☿♏	8:14 am	**5:14 am**
☽♊ ♂ ♀♐	9:16 am	**6:16 am**
☽♊ □ ♆♓	9:32 am	**6:32 am**
☽♊ ⊼ ♄♑	10:27 am	**7:27 am**
♀♐ □ ♆♓	12:06 pm	**9:06 am**
☽♊ ⊼ ♀♑	6:56 pm	**3:56 pm**
☽♊ ⊼ ☉♏	9:23 pm	**6:23 pm**

☽Ⅱ ☍ ♃♐ 4:24 am **1:24 am**

FRI 15
3rd Ⅱ

☽Ⅱ △ ♂♎ 6:40 am **3:40 am** ☽ v/c
☽ enters ♋ 11:15 am **8:15 am**
☽♋ □ ⚷♈ 2:28 pm **11:28 am**
☽♋ ⚹ ♅♉ 6:16 pm **3:16 pm**

OP: After Moon opposes Jupiter until v/c Moon. A few good
hours in the middle of the night.

☽♋ △ ☿♏ 11:08 am **8:08 am**
☽♋ △ ♆♓ 4:02 pm **1:02 pm**
☽♋ ☍ ♄♑ 5:18 pm **2:18 pm**
☽♋ ☌ ♀♐ 9:21 pm **6:21 pm**
☽♋ ☍ ♀♑ **10:15 pm**

SAT 16
3rd ♋

☽♋ ☍ ♀♑ 1:15 am
☽♋ △ ☉♏ 7:53 am **4:53 am**
☽♋ ☌ ♃♐ 11:10 am **8:10 am**
☽♋ □ ♂♎ 3:14 pm **12:14 pm** ☽ v/c
☽ enters ♌ 4:57 pm **1:57 pm**
☽♌ △ ⚷♈ 7:58 pm **4:58 pm**
☽♌ □ ♅♉ 11:35 pm **8:35 pm**

SUN 17
3rd ♋

Eastern Time plain / **Pacific Time bold**

OCTOBER						
S	M	T	W	T	F	S
		1	2	3	4	5
6	7	8	9	10	11	12
13	14	15	16	17	18	19
20	21	22	23	24	25	26
27	28	29	30	31		

NOVEMBER						
S	M	T	W	T	F	S
					1	2
3	4	5	6	7	8	9
10	11	12	13	14	15	16
17	18	19	20	21	22	23
24	25	26	27	28	29	30

DECEMBER						
S	M	T	W	T	F	S
1	2	3	4	5	6	7
8	9	10	11	12	13	14
15	16	17	18	19	20	21
22	23	24	25	26	27	28
29	30	31				

18 Mon
3rd ♌

☽♌ □ ☿♏	1:53 pm	**10:53 am**
☽♌ ⚹ ♆♓	8:47 pm	**5:47 pm**
☽♌ ⚹ ♄♑	10:21 pm	**7:21 pm**
♂ enters ♏		**11:40 pm**

19 Tue
3rd ♌
◗ 4th Quarter 27 ♌ 14

♂ enters ♏	2:40 am	
☽♌ ⚹ ♀♑	5:48 am	**2:48 am**
☽♌ △ ♀ ✶	7:04 am	**4:04 am**
☽♌ △ ♃ ✶	4:06 pm	**1:06 pm**
☽♌ □ ☉♏	4:11 pm	**1:11 pm** ☽ v/c
☽ enters ♍	8:54 pm	**5:54 pm**
☽♍ ⚹ ♂♏	9:48 pm	**6:48 pm**
☽♍ ⚹ ♀ ♈	11:45 pm	**8:45 pm**

20 Wed
4th ♍
Mercury direct

☽♍ △ ♅ ♉	3:12 am	**12:12 am**
☿ D	2:12 pm	**11:12 am**
☽♍ ⚹ ☿♏	4:32 pm	**1:32 pm**
☽♍ ☍ ♆♓	11:51 pm	**8:51 pm**
☽♍ △ ♄♑		**10:43 pm**

21 Thu
4th ♍
OP: After Moon squares Jupiter until v/c Moon. Good time to be productive or just enjoy yourself.

☽♍ △ ♄♑	1:43 am	
☽♍ △ ♀♑	8:42 am	**5:42 am**
♂♏ ⚹ ♀ ♈	2:31 pm	**11:31 am**
☽♍ □ ♀ ✶	2:39 pm	**11:39 am**
☽♍ □ ♃ ✶	7:25 pm	**4:25 pm**

☽♍ ⚹ ☉♏	10:31 pm	**7:31 pm** ☽ v/c
☽ enters ♎	11:20 pm	**8:20 pm**
☽♎ ☍ ♀ ♈		**11:02 pm**

Fri 22
4th ♎︎
Sun enters Sagittarius

☽☌ ♂ ♅ ♈︎	2:02 am	
☽☌ ⊼ ♅ ♉︎	5:21 am	**2:21 am**
☉ enters ♐︎	9:59 am	**6:59 am**
☽☌ ⊼ ♆ ♓︎		**10:43 pm**

Sat 23
4th ♎︎

OP: After Moon squares Pluto until v/c Moon. Wait two hours after the square. The Moon is Balsamic and Mercury is slow: still okay for finishing up projects that started prior to October 25.

☽☌ ∧ ♆ ♓︎	1:43 am	
☽☌ □ ♄ ♑︎	3:53 am	**12:53 am**
☽☌ □ ♀ ♑︎	10:32 am	**7:32 am**
☽☌ ⚹ ♀ ♐︎	9:00 pm	**6:00 pm**
☽☌ ⚹ ♃ ♐︎	9:49 pm	**6:49 pm** ☽ v/c
☉♐︎ △ ♂ ♈︎	11:55 pm	**8:55 pm**
☽ enters ♏︎		**9:58 pm**

Sun 24
4th ♎︎

☽ enters ♏︎	12:58 am	
☽♏︎ ⊼ ♂ ♈︎	3:37 am	**12:37 am**
☽♏︎ ☌ ♂ ♏︎	6:36 am	**3:36 am**
☽♏︎ ☌ ♅ ♉︎	6:51 am	**3:51 am**
♀♐︎ ☌ ♃ ♐︎	8:33 am	**5:33 am**
♂♏︎ ☌ ♅ ♉︎	11:51 am	**8:51 am**
☽♏︎ ☌ ☿ ♏︎	10:50 pm	**7:50 pm**

Eastern Time plain / **Pacific Time bold**

	OCTOBER								NOVEMBER								DECEMBER					
S	M	T	W	T	F	S		S	M	T	W	T	F	S		S	M	T	W	T	F	S
		1	2	3	4	5							1	2		1	2	3	4	5	6	7
6	7	8	9	10	11	12		3	4	5	6	7	8	9		8	9	10	11	12	13	14
13	14	15	16	17	18	19		10	11	12	13	14	15	16		15	16	17	18	19	20	21
20	21	22	23	24	25	26		17	18	19	20	21	22	23		22	23	24	25	26	27	28
27	28	29	30	31				24	25	26	27	28	29	30		29	30	31				

NOVEMBER

Mercury Note: Mercury finally leaves its Storm on Monday, November 25. Look over your notes on any ideas that occurred to you while Mercury was retrograde and/or slow. How do they look now?

25 MON
4th ♏︎

☽♏︎ △ ♆♓︎	3:27 am	**12:27 am**	
☽♏︎ ✳ ♄♑︎	5:59 am	**2:59 am**	
☽♏︎ ✳ ♀♑︎	12:30 pm	**9:30 am**	☽ v/c
♀ enters ♑︎	7:28 am	**4:28 pm**	
☉♐︎ ⊼ ♅♉︎	9:00 pm	**6:00 pm**	

26 TUE
4th ♏︎
● New Moon 4 ♐︎ 03

☽ enters ♐︎	3:11 am	**12:11 am**	
☽♐︎ △ ♃♈︎	5:51 am	**2:51 am**	
☽♐︎ ⊼ ♅♉︎	9:07 am	**6:07 am**	
☽♐︎ ☌ ☉♐︎	10:06 am	**7:06 am**	
♀♑︎ □ ♃♈︎		**10:28 pm**	

27 WED
1st ♐︎
NEPTUNE DIRECT

♀♑︎ □ ♃♈︎	1:28 am	
☽♐︎ □ ♆♓︎	6:37 am	**3:37 am**
♆D	7:32 am	**4:32 am**

28 THU
1st ♐︎
THANKSGIVING DAY (US)
OP: After Moon conjoins Jupiter until Moon enters Capricorn. A few good hours before dawn.

☿♏︎ △ ♆♓︎	4:51 am	**1:51 am**	
☽♐︎ ☌ ♃♐︎	5:50 am	**2:50 am**	☽ v/c
☽ enters ♑︎	7:33 am	**4:33 am**	
☽♑︎ □ ♃♈︎	10:18 am	**7:18 am**	
♀♑︎ △ ♅♉︎	1:27 pm	**10:27 am**	
☽♑︎ △ ♅♉︎	1:41 pm	**10:41 am**	
☽♑︎ ☌ ♀♑︎	1:43 pm	**10:43 am**	
☽♑︎ ✳ ♂♏︎	7:06 pm	**4:06 pm**	

☽♑ ⚹ ♆♓ 12:39 pm **9:39 am**
☽♑ ⚹ ☿♏ 3:30 pm **12:30 pm**
☽♑ ♂ ♄♑ 4:17 pm **1:17 pm**
☽♑ ♂ ♀♑ 10:57 pm **7:57 pm** ☽ v/c
☿♏ ⚹ ♄♑ **10:13 pm**

Fri 29
1st ♑

☿♏ ⚹ ♄♑ 1:13 am
☽ enters ♒ 3:13 pm **12:13 pm**
☽♒ ⚹ ♅♈ 6:06 pm **3:06 pm**
☽♒ □ ♅♉ 9:38 pm **6:38 pm**

Sat 30
1st ♑

☽♒ □ ♂♏ 6:43 am **3:43 am**
☽♒ ⚹ ☉♐ 8:43 am **5:43 am**

Sun 1
1st ♒

Eastern Time plain / **Pacific Time bold**

NOVEMBER	DECEMBER	JANUARY 2020
S M T W T F S	S M T W T F S	S M T W T F S
1 2	1 2 3 4 5 6 7	1 2 3 4
3 4 5 6 7 8 9	8 9 10 11 12 13 14	5 6 7 8 9 10 11
10 11 12 13 14 15 16	15 16 17 18 19 20 21	12 13 14 15 16 17 18
17 18 19 20 21 22 23	22 23 24 25 26 27 28	19 20 21 22 23 24 25
24 25 26 27 28 29 30	29 30 31	26 27 28 29 30 31

179

DECEMBER

2 MON
1st ≈

☽≈ □ ☿♏	7:27 am	**4:27 am** ☽ v/c
♃ enters ♑	1:20 pm	**10:20 am**
☿♏ ⚹ ♀♑		**9:23 pm**
☽ enters ♓		**11:11 pm**
☽♓ ⚹ ♃♑		**11:25 pm**

3 TUE
1st ≈
◑ 2nd Quarter 11 ♓ 49 (Pacific)

☿♏ ⚹ ♀♑	12:23 am	
☽ enters ♓	2:11 am	
☽♓ ⚹ ♃♑	2:25 am	
☽♓ ⚹ ♅♉	8:43 am	**5:43 am**
♀♑ ⚹ ♂♏	10:47 am	**7:47 am**
☽♓ △ ♂♏	9:51 pm	**6:51 pm**
☽♓ ⚹ ♀♑	10:26 pm	**7:26 pm**
☽♓ □ ☉♐		**10:58 pm**

4 WED
1st ♓
◑ 2nd Quarter 11 ♓ 49 (Eastern)
OP: After Moon sextiles Pluto today (see "Translating Darkness" on page 78) until Moon enters Aries on Thursday. Favorable for artistic pursuits and helping others.

☽♓ □ ☉♐	1:58 am	
☽♓ ☌ ♆♓	10:19 am	**7:19 am**
☽♓ ⚹ ♄♑	3:14 pm	**12:14 pm**
☽♓ ⚹ ♀♑	9:41 pm	**6:41 pm**

5 THU
2nd ♓

☽♓ △ ☿♏	3:15 am	**12:15 am** ☽ v/c
☽ enters ♈	2:44 pm	**11:44 am**
☽♈ □ ♃♑	4:09 pm	**1:09 pm**
☽♈ ☌ ♅♈	5:41 pm	**2:41 pm**

180

☽♈ ⚼ ♂♏︎ 1:57 pm **10:57 am**
☽♈ □ ♀♑ 5:57 pm **2:57 pm**
☽♈ △ ☉♐ 8:04 pm **5:04 pm**

Fri 6
2nd ♈

☽♈ □ ♄♑ 4:05 am **1:05 am**
☽♈ □ ♀♑ 10:01 am **7:01 am** ☽ v/c
☽♈ ⚼ ☿♏︎ 11:02 pm **8:02 pm**
☽ enters ♉   **11:29 pm**

Sat 7
2nd ♈

☽ enters ♉ 2:29 am
☉♐ □ ♆♓ 4:00 am **1:00 am**
☽♉ △ ♃♑ 4:58 am **1:58 am**
☽♉ ☌ ♅♉ 8:34 am **5:34 am**
♀♑ ⚹ ♆♓ 4:48 pm **1:48 pm**
♃♑ □ ♅♈ 11:27 pm **8:27 pm**

Sun 8
2nd ♈

Eastern Time plain / **Pacific Time bold**

NOVEMBER						
S	M	T	W	T	F	S
					1	2
3	4	5	6	7	8	9
10	11	12	13	14	15	16
17	18	19	20	21	22	23
24	25	26	27	28	29	30

DECEMBER						
S	M	T	W	T	F	S
1	2	3	4	5	6	7
8	9	10	11	12	13	14
15	16	17	18	19	20	21
22	23	24	25	26	27	28
29	30	31				

JANUARY 2020						
S	M	T	W	T	F	S
			1	2	3	4
5	6	7	8	9	10	11
12	13	14	15	16	17	18
19	20	21	22	23	24	25
26	27	28	29	30	31	

9 Mon
2nd ♉

OP: After Moon sextiles Neptune today (see "Translating Darkness" on page 78) until Moon enters Gemini on Tuesday. Whole day for practical thinking.

☽♉ ☍ ♂♏	4:10 am	**1:10 am**	
☿ enters ♐	4:42 am	**1:42 am**	
☽♉ ⚹ ♆♓	9:20 am	**6:20 am**	
☽♉ △ ♀♑	11:07 am	**8:07 am**	
☽♉ ⚻ ☉♐	11:53 am	**8:53 am**	
☽♉ △ ♄♑	2:54 pm	**11:54 am**	
☽♉ △ ♇♑	8:13 pm	**5:13 pm**	☽ v/c

10 Tue
2nd ♉

☿♐ △ ⚷♈	4:32 am	**1:32 am**	
☽ enters ♊	11:47 am	**8:47 am**	
☽♊ ⚹ ⚷♈	2:27 pm	**11:27 am**	
☽♊ ⚻ ♃♑	3:10 pm	**12:10 pm**	
☽♊ ☍ ☿♐	3:43 pm	**12:43 pm**	

11 Wed
2nd ♊
○ Full Moon 19 ♊ 52 (Pacific)

♀♑ ☌ ♄♑	5:05 am	**2:05 am**	
☿♐ ⚻ ♅♉	6:55 am	**3:55 am**	
☽♊ ⚻ ♂♏	3:12 pm	**12:12 pm**	
☽♊ □ ♆♓	5:11 pm	**2:11 pm**	
☽♊ ⚻ ♄♑	10:55 pm	**7:55 pm**	
☽♊ ☍ ☉♐		**9:12 pm**	☽ v/c
☽♊ ⚻ ♀♑		**9:35 pm**	

12 Thu
2nd ♊
○ Full Moon 19 ♊ 52 (Eastern)

☽♊ ☍ ☉♐	12:12 am		☽ v/c
☽♊ ⚻ ♀♑	12:35 am		
☽♊ ⚻ ♇♑	3:38 am	**12:38 am**	
☽ enters ♋	6:23 pm	**3:23 pm**	
☽♋ □ ⚷♈	8:56 pm	**5:56 pm**	
☽♋ ☍ ♃♑	10:33 pm	**7:33 pm**	
⚷ D	10:48 pm	**7:48 pm**	
☽♋ ⚹ ♅♉	11:43 pm	**8:43 pm**	

☽⊗ ⊼ ☿ ♐	4:48 am	**1:48 am**
♂♏△♆♓	6:55 am	**3:55 am**
♀♑ ☌ ♀♑	10:16 am	**7:16 am**
☽⊗ △ ♆♓	10:37 pm	**7:37 pm**
☽⊗ △ ♂♏	11:25 pm	**8:25 pm**

Fri 13
3rd ⊗

☽⊗ ☍ ♄♑	4:32 am	**1:32 am**
☽⊗ ☍ ♀♑	8:47 am	**5:47 am**
☽⊗ ⊼ ☉♐	9:35 am	**6:35 am**
☽⊗ ☍ ♀♑	10:57 am	**7:57 am** ☽ v/c
☽ enters ♌	10:56 pm	**7:56 pm**
☽♌ △ ⚷♈		**10:25 pm**

Sat 14
3rd ⊗

☽♌ △ ⚷♈	1:25 am	
☽♌ ⊼ ♃♑	3:51 am	**12:51 am**
☽♌ □ ♅♉	4:02 am	**1:02 am**
♃♑ △ ♅♉	2:01 pm	**11:01 am**
☽♌ △ ☿♐	3:18 pm	**12:18 pm**
☽♌ ⊼ ♆♓		**11:28 pm**

Sun 15
3rd ♌

Eastern Time plain / **Pacific Time bold**

NOVEMBER								DECEMBER								JANUARY 2020					
S	M	T	W	T	F	S		S	M	T	W	T	F	S		S	M	T	W	T	F	S
					1	2		1	2	3	4	5	6	7					1	2	3	4
3	4	5	6	7	8	9		8	9	10	11	12	13	14		5	6	7	8	9	10	11
10	11	12	13	14	15	16		15	16	17	18	19	20	21		12	13	14	15	16	17	18
17	18	19	20	21	22	23		22	23	24	25	26	27	28		19	20	21	22	23	24	25
24	25	26	27	28	29	30		29	30	31						26	27	28	29	30	31	

16 Mon
3rd ♌

OP: After Moon squares Mars until v/c Moon. Wait two hours after the square for a day of good accomplishments.

☽♌ ⊼ ♆♓	2:28 am	
☽♌ □ ♂♏	5:47 am	**2:47 am**
☽♌ ⊼ ♄♑	8:37 am	**5:37 am**
☽♌ ⊼ ♀♑	12:29 pm	**9:29 am**
☽♌ △ ☉♐	5:10 pm	**2:10 pm** ☽ v/c
☽♌ ⊼ ♀♑	7:26 pm	**4:26 pm**
☽ enters ♍		**11:16 pm**

17 Tue
3rd ♌

☽ enters ♍	2:16 am	
☽♍ ⊼ ♅♈	4:43 am	**1:43 am**
☽♍ △ ♅♉	7:12 am	**4:12 am**
☽♍ △ ♃♑	7:56 am	**4:56 am**
☽♍ □ ☿♐		**9:29 pm**

18 Wed
3rd ♍

◑ 4th Quarter 26 ♍ 58

OP: After Moon squares Sun today until v/c Moon on Thursday. A few good hours during the Last Quarter Moon to put the finishing touches on your plans.

☽♍ □ ☿♐	12:29 am	
☽♍ ☍ ♆♓	5:29 am	**2:29 am**
☽♍ ✳ ♂♏	11:14 am	**8:14 am**
☽♍ △ ♄♑	11:56 am	**8:56 am**
☽♍ △ ♀♑	3:29 pm	**12:29 pm**
☽♍ □ ☉♐	11:57 pm	**8:57 pm**

19 Thu
4th ♍

☽♍ △ ♀♑	3:07 am	**12:07 am** ☽ v/c
♂♏ ✳ ♄♑	5:00 am	**2:00 am**
☽ enters ♎	5:04 am	**2:04 am**
☽♎ ☍ ♅♈	7:32 am	**4:32 am**
☽♎ ⊼ ♅♉	9:55 am	**6:55 am**
☽♎ □ ♃♑	11:34 am	**8:34 am**
☿♐ □ ♆♓	11:19 pm	**8:19 pm**
♀ enters ≈		**10:42 pm**

♀ enters ≈ 1:42 am
☽☌⚷ ♆♓ 8:18 am **5:18 am**
☽☌⚹ ☿♐ 9:22 am **6:22 am**
☽☌□ ♄♑ 3:08 pm **12:08 pm**
☽☌□ ♇♑ 6:24 pm **3:24 pm**

Fri 20
4th ♎

OP: After Moon squares Pluto today until v/c Moon on Saturday. Last OP of the year is usable two hours after the square; good for work and get-togethers.

♀≈⚹ ♂♈ 6:14 am **3:14 am**
☽♎⚹ ☉♐ 6:45 am **3:45 am** ☽ v/c
☽ enters ♏ 7:57 am **4:57 am**
☽♏⚷ ♂♈ 10:27 am **7:27 am**
☽♏□ ♀≈ 10:51 am **7:51 am**
☽♏☍ ♅♉ 12:47 pm **9:47 am**
☽♏⚹ ♃♑ 3:21 pm **12:21 pm**
☉ enters ♑ 11:19 pm **8:19 pm**

Sat 21
4th ♎
WINTER SOLSTICE
YULE
SUN ENTERS CAPRICORN

♀≈□ ♅♉ 8:30 am **5:30 am**
♂♏⚹ ♀♑ 9:32 am **6:32 am**
☽♏△ ♆♓ 11:32 am **8:32 am**
☽♏⚹ ♄♑ 6:51 pm **3:51 pm**
☽♏⚹ ♀♑ 9:52 pm **6:52 pm**
☽♏☌ ♂♏ 10:27 pm **7:27 pm** ☽ v/c

Sun 22
4th ♏

Eastern Time plain / **Pacific Time bold**

NOVEMBER								DECEMBER								JANUARY 2020						
S	M	T	W	T	F	S		S	M	T	W	T	F	S		S	M	T	W	T	F	S
					1	2		1	2	3	4	5	6	7					1	2	3	4
3	4	5	6	7	8	9		8	9	10	11	12	13	14		5	6	7	8	9	10	11
10	11	12	13	14	15	16		15	16	17	18	19	20	21		12	13	14	15	16	17	18
17	18	19	20	21	22	23		22	23	24	25	26	27	28		19	20	21	22	23	24	25
24	25	26	27	28	29	30		29	30	31						26	27	28	29	30	31	

December

23 Mon

4th ♏
Hanukkah begins (at sundown on December 22)

☉♑□⚷♈	10:17 am	**7:17 am**
☽ enters ♐	11:34 am	**8:34 am**
☽♐△⚷♈	2:10 pm	**11:10 am**
☽♐⚻♅♉	4:26 pm	**1:26 pm**
☽♐⚹♀♒	7:38 pm	**4:38 pm**

24 Tue

4th ♐
Christmas Eve

☽♐□♆♓	3:56 pm	**12:56 pm**
☉♑△♅♉	4:44 pm	**1:44 pm**

25 Wed

4th ♐
Solar Eclipse | ● New Moon 4 ♑ 07 (Pacific)
Christmas Day

☽♐☌☿♐	6:18 am	**3:18 am** ☽ v/c
☽ enters ♑	4:45 pm	**1:45 pm**
☽♑□⚷♈	7:29 pm	**4:29 pm**
☽♑△♅♉	9:45 pm	**6:45 pm**
☽♑☌☉♑		**9:13 pm**
☽♑☌♃♑		**11:29 pm**

26 Thu

4th ♑
Solar Eclipse | ● New Moon 4 ♑ 07 (Eastern)
Kwanzaa begins
Boxing Day (Canada & UK)

☽♑☌☉♑	12:13 am	
☽♑☌♃♑	2:29 am	
☽♑⚹♆♓	10:23 pm	**7:23 pm**

☽♑ ☌ ♄♑	7:08 am	**4:08 am**	
☽♑ ☌ ♀♑	9:42 am	**6:42 am**	
☉♑ ☌ ♃♑	1:25 pm	**10:25 am**	
☽♑ ⚹ ♂♏	4:03 pm	**1:03 pm**	☽ v/c
☽ enters ♒		**9:21 pm**	

FRI 27
1st ♑

☽ enters ♒	12:21 am		
☽♒ ⚹ ⚷♈	3:16 am	**12:16 am**	
☽♒ □ ♅♉	5:33 am	**2:33 am**	
☽♒ ☌ ♀♒	9:07 pm	**6:07 pm**	
☿ enters ♑	11:55 pm	**8:55 pm**	

SAT 28
1st ♑

☿♑ □ ⚷♈	11:58 pm	**8:58 pm**	

SUN 29
1st ♒

Eastern Time plain / **Pacific Time bold**

	NOVEMBER								DECEMBER								JANUARY 2020					
S	M	T	W	T	F	S		S	M	T	W	T	F	S		S	M	T	W	T	F	S
					1	2		1	2	3	4	5	6	7					1	2	3	4
3	4	5	6	7	8	9		8	9	10	11	12	13	14		5	6	7	8	9	10	11
10	11	12	13	14	15	16		15	16	17	18	19	20	21		12	13	14	15	16	17	18
17	18	19	20	21	22	23		22	23	24	25	26	27	28		19	20	21	22	23	24	25
24	25	26	27	28	29	30		29	30	31						26	27	28	29	30	31	

30 Mon
1st ≈
Hanukkah ends

☽≈ □ ♂♏	5:24 am	**2:24 am** ☽ v/c
☽ enters ♓	10:41 am	**7:41 am**
☽♓ ⚹ ☿♑	3:52 pm	**12:52 pm**
☽♓ ⚹ ♅♉	4:04 pm	**1:04 pm**
☿♑ △ ♅♉	5:22 pm	**2:22 pm**
☽♓ ⚹ ♃♑	11:37 pm	**8:37 pm**

31 Tue
1st ♓
New Year's Eve

☽♓ ⚹ ☉♑	5:32 am	**2:32 am**
☽♓ ♂ ♆♓	7:15 pm	**4:15 pm**

1 Wed
1st ♓
New Year's Day
Kwanzaa ends

☽♓ ⚹ ♄♑	5:43 am	**2:43 am**
☽♓ ⚹ ♀♑	7:39 am	**4:39 am**
☽♓ △ ♂♏	9:14 pm	**6:14 pm** ☽ v/c
☽ enters ♈	11:00 pm	**8:00 pm**
☽♈ ♂ ⚷♈		**11:17 pm**

2 Thu
1st ♈
◗ 2nd Quarter 12 ♈ 15

☽♈ ♂ ⚷♈	2:17 am	
☿♑ ♂ ♃♑	11:42 am	**8:42 am**
☽♈ □ ♃♑	1:19 pm	**10:19 am**
☽♈ □ ☿♑	1:32 pm	**10:32 am**
☽♈ □ ☉♑	11:45 pm	**8:45 pm**

♂ enters ♐ 4:37 am **1:37 am**
☽♈ ✶ ♀≈ 10:38 am **7:38 am**
☽♈ □ ♄♑ 6:50 pm **3:50 pm**
☽♈ □ ♀♑ 8:18 pm **5:18 pm** ☽ v/c

FRI 3
2nd ♈

☽ enters ♉ 11:15 am **8:15 am**
☽♉ ☌ ♂♐ 1:03 pm **10:03 am**
☽♉ ☌ ♅♉ 4:31 pm **1:31 pm**
☽♉ △ ♃♑ **11:20 pm**

SAT 4
2nd ♈

☽♉ △ ♃♑ 2:20 am
☽♉ △ ☿♑ 10:18 am **7:18 am**
☽♉ △ ☉♑ 4:37 pm **1:37 pm**
♂♐ △ ♆♈ 4:53 pm **1:53 pm**
☽♉ ✶ ♆♓ 7:15 pm **4:15 pm**

SUN 5
2nd ♉

Eastern Time plain / **Pacific Time bold**

DECEMBER							JANUARY 2020							FEBRUARY 2020						
S	M	T	W	T	F	S	S	M	T	W	T	F	S	S	M	T	W	T	F	S
1	2	3	4	5	6	7				1	2	3	4							1
8	9	10	11	12	13	14	5	6	7	8	9	10	11	2	3	4	5	6	7	8
15	16	17	18	19	20	21	12	13	14	15	16	17	18	9	10	11	12	13	14	15
22	23	24	25	26	27	28	19	20	21	22	23	24	25	16	17	18	19	20	21	22
29	30	31					26	27	28	29	30	31		23	24	25	26	27	28	29

World Time Zones
Compared to Eastern Standard Time

(R)	EST (used in *Guide*)	(D)	Add 9 hours
(S)	CST/Subtract 1 hour	(D*)	Add 9.5 hours
(Q)	Add 1 hour	(E)	Add 10 hours
(P)	Add 2 hours	(E*)	Add 10.5 hours
(O)	Add 3 hours	(F)	Add 11 hours
(Z)	Add 5 hours	(F*)	Add 11.5 hours
(T)	MST/Subtract 2 hours	(G)	Add 12 hours
(U)	PST/Subtract 3 hours	(H)	Add 13 hours
(U*)	Subtract 3.5 hours	(I)	Add 14 hours
(V)	Subtract 4 hours	(I*)	Add 14.5 hours
(V*)	Subtract 4.5 hours	(K)	Add 15 hours
(W)	Subtract 5 hours	(K*)	Add 15.5 hours
(X)	Subtract 6 hours	(L)	Add 16 hours
(Y)	Subtract 7 hours	(L*)	Add 16.5 hours
(A)	Add 6 hours	(M)	Add 17 hours
(B)	Add 7 hours	(M*)	Add 18 hours
(C)	Add 8 hours	(P*)	Add 2.5 hours
(C*)	Add 8.5 hours		

Eastern Standard Time = Universal Time (Greenwich Mean Time) + or − the value from the table.

World Map of Time Zones

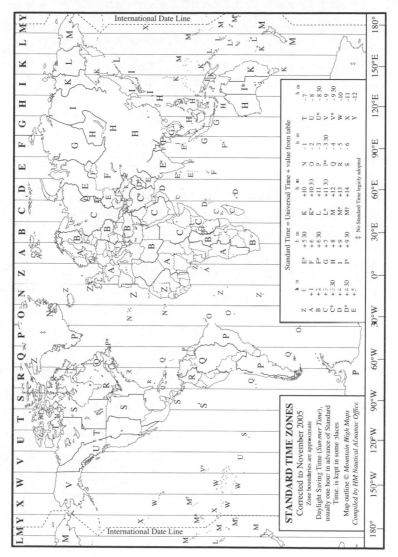

STANDARD TIME ZONES
Corrected to November 2005
Zone boundaries are approximate
Daylight Saving Time (*Summer Time*),
usually one hour in advance of Standard
Time, is kept in some places
Map outline © *Mountain High Maps*
Compiled by *HM Nautical Almanac Office*

Standard Time = Universal Time + value from table

	h m		h m		h m
Z	0	E*	+5 30	K	+10
A	+1	F	+6	K*	+10 30
B	+2	F*	+6 30	L	+11
C	+3	G	+7	L*	+11 30
C*	+3 30	H	+8	M	+12
D	+4	I	+9	M*	+13
D*	+4 30	I*	+9 30	M†	+14
E	+5				

	h m		h m		h m
N	−1	T	−7		
O	−2	U	−8		
P	−3	U*	−8 30		
P*	−3 30	V	−9		
Q	−4	V*	−9 30		
R	−5	W	−10		
S	−6	X	−11		
		Y	−12		

† No Standard Time legally adopted

International Date Line

2019 Ephemeris Tables

DATE	SID.TIME	SUN	MOON	NODE	MERCURY	VENUS	MARS	JUPITER	SATURN	URANUS	NEPTUNE	PLUTO	CERES	PALLAS	JUNO	VESTA	CHIRON
1 T	6 41 26	10♑15 24	12♏,22	26♋52 R	23✗51	23♏,30	29♓56	11✗46	11♑23	28♈37 R	14♓05	20♑36	21♏,00	21♎32	20♉37	14≈28	28♓08
2 W	6 45 22	11 16 34	25 15	26 50	25 19	24 29	0♈36	11 59	11 30	28 37	14 06	20 38	21 23	21 49	20 41	14 57	28 09
3 Th	6 49 19	12 17 45	7✗53	26 48	26 48	25 28	1 17	12 11	11 37	28 36	14 07	20 40	21 46	22 06	20 46	15 26	28 11
4 F	6 53 15	13 18 55	20 20	26 45	28 17	26 28	1 57	12 24	11 44	28 36	14 09	20 42	22 09	22 23	20 52	15 56	28 12
5 Sa	6 57 12	14 20 06	2♑35	26 44	29 46	27 29	2 38	12 36	11 51	28 36	14 10	20 44	22 32	22 40	20 58	16 25	28 13
6 Su	7 1 8	15 21 17	14 41	26 43	1♑16	28 30	3 18	12 49	11 58	28 36 D	14 11	20 46	22 55	22 56	21 05	16 55	28 15
7 M	7 5 5	16 22 28	26 39	26 43 D	2 47	29 31	3 58	13 01	12 05	28 36	14 13	20 48	23 18	23 12	21 12	17 24	28 16
8 T	7 9 1	17 23 39	8≈31	26 43	4 18	0✗33	4 39	13 13	12 12	28 36	14 14	20 50	23 40	23 28	21 20	17 54	28 18
9 W	7 12 58	18 24 49	20 19	26 44	5 49	1 35	5 19	13 25	12 19	28 36	14 16	20 52	24 03	23 44	21 28	18 23	28 20
10 Th	7 16 55	19 25 59	2♓06	26 44	7 21	2 37	6 00	13 37	12 26	28 36	14 17	20 54	24 25	23 59	21 37	18 53	28 21
11 F	7 20 51	20 27 09	13 55	26 45	8 53	3 40	6 41	13 50	12 33	28 36	14 19	20 56	24 47	24 14	21 46	19 22	28 23
12 Sa	7 24 48	21 28 18	25 51	26 46	10 26	4 43	7 21	14 02	12 40	28 37	14 20	20 58	25 09	24 29	21 56	19 52	28 25
13 Su	7 28 44	22 29 26	7♈56	26 46	11 59	5 46	8 02	14 14	12 47	28 37	14 22	21 00	25 31	24 44	22 06	20 22	28 27
14 M	7 32 41	23 30 34	20 16	26 46 R	13 32	6 50	8 42	14 25	12 55	28 37	14 23	21 02	25 53	24 58	22 17	20 51	28 28
15 T	7 36 37	24 31 42	2♉55	26 46	15 06	7 54	9 23	14 37	13 02	28 38	14 25	21 04	26 15	25 12	22 28	21 21	28 30
16 W	7 40 34	25 32 48	15 57	26 46	16 41	8 58	10 03	14 49	13 09	28 38	14 26	21 06	26 36	25 25	22 40	21 51	28 32
17 Th	7 44 30	26 33 54	29 26	26 46 D	18 16	10 03	10 44	15 01	13 15	28 39	14 28	21 08	26 58	25 39	22 52	22 20	28 34
18 F	7 48 27	27 34 59	13♊21	26 46	19 51	11 08	11 25	15 12	13 22	28 39	14 30	21 10	27 19	25 52	23 05	22 50	28 36
19 Sa	7 52 24	28 36 04	27 44	26 46	21 28	12 13	12 05	15 24	13 29	28 40	14 32	21 12	27 40	26 04	23 18	23 20	28 38
20 Su	7 56 20	29 37 07	12♋29	26 47 R	23 04	13 18	12 46	15 35	13 36	28 41	14 33	21 14	28 02	26 17	23 31	23 49	28 41
21 M	8 0 17	0≈38 11	27 32	26 47	24 41	14 24	13 27	15 47	13 43	28 41	14 35	21 16	28 22	26 29	23 45	24 19	28 43
22 T	8 4 13	1 39 13	12♌43	26 46	26 19	15 29	14 07	15 58	13 50	28 42	14 37	21 18	28 43	26 40	23 59	24 49	28 45
23 W	8 8 10	2 40 15	27 57	26 46	27 57	16 36	14 48	16 09	13 57	28 43	14 38	21 20	29 04	26 52	24 13	25 18	28 47
24 Th	8 12 6	3 41 16	12♍52	26 45	29 36	17 42	15 29	16 20	14 04	28 44	14 40	21 22	29 24	27 03	24 28	25 48	28 49
25 F	8 16 3	4 42 16	27 34	26 44	1≈15	18 48	16 09	16 31	14 11	28 45	14 42	21 24	29 45	27 13	24 44	26 18	28 52
26 Sa	8 19 59	5 43 16	11♎52	26 44	2 55	19 55	16 50	16 42	14 17	28 46	14 44	21 26	0✗05	27 24	24 59	26 48	28 54
27 Su	8 23 56	6 44 15	25 45	26 43 D	4 36	21 02	17 30	16 53	14 24	28 47	14 46	21 28	0 25	27 34	25 16	27 17	28 57
28 M	8 27 53	7 45 14	9♏,12	26 43	6 17	22 09	18 11	17 04	14 31	28 48	14 48	21 30	0 45	27 43	25 32	27 47	28 59
29 T	8 31 49	8 46 13	22 15	26 43	7 59	23 17	18 52	17 15	14 38	28 49	14 50	21 32	1 05	27 52	25 49	28 17	29 02
30 W	8 35 46	9 47 10	4✗58	26 44	9 42	24 24	19 32	17 25	14 44	28 50	14 52	21 34	1 24	28 01	26 06	28 47	29 04
31 Th	8 39 42	10 48 07	17 24	26 45	11 25	25 32	20 13	17 36	14 51	28 51	14 54	21 36	1 44	28 10	26 23	29 16	29 07

Tables are calculated for midnight Greenwich Mean Time

February 2019

DATE	SID.TIME	SUN	MOON	NODE	MERCURY	VENUS	MARS	JUPITER	SATURN	URANUS	NEPTUNE	PLUTO	CERES	PALLAS	JUNO	VESTA	CHIRON
1 F	8 43 39	11≈49 04	29♐36	26♋47	13≈09	26♐40	20♈54	17♐46	14♑57	28♈52	14♓56	21♑38	2♐03	28≏18	26♉41	29≈46	29♓09
2 Sa	8 47 35	12 49 59	11♑38	26 48	14 54	27 48	21 34	17 56	15 04	28 54	14 58	21 40	2 22	28 25	26 59	0♓16	29 12
3 Su	8 51 32	13 50 54	23 33	26 48 ℞	16 39	28 56	22 15	18 07	15 11	28 55	15 00	21 42	2 41	28 32	27 18	0 46	29 15
4 M	8 55 28	14 51 47	5≈24	26 48	18 25	0♑04	22 56	18 17	15 17	28 57	15 02	21 43	2 59	28 39	27 37	1 16	29 17
5 T	8 59 25	15 52 40	17 12	26 47	20 12	1 13	23 36	18 27	15 24	28 58	15 04	21 45	3 18	28 46	27 56	1 45	29 20
6 W	9 3 22	16 53 31	29 00	26 45	21 59	2 21	24 17	18 37	15 30	28 59	15 06	21 47	3 36	28 52	28 15	2 15	29 23
7 Th	9 7 18	17 54 21	10♓50	26 41	23 46	3 30	24 57	18 47	15 36	29 01	15 08	21 49	3 55	28 57	28 35	2 45	29 26
8 F	9 11 15	18 55 09	22 44	26 38	25 34	4 39	25 38	18 56	15 43	29 03	15 10	21 51	4 12	29 02	28 55	3 15	29 29
9 Sa	9 15 11	19 55 56	4♈44	26 34	27 22	5 48	26 19	19 06	15 49	29 04	15 12	21 53	4 30	29 07	29 15	3 45	29 32
10 Su	9 19 8	20 56 42	16 53	26 30	29 11	6 57	26 59	19 15	15 55	29 06	15 14	21 55	4 48	29 11	29 35	4 14	29 34
11 M	9 23 4	21 57 26	29 14	26 27	1♓00	8 07	27 40	19 25	16 01	29 08	15 16	21 56	5 05	29 15	29 56	4 44	29 37
12 T	9 27 1	22 58 09	11♉51	26 25 D	2 48	9 16	28 21	19 34	16 08	29 09	15 18	21 58	5 22	29 19	0♊17	5 14	29 40
13 W	9 30 57	23 58 50	24 46	26 25	4 36	10 25	29 01	19 43	16 14	29 11	15 20	22 00	5 39	29 22	0 39	5 44	29 43
14 Th	9 34 54	24 59 30	8♊04	26 25	6 24	11 35	29 42	19 52	16 20	29 13	15 23	22 02	5 56	29 24	1 00	6 13	29 46
15 F	9 38 51	26 00 07	21 46	26 27	8 12	12 45	0♉22	20 01	16 26	29 15	15 25	22 04	6 13	29 26	1 22	6 43	29 49
16 Sa	9 42 47	27 00 43	5♋55	26 28	9 58	13 55	1 03	20 10	16 32	29 17	15 27	22 05	6 29	29 28	1 44	7 13	29 53
17 Su	9 46 44	28 01 18	20 29	26 29 ℞	11 43	15 04	1 43	20 19	16 38	29 19	15 29	22 07	6 45	29 29	2 06	7 43	29 56
18 M	9 50 40	29 01 50	5♌25	26 29	13 26	16 14	2 24	20 27	16 44	29 21	15 31	22 09	7 01	29 29 ℞	2 29	8 12	29 59
19 T	9 54 37	0♓02 21	20 36	26 27	15 07	17 25	3 04	20 35	16 49	29 23	15 34	22 10	7 17	29 29	2 51	8 42	0♈02
20 W	9 58 33	1 02 51	5♍52	26 24	16 45	18 35	3 45	20 44	16 55	29 25	15 36	22 12	7 32	29 28	3 14	9 12	0 05
21 Th	10 2 30	2 03 18	21 04	26 19	18 20	19 45	4 25	20 52	17 01	29 27	15 38	22 14	7 48	29 27	3 37	9 41	0 08
22 F	10 6 26	3 03 44	6♎01	26 13	19 52	20 55	5 06	21 00	17 06	29 30	15 40	22 15	8 03	29 25	4 01	10 11	0 12
23 Sa	10 10 23	4 04 09	20 35	26 08	21 19	22 06	5 46	21 08	17 12	29 32	15 42	22 17	8 17	29 22	4 24	10 41	0 15
24 Su	10 14 20	5 04 33	4♏41	26 03	22 41	23 16	6 26	21 16	17 18	29 34	15 45	22 19	8 32	29 22	4 48	11 10	0 18
25 M	10 18 16	6 04 55	18 18	26 00	23 57	24 27	7 07	21 23	17 23	29 37	15 47	22 20	8 46	29 19	5 12	11 40	0 21
26 T	10 22 13	7 05 15	1♐27	25 58 D	25 07	25 38	7 47	21 31	17 29	29 39	15 49	22 22	9 00	29 16	5 36	12 10	0 25
27 W	10 26 9	8 05 35	14 10	25 58	26 10	26 49	8 28	21 38	17 34	29 41	15 51	22 23	9 14	29 12	6 00	12 39	0 28
28 Th	10 30 6	9 05 52	26 33	25 59	27 08	27 59	9 08	21 45	17 39	29 44	15 54	22 25	9 28	29 08	6 25	13 09	0 31

DATE	SID.TIME	SUN	MOON	NODE	MERCURY	VENUS	MARS	JUPITER	SATURN	URANUS	NEPTUNE	PLUTO	CERES	PALLAS	JUNO	VESTA	CHIRON
1 F	10 34 2	10 ♓ 06 09	8 ♑ 39	26 ♋ 01	27 ♓ 54	29 ♑ 10	9 ♉ 48	21 ♐ 52	17 ♑ 44	29 ♈ 46	15 ♓ 56	22 ♑ 26	9 ♐ 41	29 ♎ 03 Rx	6 ♊ 49	13 ♓ 38	0 ♈ 35
2 Sa	10 37 59	11 06 24	20 35	26 02 Rx	28 33	0 ♒ 21	10 29	21 59	17 50	29 49	15 58	22 28	9 54	28 57	7 14	14 08	0 38
3 Su	10 41 55	12 06 37	2 ♒ 24	26 02	29 03	1 33	11 09	22 06	17 55	29 51	16 01	22 29	10 07	28 52	7 39	14 37	0 42
4 M	10 45 52	13 06 49	14 11	26 00	29 24	2 44	11 49	22 13	18 00	29 54	16 03	22 31	10 19	28 45	8 04	15 07	0 45
5 T	10 49 49	14 06 58	25 58	25 56	29 ♓ 36 Rx	3 55	12 30	22 19	18 05	29 56	16 05	22 32	10 31	28 38	8 29	15 37	0 48
6 W	10 53 45	15 07 07	7 ♓ 49	25 49	29 39	5 06	13 10	22 25	18 10	29 59	16 07	22 34	10 43	28 31	8 55	16 06	0 52
7 Th	10 57 42	16 07 13	19 45	25 40	29 32	6 17	13 50	22 32	18 14	0 ♉ 02	16 10	22 35	10 55	28 23	9 20	16 35	0 55
8 F	11 1 38	17 07 17	1 ♈ 47	25 31	29 16	7 29	14 30	22 38	18 19	0 04	16 12	22 36	11 06	28 14	9 46	17 05	0 59
9 Sa	11 5 35	18 07 20	13 58	25 20	28 52	8 40	15 10	22 44	18 24	0 07	16 14	22 38	11 17	28 05	10 12	17 34	1 02
10 Su	11 9 31	19 07 20	26 17	25 10	28 20	9 52	15 51	22 49	18 28	0 10	16 16	22 39	11 28	27 56	10 38	18 04	1 06
11 M	11 13 28	20 07 18	8 ♉ 48	25 02	27 41	11 03	16 31	22 55	18 33	0 13	16 19	22 40	11 39	27 46	11 04	18 33	1 09
12 T	11 17 24	21 07 15	21 30	24 56	26 56	12 15	17 11	23 00	18 38	0 16	16 21	22 41	11 49	27 35	11 30	19 03	1 13
13 W	11 21 21	22 07 09	4 ♊ 27	24 52	26 06	13 26	17 51	23 05	18 42	0 18	16 23	22 43	11 59	27 24	11 56	19 32	1 16
14 Th	11 25 17	23 07 01	17 41	24 50 D	25 12	14 38	18 31	23 10	18 46	0 21	16 26	22 44	12 08	27 13	12 23	20 01	1 20
15 F	11 29 14	24 06 51	1 ♋ 15	24 50	24 16	15 50	19 11	23 15	18 50	0 24	16 28	22 45	12 17	27 01	12 49	20 30	1 23
16 Sa	11 33 11	25 06 38	15 09	24 51 Rx	23 18	17 01	19 51	23 20	18 55	0 27	16 30	22 46	12 26	26 49	13 16	21 00	1 27
17 Su	11 37 7	26 06 23	29 26	24 51	22 21	18 13	20 31	23 25	18 59	0 30	16 32	22 47	12 35	26 36	13 43	21 29	1 30
18 M	11 41 4	27 06 06	14 ♌ 03	24 50	21 25	19 25	21 11	23 29	19 03	0 33	16 35	22 48	12 43	26 23	14 10	21 58	1 34
19 T	11 45 0	28 05 47	28 57	24 46	20 31	20 37	21 51	23 33	19 07	0 36	16 37	22 49	12 51	26 09	14 37	22 27	1 37
20 W	11 48 57	29 05 26	14 ♍ 00	24 39	19 41	21 49	22 31	23 37	19 11	0 39	16 39	22 50	12 59	25 55	15 04	22 57	1 41
21 Th	11 52 53	0 ♈ 05 02	29 05	24 30	18 55	23 01	23 11	23 41	19 14	0 42	16 41	22 51	13 06	25 41	15 31	23 26	1 45
22 F	11 56 50	1 04 36	14 ♎ 01	24 20	18 14	24 13	23 51	23 45	19 18	0 45	16 44	22 52	13 13	25 26	15 58	23 55	1 48
23 Sa	12 0 46	2 04 09	28 38	24 10	17 38	25 25	24 31	23 48	19 22	0 48	16 46	22 53	13 20	25 11	16 26	24 24	1 52
24 Su	12 4 43	3 03 39	12 ♏ 51	24 01	17 08	26 37	25 11	23 52	19 25	0 52	16 48	22 54	13 26	24 56	16 53	24 53	1 55
25 M	12 8 40	4 03 08	26 35	23 53	16 44	27 49	25 51	23 55	19 29	0 55	16 50	22 55	13 32	24 40	17 21	25 22	1 59
26 T	12 12 36	5 02 35	9 ♐ 50	23 48	16 25	29 01	26 31	23 58	19 32	0 58	16 52	22 56	13 37	24 24	17 48	25 51	2 02
27 W	12 16 33	6 02 00	22 39	23 45	16 13	0 ♓ 13	27 11	24 01	19 35	1 01	16 55	22 57	13 43	24 07	18 16	26 20	2 06
28 Th	12 20 29	7 01 24	5 ♑ 04	23 45 D	16 07 D	1 25	27 50	24 03	19 38	1 04	16 57	22 58	13 48	23 50	18 44	26 49	2 09
29 F	12 24 26	8 00 45	17 12	23 45 Rx	16 06	2 37	28 30	24 06	19 41	1 07	16 59	22 59	13 52	23 33	19 12	27 18	2 13
30 Sa	12 28 22	9 00 05	29 08	23 45	16 11	3 49	29 10	24 08	19 44	1 11	17 01	22 59	13 56	23 16	19 40	27 46	2 16
31 Su	12 32 19	9 59 23	10 ♒ 56	23 43	16 22	5 02	29 50	24 10	19 47	1 14	17 03	23 00	14 00	22 58	20 08	28 15	2 20

Tables are calculated for midnight Greenwich Mean Time

DATE	SID.TIME	SUN	MOON	NODE	MERCURY	VENUS	MARS	JUPITER	SATURN	URANUS	NEPTUNE	PLUTO	CERES	PALLAS	JUNO	VESTA	CHIRON
1 M	12 36 15	10 ♈ 58 40	22 ♒ 43	23 ♋ 40 ℞	16 ♓ 38	6 ♓ 14	0 ♊ 29	24 ♐ 12	19 ♑ 50	1 ♉ 17	17 ♓ 05	23 ♑ 01	14 ♐ 03	22 ♎ 41 ℞	20 ♊ 36	28 ♓ 44	2 ♈ 23
2 T	12 40 12	11 57 54	4 ♓ 32	23 34	16 59	7 26	1 08	24 14	19 53	1 20	17 07	23 01	14 06	22 23	21 04	29 13	2 27
3 W	12 44 9	12 57 06	16 27	23 25	17 24	8 39	1 48	24 15	19 56	1 24	17 10	23 02	14 09	22 05	21 32	29 42	2 31
4 Th	12 48 5	13 56 17	28 31	23 14	17 54	9 51	2 28	24 17	19 58	1 27	17 12	23 03	14 11	21 46	22 00	0 ♈ 10	2 34
5 F	12 52 2	14 55 26	10 ♈ 44	23 00	18 28	11 03	3 08	24 18	20 01	1 30	17 14	23 03	14 13	21 28	22 29	0 39	2 37
6 Sa	12 55 58	15 54 32	23 09	22 46	19 07	12 16	3 48	24 19	20 03	1 34	17 16	23 04	14 14	21 09	22 57	1 07	2 41
7 Su	12 59 55	16 53 37	5 ♉ 44	22 33	19 49	13 28	4 27	24 20	20 05	1 37	17 18	23 04	14 15	20 51	23 26	1 36	2 44
8 M	13 3 51	17 52 39	18 31	22 21	20 35	14 41	5 07	24 20	20 07	1 40	17 20	23 05	14 16	20 32	23 54	2 05	2 48
9 T	13 7 48	18 51 39	1 ♊ 30	22 12	21 24	15 53	5 46	24 21	20 09	1 44	17 22	23 05	14 16 ℞	20 13	24 23	2 33	2 51
10 W	13 11 44	19 50 37	14 39	22 06	22 16	17 06	6 26	24 21	20 11	1 47	17 24	23 06	14 16	19 55	24 51	3 01	2 55
11 Th	13 15 41	20 49 33	28 01	22 03	23 12	18 18	7 06	24 21 ℞	20 13	1 51	17 26	23 06	14 16	19 36	25 20	3 30	2 58
12 F	13 19 37	21 48 27	11 ♋ 36	22 02	24 10	19 31	7 45	24 21	20 15	1 54	17 28	23 07	14 15	19 17	25 49	3 58	3 02
13 Sa	13 23 34	22 47 18	25 26	22 02	25 11	20 43	8 25	24 21	20 17	1 57	17 30	23 07	14 13	18 59	26 17	4 27	3 05
14 Su	13 27 31	23 46 07	9 ♌ 30	22 01	26 15	21 56	9 04	24 20	20 19	2 01	17 32	23 07	14 12	18 40	26 46	4 55	3 08
15 M	13 31 27	24 44 54	23 50	21 59	27 22	23 08	9 43	24 19	20 20	2 04	17 34	23 08	14 10	18 22	27 15	5 23	3 12
16 T	13 35 24	25 43 38	8 ♍ 22	21 55	28 31	24 20	10 23	24 18	20 21	2 08	17 35	23 08	14 07	18 04	27 44	5 51	3 15
17 W	13 39 20	26 42 20	23 02	21 48	29 42	25 33	11 02	24 17	20 23	2 11	17 37	23 08	14 04	17 45	28 13	6 19	3 18
18 Th	13 43 17	27 41 00	7 ♎ 44	21 38	0 ♈ 55	26 46	11 41	24 16	20 24	2 15	17 39	23 09 ℞	14 01	17 27	28 42	6 48	3 22
19 F	13 47 13	28 39 38	22 22	21 27	2 11	27 58	12 21	24 15	20 25	2 18	17 41	23 09	13 57	17 10	29 11	7 16	3 25
20 Sa	13 51 10	29 38 14	6 ♏ 46	21 15	3 29	29 11	13 00	24 13	20 26	2 21	17 43	23 09	13 53	16 52	29 40	7 44	3 28
21 Su	13 55 6	0 ♉ 36 48	20 50	21 05	4 49	0 ♈ 24	13 39	24 11	20 27	2 25	17 45	23 09	13 49	16 35	0 ♋ 09	8 12	3 32
22 M	13 59 3	1 35 20	4 ♐ 31	20 56	6 11	1 36	14 19	24 09	20 28	2 28	17 46	23 09	13 44	16 17	0 38	8 40	3 35
23 T	14 3 0	2 33 50	17 46	20 49	7 35	2 49	14 58	24 07	20 29	2 32	17 48	23 09	13 39	16 01	1 07	9 07	3 38
24 W	14 6 56	3 32 19	0 ♑ 37	20 46	9 01	4 02	15 37	24 05	20 29	2 35	17 50	23 09 ℞	13 33	15 44	1 36	9 35	3 41
25 Th	14 10 53	4 30 47	13 05	20 44 D	10 28	5 14	16 16	24 02	20 30	2 39	17 52	23 09	13 27	15 28	2 05	10 03	3 44
26 F	14 14 49	5 29 12	25 16	20 44 ℞	11 58	6 27	16 55	23 59	20 30	2 42	17 53	23 09	13 21	15 12	2 35	10 31	3 47
27 Sa	14 18 46	6 27 36	7 ♒ 14	20 44	13 30	7 40	17 35	23 56	20 31	2 46	17 55	23 09	13 14	14 56	3 04	10 58	3 51
28 Su	14 22 42	7 25 59	19 05	20 44	15 03	8 53	18 14	23 53	20 31	2 49	17 57	23 09	13 07	14 41	3 33	11 26	3 54
29 M	14 26 39	8 24 19	0 ♓ 54	20 41	16 38	10 05	18 53	23 50	20 31	2 52	17 58	23 09	13 00	14 26	4 02	11 54	3 57
30 T	14 30 35	9 22 39	12 46	20 37	18 15	11 18	19 32	23 47	20 31 ℞	2 56	18 00	23 09	12 52	14 11	4 31	12 21	4 00

May 2019

DATE	SID.TIME	SUN	MOON	NODE	MERCURY	VENUS	MARS	JUPITER	SATURN	URANUS	NEPTUNE	PLUTO	CERES	PALLAS	JUNO	VESTA	CHIRON
1 W	14 34 32	10♉20 56	24♓45	20♋30 ℞	19♈54	12♈31	20♊11	23♐43 ℞	20♑31 ℞	2♉59	18♓01	23♑09 ℞	12♐44 ℞	13♎57 ℞	5♋01	12♈49	4♈03
2 Th	14 38 29	11 19 12	6♈56	20 20	21 35	13 44	20 50	23 39	20 31	3 03	18 03	23 08	12 36	13 43	5 30	13 16	4 06
3 F	14 42 25	12 17 27	19 19	20 09	23 17	14 56	21 29	23 35	20 31	3 06	18 04	23 08	12 27	13 30	5 59	13 43	4 09
4 Sa	14 46 22	13 15 40	1♉58	19 57	25 02	16 09	22 08	23 31	20 30	3 10	18 06	23 08	12 18	13 17	6 29	14 11	4 12
5 Su	14 50 18	14 13 51	14 51	19 46	26 48	17 22	22 47	23 27	20 30	3 13	18 07	23 08	12 08	13 04	6 58	14 38	4 15
6 M	14 54 15	15 12 00	27 59	19 36	28 36	18 35	23 26	23 22	20 29	3 16	18 09	23 07	11 59	12 52	7 27	15 05	4 17
7 T	14 58 11	16 10 08	11♊19	19 28	0♉26	19 48	24 05	23 18	20 29	3 20	18 10	23 07	11 49	12 40	7 57	15 32	4 20
8 W	15 2 8	17 08 14	24 50	19 23	2 17	21 00	24 44	23 13	20 28	3 23	18 12	23 07	11 38	12 29	8 26	15 59	4 23
9 Th	15 6 4	18 06 18	8♋30	19 21 D	4 11	22 13	25 23	23 08	20 27	3 27	18 13	23 06	11 28	12 18	8 56	16 26	4 26
10 F	15 10 1	19 04 21	22 20	19 20	6 06	23 26	26 02	23 03	20 26	3 30	18 14	23 06	11 17	12 08	9 25	16 53	4 29
11 Sa	15 13 58	20 02 21	6♌17	19 21	8 03	24 39	26 41	22 58	20 25	3 33	18 16	23 05	11 06	11 58	9 54	17 20	4 31
12 Su	15 17 54	21 00 20	20 21	19 21 ℞	10 02	25 52	27 20	22 53	20 24	3 37	18 17	23 05	10 55	11 49	10 24	17 47	4 34
13 M	15 21 51	21 58 16	4♍31	19 21	12 03	27 05	27 58	22 47	20 23	3 40	18 18	23 04	10 43	11 40	10 53	18 14	4 37
14 T	15 25 47	22 56 11	18 47	19 18	14 05	28 17	28 37	22 41	20 22	3 43	18 20	23 04	10 31	11 32	11 23	18 41	4 39
15 W	15 29 44	23 54 04	3♎04	19 13	16 09	29 30	29 16	22 36	20 21	3 46	18 21	23 03	10 19	11 24	11 52	19 07	4 42
16 Th	15 33 40	24 51 55	17 20	19 06	18 15	0♉43	29 55	22 30	20 19	3 50	18 22	23 03	10 07	11 16	12 22	19 34	4 44
17 F	15 37 37	25 49 44	1♏31	18 58	20 22	1 56	0♋34	22 24	20 17	3 53	18 23	23 02	9 55	11 09	12 51	20 00	4 47
18 Sa	15 41 33	26 47 32	15 30	18 50	22 30	3 09	1 12	22 18	20 16	3 56	18 24	23 01	9 42	11 03	13 20	20 27	4 49
19 Su	15 45 30	27 45 19	29 14	18 42	24 39	4 22	1 51	22 12	20 14	3 59	18 25	23 01	9 30	10 57	13 50	20 53	4 52
20 M	15 49 27	28 43 04	12♐40	18 35	26 50	5 35	2 30	22 05	20 12	4 03	18 26	23 00	9 17	10 51	14 19	21 19	4 54
21 T	15 53 23	29 40 48	25 45	18 31	29 01	6 48	3 09	21 59	20 10	4 06	18 27	22 59	9 04	10 46	14 49	21 46	4 56
22 W	15 57 20	0♊38 30	8♑30	18 28 D	1♊12	8 01	3 47	21 52	20 08	4 09	18 28	22 59	8 51	10 42	15 18	22 12	4 59
23 Th	16 1 16	1 36 12	20 56	18 28	3 24	9 14	4 26	21 46	20 06	4 12	18 29	22 58	8 38	10 38	15 48	22 38	5 01
24 F	16 5 13	2 33 52	3♒07	18 29	5 35	10 27	5 05	21 39	20 04	4 15	18 30	22 57	8 25	10 34	16 17	23 04	5 03
25 Sa	16 9 9	3 31 32	15 06	18 30	7 46	11 39	5 43	21 32	20 02	4 18	18 31	22 56	8 11	10 31	16 46	23 30	5 05
26 Su	16 13 6	4 29 10	26 59	18 31 ℞	9 57	12 52	6 22	21 25	19 59	4 22	18 32	22 55	7 58	10 29	17 16	23 56	5 08
27 M	16 17 2	5 26 47	8♓49	18 32	12 07	14 05	7 00	21 18	19 57	4 25	18 33	22 55	7 45	10 26	17 45	24 22	5 10
28 T	16 20 59	6 24 23	20 43	18 30	14 15	15 18	7 39	21 11	19 54	4 28	18 34	22 54	7 31	10 25	18 15	24 47	5 12
29 W	16 24 56	7 21 59	2♈46	18 27	16 23	16 31	8 17	21 04	19 52	4 31	18 34	22 53	7 18	10 24	18 44	25 13	5 14
30 Th	16 28 52	8 19 33	15 00	18 23	18 28	17 44	8 56	20 56	19 49	4 34	18 35	22 52	7 04	10 23	19 13	25 39	5 16
31 F	16 32 49	9 17 06	27 30	18 17	20 32	18 57	9 34	20 49	19 46	4 37	18 36	22 51	6 51	10 23 D	19 43	26 04	5 18

Tables are calculated for midnight Greenwich Mean Time

DATE	SID.TIME	SUN	MOON	NODE	MERCURY	VENUS	MARS	JUPITER	SATURN	URANUS	NEPTUNE	PLUTO	CERES	PALLAS	JUNO	VESTA	CHIRON
1 Sa	16 36 45	10♊39	10♉19	18♋11R	22♊34	20♉10	10♋13	20♐42R	19♑43R	4♉40	18♓37	22♑50R	6♐38R	10♎23	20♋12	26♈29	5♈20
2 Su	16 40 42	11 12 11	23 26	18 05	24 33	21 24	10 52	20 34	19 41	4 43	18 37	22 49	6 24	10 23	20 42	26 55	5 22
3 M	16 44 38	12 09 42	6♊52	17 59	26 31	22 37	11 30	20 27	19 38	4 46	18 38	22 48	6 11	10 24	21 11	27 20	5 23
4 T	16 48 35	13 07 12	20 34	17 55	28 26	23 50	12 09	20 19	19 34	4 48	18 38	22 47	5 58	10 26	21 40	27 45	5 25
5 W	16 52 31	14 04 40	4♋30	17 53 D	0♋18	25 03	12 47	20 12	19 31	4 51	18 39	22 46	5 45	10 28	22 10	28 10	5 27
6 Th	16 56 28	15 02 08	18 36	17 52	2 08	26 16	13 26	20 04	19 28	4 54	18 40	22 45	5 32	10 30	22 39	28 35	5 29
7 F	17 0 25	15 59 35	2♌49	17 53	3 56	27 29	14 04	19 57	19 25	4 57	18 40	22 44	5 19	10 33	23 08	29 00	5 30
8 Sa	17 4 21	16 57 01	17 04	17 54	5 41	28 42	14 42	19 49	19 22	5 00	18 40	22 43	5 07	10 36	23 38	29 25	5 32
9 Su	17 8 18	17 54 25	1♍20	17 56	7 23	29 55	15 21	19 41	19 18	5 02	18 41	22 42	4 54	10 40	24 07	29 50	5 33
10 M	17 12 14	18 51 48	15 34	17 56R	9 03	1♊08	15 59	19 34	19 15	5 05	18 41	22 40	4 42	10 44	24 36	0♉14	5 35
11 T	17 16 11	19 49 10	29 43	17 56	10 40	2 21	16 38	19 26	19 11	5 08	18 42	22 39	4 30	10 49	25 05	0 39	5 36
12 W	17 20 7	20 46 31	13♎46	17 55	12 14	3 34	17 16	19 18	19 08	5 10	18 42	22 38	4 18	10 53	25 35	1 03	5 38
13 Th	17 24 4	21 43 51	27 40	17 52	13 45	4 48	17 54	19 11	19 04	5 13	18 42	22 37	4 06	10 59	26 04	1 28	5 39
14 F	17 28 0	22 41 10	11♏25	17 49	15 14	6 01	18 33	19 03	19 00	5 16	18 43	22 36	3 55	11 04	26 33	1 52	5 40
15 Sa	17 31 57	23 38 28	24 57	17 45	16 40	7 14	19 11	18 55	18 57	5 18	18 43	22 34	3 44	11 10	27 02	2 16	5 41
16 Su	17 35 54	24 35 46	8♐16	17 42	18 03	8 27	19 49	18 48	18 53	5 21	18 43	22 33	3 33	11 17	27 31	2 40	5 43
17 M	17 39 50	25 33 02	21 19	17 39	19 24	9 40	20 28	18 40	18 49	5 23	18 43	22 32	3 22	11 24	28 00	3 04	5 44
18 T	17 43 47	26 30 19	4♑07	17 37	20 41	10 53	21 06	18 33	18 45	5 26	18 43	22 31	3 12	11 31	28 30	3 28	5 45
19 W	17 47 43	27 27 34	16 40	17 37 D	21 56	12 07	21 44	18 25	18 41	5 28	18 43	22 29	3 01	11 38	28 59	3 52	5 46
20 Th	17 51 40	28 24 49	28 59	17 37	23 07	13 20	22 22	18 18	18 37	5 31	18 43	22 28	2 51	11 46	29 28	4 16	5 47
21 F	17 55 36	29 22 04	11♒06	17 38	24 16	14 33	23 01	18 10	18 33	5 33	18 43R	22 27	2 42	11 54	29 57	4 39	5 48
22 Sa	17 59 33	0♋19 19	23 03	17 40	25 21	15 46	23 39	18 03	18 29	5 35	18 43	22 26	2 33	12 03	0♌26	5 03	5 49
23 Su	18 3 30	1 16 33	4♓56	17 41	26 24	17 00	24 17	17 56	18 25	5 37	18 43	22 24	2 23	12 12	0 55	5 26	5 50
24 M	18 7 26	2 13 47	16 47	17 42	27 23	18 13	24 55	17 49	18 21	5 40	18 43	22 23	2 15	12 21	1 24	5 49	5 51
25 T	18 11 23	3 11 00	28 41	17 43R	28 18	19 26	25 34	17 41	18 17	5 42	18 43	22 22	2 06	12 30	1 53	6 12	5 51
26 W	18 15 19	4 08 14	10♈44	17 43	29 11	20 39	26 12	17 34	18 13	5 44	18 43	22 20	1 58	12 40	2 22	6 35	5 52
27 Th	18 19 16	5 05 28	22 59	17 42	29 59	21 53	26 50	17 27	18 08	5 46	18 43	22 19	1 51	12 50	2 51	6 58	5 53
28 F	18 23 12	6 02 42	5♉30	17 41	0♋44	23 06	27 23	17 20	18 04	5 48	18 43	22 17	1 43	13 01	3 20	7 21	5 53
29 Sa	18 27 9	6 59 55	18 22	17 40	1 26	24 20	28 07	17 13	18 00	5 50	18 43	22 16	1 36	13 11	3 49	7 44	5 54
30 Su	18 31 5	7 57 09	1♊36	17 38	2 03	25 33	28 45	17 07	17 56	5 52	18 42	22 15	1 29	13 22	4 18	8 06	5 54

DATE	SID.TIME	SUN	MOON	NODE	MERCURY	VENUS	MARS	JUPITER	SATURN	URANUS	NEPTUNE	PLUTO	CERES	PALLAS	JUNO	VESTA	CHIRON
1 M	18 35 2	8♋54 23	15♊12	17♋37R	2♌36	26♊46	29♋23	17✗00R	17♑51R	5♉54	18♓42R	22♑13R	1✗23R	13♎34	4♌46	8♉28	5♈55
2 T	18 38 59	9 51 37	29 11	17 37	3 06	28 00	0♌01	16 53	17 47	5 56	18 42	22 12	1 17	13 45	5 15	8 51	5 55
3 W	18 42 55	10 48 50	13♋28	17 36D	3 31	29 13	0 39	16 47	17 43	5 58	18 41	22 10	1 11	13 57	5 44	9 13	5 55
4 Th	18 46 52	11 46 04	27 59	17 36	3 51	0♋27	1 17	16 41	17 38	6 00	18 41	22 09	1 06	14 10	6 13	9 35	5 56
5 F	18 50 48	12 43 18	12♌38	17 37	4 07	1 40	1 56	16 34	17 34	6 02	18 41	22 08	1 01	14 22	6 42	9 57	5 56
6 Sa	18 54 45	13 40 31	27 18	17 37	4 19	2 54	2 34	16 28	17 29	6 04	18 40	22 06	0 57	14 35	7 10	10 19	5 56
7 Su	18 58 41	14 37 44	11♍54	17 37	4 26R	4 07	3 12	16 22	17 25	6 05	18 40	22 05	0 52	14 48	7 39	10 40	5 56
8 M	19 2 38	15 34 57	26 21	17 38	4 28	5 21	3 50	16 16	17 21	6 07	18 39	22 03	0 49	15 01	8 08	11 02	5 56R
9 T	19 6 34	16 32 09	10♎35	17 38R	4 25	6 34	4 28	16 11	17 16	6 09	18 39	22 02	0 45	15 15	8 36	11 23	5 56
10 W	19 10 31	17 29 21	24 33	17 38D	4 18	7 48	5 06	16 05	17 12	6 10	18 38	22 00	0 42	15 29	9 05	11 44	5 56
11 Th	19 14 28	18 26 33	8♏16	17 38	4 06	9 01	5 44	16 00	17 07	6 12	18 37	21 59	0 39	15 43	9 34	12 05	5 56
12 F	19 18 24	19 23 45	21 42	17 38	3 50	10 15	6 23	15 54	17 03	6 13	18 37	21 57	0 37	15 57	10 02	12 26	5 56
13 Sa	19 22 21	20 20 58	4✗52	17 38	3 29	11 28	7 01	15 49	16 58	6 15	18 36	21 56	0 35	16 11	10 31	12 47	5 56
14 Su	19 26 17	21 18 10	17 47	17 38	3 04	12 42	7 39	15 44	16 54	6 16	18 35	21 54	0 33	16 26	10 59	13 08	5 56
15 M	19 30 14	22 15 22	0♑29	17 39	2 36	13 56	8 17	15 39	16 50	6 18	18 35	21 53	0 32	16 41	11 28	13 28	5 55
16 T	19 34 10	23 12 34	12 58	17 39R	2 04	15 09	8 55	15 34	16 45	6 19	18 34	21 52	0 31	16 56	11 56	13 48	5 55
17 W	19 38 7	24 09 47	25 16	17 39	1 29	16 23	9 33	15 30	16 41	6 20	18 33	21 50	0 31D	17 12	12 25	14 08	5 55
18 Th	19 42 3	25 07 00	7♒25	17 39	0 51	17 36	10 11	15 25	16 37	6 21	18 32	21 49	0 31	17 27	12 53	14 28	5 54
19 F	19 46 0	26 04 14	19 25	17 38	0 12	18 50	10 49	15 21	16 32	6 23	18 32	21 47	0 31	17 43	13 21	14 48	5 54
20 Sa	19 49 57	27 01 28	1♓20	17 37	29♋31	20 04	11 27	15 17	16 28	6 24	18 31	21 46	0 32	17 59	13 50	15 08	5 53
21 Su	19 53 53	27 58 42	13 11	17 35	28 50	21 18	12 05	15 13	16 24	6 25	18 30	21 44	0 33	18 16	14 18	15 27	5 53
22 M	19 57 50	28 55 58	25 02	17 34	28 09	22 31	12 43	15 09	16 19	6 26	18 29	21 43	0 34	18 32	14 46	15 47	5 52
23 T	20 1 46	29 53 13	6♈56	17 32	27 29	23 45	13 21	15 06	16 15	6 27	18 28	21 41	0 36	18 49	15 15	16 06	5 51
24 W	20 5 43	0♌50 30	18 58	17 31	26 51	24 59	13 59	15 02	16 11	6 28	18 27	21 40	0 38	19 06	15 43	16 25	5 51
25 Th	20 9 39	1 47 48	1♉11	17 31D	26 15	26 13	14 38	14 59	16 07	6 29	18 26	21 39	0 40	19 23	16 11	16 44	5 50
26 F	20 13 36	2 45 06	13 40	17 31	25 41	27 26	15 16	14 56	16 03	6 30	18 25	21 37	0 43	19 40	16 39	17 02	5 49
27 Sa	20 17 32	3 42 26	26 28	17 32	25 12	28 40	15 54	14 53	15 58	6 31	18 24	21 36	0 46	19 57	17 07	17 21	5 48
28 Su	20 21 29	4 39 46	9♊41	17 33	24 47	29 54	16 32	14 50	15 54	6 31	18 23	21 34	0 49	20 15	17 35	17 39	5 47
29 M	20 25 26	5 37 08	23 18	17 35	24 26	1♌08	17 10	14 47	15 50	6 32	18 22	21 33	0 53	20 33	18 03	17 57	5 46
30 T	20 29 22	6 34 30	7♋22	17 36R	24 11	2 22	17 48	14 45	15 46	6 33	18 21	21 31	0 57	20 51	18 31	18 15	5 45
31 W	20 33 19	7 31 53	21 50	17 36	24 01	3 36	18 26	14 43	15 42	6 33	18 20	21 30	1 02	21 09	18 59	18 32	5 44

Tables are calculated for midnight Greenwich Mean Time

August 2019

DATE	SID.TIME	SUN	MOON	NODE	MERCURY	VENUS	MARS	JUPITER	SATURN	URANUS	NEPTUNE	PLUTO	CERES	PALLAS	JUNO	VESTA	CHIRON
1 Th	20 37 15	8 Ω 29 18	6 Ω 38	17 ♋ 35 R	23 ♋ 57 D	4 Ω 50	19 Ω 04	14 ♐ 41 R	15 ♑ 38 R	6 ♉ 34	18 ♓ 19 R	21 ♑ 29 R	1 ♈ 06	21 ♎ 27	19 Ω 27	18 Ω 50	5 ♈ 43 R
2 F	20 41 12	9 26 43	21 38	17 33	23 59	6 04	19 42	14 39	15 35	6 34	18 17	21 27	1 12	21 46	19 55	19 07	5 42
3 Sa	20 45 8	10 24 08	6 ♍ 41	17 31	24 07	7 18	20 20	14 37	15 31	6 35	18 16	21 26	1 17	22 04	20 23	19 24	5 40
4 Su	20 49 5	11 21 35	21 40	17 28	24 22	8 32	20 58	14 36	15 27	6 35	18 15	21 25	1 23	22 23	20 51	19 41	5 39
5 M	20 53 1	12 19 02	6 ♎ 25	17 25	24 43	9 46	21 36	14 34	15 23	6 36	18 14	21 23	1 29	22 42	21 19	19 58	5 38
6 T	20 56 58	13 16 30	20 52	17 22	25 11	11 00	22 14	14 33	15 20	6 36	18 12	21 22	1 35	23 01	21 47	20 14	5 37
7 W	21 0 55	14 13 58	4 ♏ 55	17 21 D	25 45	12 14	22 53	14 32	15 16	6 36	18 11	21 21	1 42	23 20	22 14	20 30	5 35
8 Th	21 4 51	15 11 27	18 35	17 20	26 26	13 28	23 31	14 31	15 12	6 37	18 10	21 19	1 49	23 40	22 42	20 46	5 34
9 F	21 8 48	16 08 57	1 ♐ 52	17 21	27 13	14 42	24 09	14 31	15 09	6 37	18 09	21 18	1 56	23 59	23 10	21 02	5 32
10 Sa	21 12 44	17 06 28	14 49	17 23	28 07	15 56	24 47	14 31	15 06	6 37	18 07	21 17	2 04	24 19	23 37	21 17	5 31
11 Su	21 16 41	18 04 00	27 29	17 24	29 06	17 10	25 25	14 30 D	15 02	6 37	18 06	21 15	2 12	24 39	24 05	21 32	5 29
12 M	21 20 37	19 01 33	9 ♑ 54	17 25 R	0 Ω 12	18 24	26 03	14 30	14 59	6 37 R	18 04	21 14	2 20	24 59	24 32	21 47	5 27
13 T	21 24 34	19 59 06	22 08	17 26	1 24	19 38	26 41	14 30	14 56	6 37	18 03	21 13	2 28	25 19	25 00	22 02	5 26
14 W	21 28 30	20 56 41	4 ♒ 13	17 24	2 41	20 52	27 19	14 31	14 53	6 37	18 02	21 12	2 37	25 39	25 27	22 17	5 24
15 Th	21 32 27	21 54 16	16 12	17 21	4 03	22 07	27 57	14 31	14 50	6 37	18 00	21 10	2 46	26 00	25 55	22 31	5 22
16 F	21 36 24	22 51 53	28 06	17 17	5 31	23 21	28 35	14 32	14 47	6 37	17 59	21 09	2 55	26 20	26 22	22 45	5 20
17 Sa	21 40 20	23 49 31	9 ♓ 58	17 11	7 03	24 35	29 13	14 33	14 44	6 36	17 57	21 08	3 05	26 41	26 50	22 59	5 19
18 Su	21 44 17	24 47 11	21 49	17 04	8 40	25 49	29 52	14 34	14 41	6 36	17 56	21 07	3 15	27 02	27 17	23 12	5 17
19 M	21 48 13	25 44 51	3 ♈ 42	16 57	10 21	27 03	0 ♍ 30	14 35	14 38	6 36	17 54	21 06	3 25	27 23	27 44	23 25	5 15
20 T	21 52 10	26 42 34	15 37	16 51	12 05	28 18	1 08	14 37	14 35	6 35	17 53	21 05	3 35	27 44	28 11	23 38	5 13
21 W	21 56 6	27 40 17	27 40	16 45	13 53	29 32	1 46	14 38	14 33	6 34	17 51	21 04	3 46	28 05	28 39	23 51	5 11
22 Th	22 0 3	28 38 03	9 ♉ 52	16 42	15 44	0 ♍ 46	2 24	14 40	14 30	6 34	17 50	21 02	3 57	28 26	29 06	24 03	5 09
23 F	22 3 59	29 35 50	22 19	16 40 D	17 37	2 00	3 02	14 42	14 28	6 33	17 48	21 01	4 08	28 47	29 33	24 15	5 07
24 Sa	22 7 56	0 ♍ 33 39	5 ♊ 03	16 40	19 31	3 15	3 40	14 45	14 25	6 33	17 47	21 00	4 19	29 09	0 ♍ 00	24 27	5 05
25 Su	22 11 53	1 31 30	18 09	16 41	21 28	4 29	4 19	14 47	14 23	6 32	17 45	20 59	4 31	29 30	0 27	24 38	5 03
26 M	22 15 49	2 29 22	1 ♋ 40	16 42	23 25	5 43	4 57	14 49	14 21	6 31	17 44	20 58	4 43	29 52	0 54	24 50	5 00
27 T	22 19 46	3 27 16	15 38	16 43 R	25 24	6 58	5 35	14 52	14 19	6 31	17 42	20 57	4 55	0 ♏ 14	1 21	25 00	4 58
28 W	22 23 42	4 25 12	0 Ω 04	16 42	27 22	8 12	6 13	14 55	14 16	6 30	17 40	20 56	5 07	0 36	1 48	25 11	4 56
29 Th	22 27 39	5 23 10	14 54	16 39	29 21	9 26	6 51	14 58	14 14	6 29	17 39	20 55	5 19	0 58	2 15	25 21	4 54
30 F	22 31 35	6 21 09	0 ♍ 02	16 34	1 ♍ 20	10 41	7 29	15 01	14 13	6 29	17 37	20 54	5 32	1 20	2 42	25 31	4 51
31 Sa	22 35 32	7 19 10	15 18	16 28	3 19	11 55	8 08	15 05	14 11	6 28	17 36	20 54	5 45	1 42	3 08	25 41	4 49

DATE	SID.TIME	SUN	MOON	NODE	MERCURY	VENUS	MARS	JUPITER	SATURN	URANUS	NEPTUNE	PLUTO	CERES	PALLAS	JUNO	VESTA	CHIRON
1 Su	22 39 28	8♍17 13	0≏33	16♋20R	5♍17	13♍10	8♍46	15✗08	14♑09R	6♉27R	17♓34R	20♑53R	5✗58	2♏04	3♍35	25♉50	4♈47R
2 M	22 43 25	9 15 16	15 35	16 12	7 15	14 24	9 24	15 12	14 08	6 26	17 32	20 52	6 12	2 27	4 02	25 59	4 44
3 T	22 47 22	10 13 22	0♏15	16 06	9 12	15 38	10 02	15 16	14 06	6 25	17 31	20 51	6 25	2 49	4 28	26 07	4 42
4 W	22 51 18	11 11 29	14 29	16 01	11 07	16 53	10 41	15 20	14 05	6 24	17 29	20 50	6 39	3 12	4 55	26 15	4 40
5 Th	22 55 15	12 09 37	28 14	15 58	13 02	18 07	11 19	15 25	14 03	6 23	17 27	20 49	6 53	3 34	5 21	26 23	4 37
6 F	22 59 11	13 07 46	11✗32	15 57D	14 56	19 22	11 57	15 29	14 02	6 22	17 26	20 49	7 08	3 57	5 48	26 31	4 35
7 Sa	23 3 8	14 05 58	24 25	15 57	16 49	20 36	12 35	15 34	14 01	6 21	17 24	20 48	7 22	4 20	6 14	26 38	4 32
8 Su	23 7 4	15 04 10	6♑57	15 58R	18 41	21 51	13 14	15 38	14 00	6 19	17 22	20 47	7 37	4 43	6 41	26 45	4 30
9 M	23 11 1	16 02 24	19 14	15 58	20 32	23 05	13 52	15 43	13 59	6 18	17 21	20 46	7 51	5 06	7 07	26 51	4 27
10 T	23 14 57	17 00 40	1≈18	15 57	22 22	24 20	14 30	15 49	13 58	6 17	17 19	20 46	8 06	5 29	7 33	26 57	4 25
11 W	23 18 54	17 58 57	13 15	15 53	24 10	25 34	15 09	15 54	13 57	6 16	17 17	20 45	8 22	5 52	7 59	27 03	4 22
12 Th	23 22 51	18 57 16	25 08	15 47	25 57	26 48	15 47	15 59	13 57	6 14	17 16	20 45	8 37	6 15	8 26	27 08	4 20
13 F	23 26 47	19 55 37	6♓59	15 39	27 43	28 03	16 25	16 05	13 56	6 13	17 14	20 44	8 53	6 39	8 52	27 13	4 17
14 Sa	23 30 44	20 53 59	18 50	15 28	29 29	29 17	17 03	16 11	13 56	6 11	17 13	20 43	9 08	7 02	9 18	27 17	4 14
15 Su	23 34 40	21 52 23	0♈43	15 15	1≏12	0≏32	17 42	16 17	13 55	6 10	17 11	20 43	9 24	7 25	9 44	27 21	4 12
16 M	23 38 37	22 50 49	12 40	15 03	2 55	1 46	18 20	16 23	13 55	6 08	17 09	20 42	9 40	7 49	10 10	27 25	4 09
17 T	23 42 33	23 49 17	24 42	14 51	4 37	3 01	18 59	16 29	13 55D	6 06	17 08	20 42	9 57	8 13	10 36	27 28	4 06
18 W	23 46 30	24 47 47	6♉50	14 41	6 18	4 15	19 37	16 35	13 55	6 05	17 06	20 41	10 13	8 36	11 01	27 31	4 04
19 Th	23 50 26	25 46 19	19 07	14 33	7 57	5 30	20 15	16 42	13 55	6 03	17 04	20 41	10 29	9 00	11 27	27 33	4 01
20 F	23 54 23	26 44 53	1♊36	14 28	9 36	6 44	20 54	16 48	13 55	6 01	17 03	20 41	10 46	9 24	11 53	27 35	3 58
21 Sa	23 58 19	27 43 30	14 19	14 25	11 14	7 59	21 32	16 55	13 55	6 00	17 01	20 40	11 03	9 48	12 19	27 37	3 56
22 Su	0 2 16	28 42 09	27 20	14 24D	12 50	9 14	22 11	17 02	13 55	5 58	16 59	20 40	11 20	10 12	12 44	27 38	3 53
23 M	0 6 13	29 40 50	10♋43	14 25R	14 26	10 28	22 49	17 09	13 56	5 56	16 58	20 40	11 37	10 36	13 10	27 39	3 50
24 T	0 10 9	0≏39 33	24 31	14 24D	16 01	11 43	23 28	17 16	13 56	5 54	16 56	20 39	11 55	11 00	13 35	27 39R	3 48
25 W	0 14 6	1 38 19	8♌45	14 23	17 34	12 57	24 06	17 24	13 57	5 52	16 55	20 39	12 12	11 24	14 01	27 39	3 45
26 Th	0 18 2	2 37 07	23 24	14 18	19 07	14 12	24 44	17 31	13 57	5 50	16 53	20 39	12 30	11 48	14 26	27 38	3 42
27 F	0 21 59	3 35 57	8♍24	14 11	20 39	15 26	25 23	17 39	13 58	5 48	16 52	20 39	12 48	12 12	14 51	27 37	3 39
28 Sa	0 25 55	4 34 49	23 37	14 02	22 10	16 41	26 02	17 47	13 59	5 46	16 50	20 38	13 06	12 37	15 17	27 36	3 37
29 Su	0 29 52	5 33 43	8≏52	13 51	23 40	17 56	26 40	17 55	14 00	5 44	16 48	20 38	13 24	13 01	15 42	27 34	3 34
30 M	0 33 48	6 32 39	23 58	13 40	25 09	19 10	27 19	18 03	14 01	5 42	16 47	20 38	13 42	13 25	16 07	27 32	3 31

Tables are calculated for midnight Greenwich Mean Time

October 2019

DATE	SID.TIME	SUN	MOON	NODE	MERCURY	VENUS	MARS	JUPITER	SATURN	URANUS	NEPTUNE	PLUTO	CERES	PALLAS	JUNO	VESTA	CHIRON
1 T	0 37 45	7≏31 37	8♏,47	13♋30R.	26≏25	20≏25	27♍57	18✗11	14♑02	5♉40R.	16♓45R.	20♑38R.	14✗00	13♏,50	16♍32	27♉29R.	3♈29R.
2 W	0 41 42	8 30 37	23 09	13 22	28 04	21 39	28 36	18 19	14 04	5 38	16 44	20 38	14 19	14 14	16 57	27 25	3 26
3 Th	0 45 38	9 29 38	7✗02	13 16	29 31	22 54	29 14	18 28	14 05	5 36	16 42	20 38D	14 37	15 04	17 22	27 18	3 23
4 F	0 49 35	10 28 42	20 25	13 13	0♏,56	24 09	29 53	18 36	14 07	5 34	16 41	20 38	14 56	15 04	17 47	27 18	3 20
5 Sa	0 53 31	11 27 47	3♑21	13 12	2 20	25 23	0≏32	18 45	14 08	5 32	16 39	20 38	15 15	15 28	18 11	27 13	3 18
6 Su	0 57 28	12 26 55	15 53	13 12	3 43	26 38	1 10	18 54	14 10	5 30	16 38	20 38	15 34	15 53	18 36	27 08	3 15
7 M	1 1 24	13 26 04	28 08	13 12	5 06	27 52	1 49	19 03	14 12	5 27	16 36	20 38	15 53	16 18	19 01	27 02	3 12
8 T	1 5 21	14 25 14	10≈10	13 10	6 27	29 07	2 28	19 12	14 14	5 25	16 35	20 38	16 12	16 43	19 25	26 56	3 10
9 W	1 9 17	15 24 27	22 04	13 06	7 46	0♏,21	3 06	19 21	14 16	5 23	16 34	20 39	16 32	17 08	19 50	26 50	3 07
10 Th	1 13 14	16 23 41	3♓54	12 59	9 05	1 36	3 45	19 30	14 18	5 21	16 32	20 39	16 51	17 33	20 14	26 43	3 05
11 F	1 17 11	17 22 57	15 45	12 49	10 23	2 51	4 24	19 40	14 20	5 18	16 31	20 39	17 11	17 57	20 39	26 36	3 02
12 Sa	1 21 7	18 22 15	27 38	12 37	11 39	4 05	5 02	19 49	14 22	5 16	16 30	20 39	17 30	18 22	21 03	26 28	2 59
13 Su	1 25 4	19 21 35	9♈36	12 23	12 54	5 20	5 41	19 59	14 24	5 14	16 28	20 39	17 50	18 47	21 27	26 20	2 57
14 M	1 29 0	20 20 57	21 41	12 09	14 07	6 34	6 20	20 09	14 27	5 11	16 27	20 40	18 10	19 13	21 51	26 11	2 54
15 T	1 32 57	21 20 21	3♉53	11 55	15 18	7 49	6 59	20 18	14 29	5 09	16 26	20 40	18 30	19 38	22 15	25 53	2 52
16 W	1 36 53	22 19 47	16 13	11 44	16 28	9 03	7 37	20 28	14 32	5 07	16 24	20 40	18 50	20 03	22 39	25 43	2 49
17 Th	1 40 50	23 19 15	28 41	11 35	17 36	10 18	8 16	20 38	14 35	5 04	16 23	20 41	19 10	20 28	23 03	25 33	2 47
18 F	1 44 46	24 18 45	11♊20	11 28	18 42	11 33	8 55	20 49	14 37	5 02	16 22	20 41	19 30	20 53	23 27	25 23	2 44
19 Sa	1 48 43	25 18 18	24 11	11 25	19 45	12 47	9 34	20 59	14 40	4 59	16 21	20 42	19 51	21 18	23 51	25 23	2 42
20 Su	1 52 39	26 17 53	7♋17	10 54	20 46	14 02	10 13	21 09	14 43	4 57	16 19	20 42	20 11	21 44	24 14	25 12	2 39
21 M	1 56 36	27 17 31	20 39	10 44	21 45	15 16	10 52	21 20	14 46	4 55	16 18	20 43	20 32	22 09	24 38	25 00	2 37
22 T	2 0 33	28 17 10	4♌20	10 34	22 40	16 31	11 31	21 30	14 50	4 52	16 17	20 43	20 53	22 34	25 01	24 49	2 34
23 W	2 4 29	29 16 52	18 21	10 23	23 32	17 45	12 09	21 41	14 53	4 50	16 16	20 44	21 13	23 00	25 25	24 37	2 32
24 Th	2 8 26	0♏,16 37	2♍43	11 19	24 20	19 00	12 48	21 52	14 56	4 47	16 15	20 44	21 34	23 25	25 48	24 34	2 30
25 F	2 12 22	1 16 23	17 24	11 13	25 04	20 15	13 27	22 03	15 00	4 45	16 14	20 45	21 55	23 51	26 11	24 12	2 27
26 Sa	2 16 19	2 16 12	2≏17	11 05	25 44	21 29	14 06	22 14	15 03	4 42	16 13	20 46	22 16	24 16	26 34	23 59	2 25
27 Su	2 20 15	3 16 02	17 16	10 54	26 19	22 44	14 45	22 25	15 07	4 40	16 12	20 46	22 37	24 41	26 57	23 45	2 23
28 M	2 24 12	4 15 55	2♏,10	10 44	26 48	23 58	15 24	22 36	15 10	4 37	16 11	20 47	22 59	25 07	27 20	23 32	2 21
29 T	2 28 8	5 15 50	16 51	10 34	27 11	25 13	16 03	22 47	15 14	4 35	16 10	20 48	23 20	25 33	27 43	23 18	2 19
30 W	2 32 5	6 15 47	1✗12	10 26	27 27	26 27	16 42	22 58	15 18	4 32	16 09	20 49	23 41	25 58	28 06	23 04	2 16
31 Th	2 36 2	7 15 45	15 06	10 21	27 37R.	27 42	17 22	23 10	15 22	4 30	16 08	20 49	24 03	26 24	28 28	22 49	2 14

201

DATE	SID.TIME	SUN	MOON	NODE	MERCURY	VENUS	MARS	JUPITER	SATURN	URANUS	NEPTUNE	PLUTO	CERES	PALLAS	JUNO	VESTA	CHIRON
1 F	2 39 58	8♏,15 46	28 ♐ 33	10♋19 D	27♏,38 Rx	28♏,57	18♎01	23♐21	15♑26	4♉28 Rx	16♓07 Rx	20♑50	24♐24	26♏,49	28♍51	22♉35 Rx	2♈12 Rx
2 Sa	2 43 55	9 15 48	11♑33	10 18	27 31	0♐11	18 40	23 33	15 30	4 25	16 06	20 51	24 46	27 15	29 13	22 20	2 10
3 Su	2 47 51	10 15 51	24 10	10 18	27 14	1 26	19 19	23 44	15 34	4 23	16 06	20 52	25 08	27 41	29 36	22 05	2 08
4 M	2 51 48	11 15 56	6≈27	10 19 Rx	26 49	2 40	19 58	23 56	15 38	4 20	16 05	20 53	25 29	28 06	29 58	21 50	2 06
5 T	2 55 44	12 16 03	18 31	10 19	26 13	3 55	20 37	24 08	15 43	4 18	16 04	20 54	25 51	28 32	0♎20	21 35	2 04
6 W	2 59 41	13 16 11	0♓26	10 17	25 28	5 09	21 16	24 20	15 47	4 15	16 03	20 55	26 13	28 58	0 42	21 20	2 02
7 Th	3 3 37	14 16 21	12 17	10 13	24 34	6 24	21 56	24 32	15 52	4 13	16 03	20 56	26 35	29 23	1 04	21 04	2 01
8 F	3 7 34	15 16 32	24 08	10 07	23 31	7 38	22 35	24 44	15 56	4 10	16 02	20 57	26 57	29 49	1 26	20 48	1 59
9 Sa	3 11 31	16 16 45	6♈05	9 58	22 21	8 53	23 14	24 56	16 01	4 08	16 01	20 58	27 19	0♐15	1 47	20 33	1 57
10 Su	3 15 27	17 17 00	18 08	9 49	21 06	10 07	23 53	25 08	16 05	4 06	16 01	20 59	27 41	0 40	2 09	20 17	1 55
11 M	3 19 24	18 17 16	0♉22	9 39	19 47	11 22	24 32	25 20	16 10	4 03	16 00	21 00	28 04	1 06	2 30	20 01	1 54
12 T	3 23 20	19 17 34	12 46	9 29	18 27	12 36	25 12	25 32	16 15	4 01	16 00	21 01	28 26	1 32	2 51	19 46	1 52
13 W	3 27 17	20 17 53	25 21	9 20	17 09	13 51	25 51	25 45	16 20	3 59	15 59	21 02	28 48	1 58	3 13	19 30	1 50
14 Th	3 31 13	21 18 14	8♊08	9 14	15 54	15 05	26 30	25 57	16 25	3 56	15 59	21 03	29 11	2 23	3 34	19 14	1 49
15 F	3 35 10	22 18 37	21 07	9 10	14 47	16 20	27 10	26 10	16 30	3 54	15 58	21 05	29 33	2 49	3 55	18 59	1 47
16 Sa	3 39 6	23 19 02	4♋16	9 09 D	13 47	17 34	27 49	26 22	16 35	3 52	15 58	21 06	29 56	3 15	4 16	18 43	1 46
17 Su	3 43 3	24 19 29	17 37	9 09	12 58	18 49	28 29	26 35	16 40	3 49	15 57	21 07	0♑18	3 41	4 36	18 28	1 45
18 M	3 47 0	25 19 58	1♌10	9 10	12 20	20 03	29 08	26 47	16 45	3 47	15 57	21 08	0 41	4 07	4 57	18 12	1 43
19 T	3 50 56	26 20 28	14 55	9 11 Rx	11 54	21 18	29 47	27 00	16 51	3 45	15 57	21 10	1 04	4 32	5 17	17 57	1 42
20 W	3 54 53	27 21 00	28 53	9 12	11 39 D	22 32	0♏,27	27 13	16 56	3 43	15 57	21 11	1 26	4 58	5 38	17 42	1 41
21 Th	3 58 49	28 21 34	13♍03	9 11	11 35	23 46	1 06	27 26	17 02	3 41	15 56	21 12	1 49	5 24	5 58	17 27	1 39
22 F	4 2 46	29 22 10	27 24	9 08	11 43	25 01	1 46	27 39	17 07	3 38	15 56	21 14	2 12	5 50	6 18	17 12	1 38
23 Sa	4 6 42	0♐22 47	11♎52	9 04	12 01	26 15	2 25	27 51	17 13	3 36	15 56	21 15	2 35	6 16	6 38	16 58	1 37
24 Su	4 10 39	1 23 26	26 23	8 58	12 28	27 30	3 05	28 04	17 18	3 34	15 56	21 17	2 58	6 41	6 58	16 43	1 36
25 M	4 14 35	2 24 07	10♏,52	8 52	13 03	28 44	3 44	28 17	17 24	3 32	15 56	21 18	3 21	7 07	7 17	16 29	1 35
26 T	4 18 32	3 24 49	25 10	8 46	13 46	29 59	4 24	28 30	17 30	3 30	15 56	21 19	3 44	7 33	7 37	16 15	1 34
27 W	4 22 29	4 25 33	9♐14	8 42	14 36	1♑13	5 04	28 44	17 35	3 28	15 56 D	21 21	4 07	7 59	7 56	16 02	1 33
28 Th	4 26 25	5 26 18	22 58	8 39	15 31	2 27	5 43	28 57	17 41	3 26	15 56	21 22	4 30	8 25	8 15	15 48	1 32
29 F	4 30 22	6 27 05	6♑20	8 38 D	16 32	3 42	6 23	29 10	17 47	3 24	15 56	21 24	4 53	8 51	8 35	15 35	1 32
30 Sa	4 34 18	7 27 52	19 20	8 39	17 37	4 56	7 03	29 23	17 53	3 22	15 56	21 26	5 16	9 16	8 53	15 22	1 31

Tables are calculated for midnight Greenwich Mean Time

202

DATE	SID.TIME	SUN	MOON	NODE	MERCURY	VENUS	MARS	JUPITER	SATURN	URANUS	NEPTUNE	PLUTO	CERES	PALLAS	JUNO	VESTA	CHIRON
1 Su	4 38 15	8✗28 41	1≈58	8♋40	18♏46	6♑10	7♏42	29✗36	17♑59	3♉20R	15♓56	21♑27	5♑40	9✗42	9♎12	15♉10R	1♈30R
2 M	4 42 11	9 29 30	14 19	8 42	19 58	7 25	8 22	29 50	18 05	3 18	15 56	21 29	6 03	10 08	9 31	14 58	1 29
3 T	4 46 8	10 30 21	26 25	8 43	21 13	8 39	9 02	0♑03	18 11	3 17	15 56	21 30	6 26	10 34	9 49	14 46	1 28
4 W	4 50 5	11 31 12	8♓22	8 44R	22 31	9 53	9 42	0 17	18 17	3 15	15 56	21 32	6 50	10 59	10 07	14 35	1 28
5 Th	4 54 1	12 32 04	20 14	8 44	23 51	11 08	10 21	0 30	18 23	3 13	15 57	21 34	7 13	11 25	10 26	14 24	1 27
6 F	4 57 58	13 32 57	2♈07	8 42	25 12	12 22	11 01	0 43	18 30	3 11	15 57	21 35	7 37	11 51	10 44	14 13	1 27
7 Sa	5 1 54	14 33 51	14 04	8 40	26 35	13 36	11 41	0 57	18 36	3 10	15 57	21 37	8 00	12 17	11 01	14 03	1 27
8 Su	5 5 51	15 34 45	26 11	8 37	28 00	14 50	12 21	1 10	18 42	3 08	15 57	21 39	8 23	12 42	11 19	13 53	1 27
9 M	5 9 47	16 35 40	8♉30	8 33	29 25	16 05	13 01	1 24	18 49	3 06	15 58	21 40	8 47	13 08	11 36	13 43	1 27
10 T	5 13 44	17 36 37	21 04	8 29	0✗52	17 19	13 40	1 38	18 55	3 05	15 58	21 42	9 11	13 34	11 53	13 34	1 26
11 W	5 17 40	18 37 34	3♊53	8 26	2 19	18 33	14 20	1 51	19 01	3 03	15 59	21 44	9 34	13 59	12 11	13 26	1 26
12 Th	5 21 37	19 38 31	16 59	8 24	3 47	19 47	15 00	2 05	19 08	3 02	15 59	21 45	9 58	14 25	12 27	13 18	1 26
13 F	5 25 34	20 39 30	0♋21	8 23D	5 16	21 01	15 40	2 18	19 14	3 00	15 59	21 47	10 21	14 50	12 44	13 10	1 26D
14 Sa	5 29 30	21 40 30	13 56	8 23	6 45	22 15	16 20	2 32	19 21	2 59	16 00	21 49	10 45	15 16	13 01	13 03	1 26
15 Su	5 33 27	22 41 30	27 43	8 24	8 14	23 29	17 00	2 46	19 27	2 58	16 01	21 51	11 09	15 41	13 17	12 56	1 26
16 M	5 37 23	23 42 32	11♌40	8 25	9 44	24 43	17 40	2 59	19 34	2 56	16 01	21 53	11 32	16 07	13 33	12 49	1 26
17 T	5 41 20	24 43 34	25 44	8 26	11 15	25 57	18 20	3 13	19 41	2 55	16 02	21 54	11 56	16 33	13 49	12 43	1 26
18 W	5 45 16	25 44 37	9♍52	8 27	12 46	27 11	19 00	3 27	19 47	2 54	16 03	21 56	12 20	16 58	14 05	12 38	1 27
19 Th	5 49 13	26 45 42	24 03	8 27R	14 17	28 25	19 40	3 41	19 54	2 53	16 04	21 58	12 44	17 23	14 20	12 32	1 27
20 F	5 53 9	27 46 47	8♎14	8 27	15 48	29 39	20 20	3 54	20 01	2 51	16 04	22 00	13 08	17 49	14 35	12 28	1 27
21 Sa	5 57 6	28 47 53	22 23	8 26	17 20	0≈53	21 00	4 08	20 08	2 50	16 05	22 02	13 31	18 14	14 51	12 23	1 28
22 Su	6 1 3	29 48 59	6♏28	8 25	18 55	2 07	21 41	4 22	20 14	2 49	16 06	22 04	13 55	18 40	15 05	12 20	1 28
23 M	6 4 59	0♑50 07	20 27	8 24	20 23	3 21	22 21	4 36	20 21	2 48	16 07	22 06	14 19	19 05	15 20	12 16	1 29
24 T	6 8 56	1 51 15	4✗15	8 24	21 56	4 35	23 01	4 50	20 28	2 47	16 08	22 08	14 43	19 30	15 35	12 13	1 29
25 W	6 12 52	2 52 24	17 52	8 23	23 28	5 49	23 41	5 03	20 35	2 47	16 09	22 09	15 07	19 56	15 49	12 11	1 30
26 Th	6 16 49	3 53 34	1♑14	8 23D	25 01	7 03	24 21	5 17	20 42	2 46	16 09	22 11	15 31	20 21	16 03	12 09	1 31
27 F	6 20 45	4 54 44	14 21	8 23	26 34	8 16	25 02	5 31	20 49	2 45	16 10	22 13	15 55	20 46	16 17	12 07	1 31
28 Sa	6 24 42	5 55 54	27 11	8 23	28 07	9 30	25 42	5 45	20 56	2 44	16 11	22 15	16 19	21 11	16 30	12 06	1 32
29 Su	6 28 38	6 57 04	9≈45	8 23	29 41	10 44	26 22	5 59	21 03	2 43	16 13	22 17	16 42	21 36	16 43	12 06D	1 33
30 M	6 32 35	7 58 14	22 04	8 23R	1♑15	11 57	27 02	6 13	21 10	2 43	16 14	22 19	17 06	22 01	16 56	12 05	1 34
31 T	6 36 32	8 59 24	4♓10	8 23	2 49	13 11	27 43	6 26	21 17	2 42	16 15	22 21	17 30	22 27	17 09	12 06	1 35

The Planetary Hours

The selection of an auspicious time for starting any activity is an important matter. Its existence tends to take on a nature corresponding to the conditions under which it was begun. Each hour is ruled by a planet, and the nature of any hour corresponds to the nature of the planet ruling it. The nature of the planetary hours is the same as the description of each of the planets. Uranus, Neptune, and Pluto are considered here as higher octaves of Mercury, Venus, and Mars.

Sunrise Hour	Sun	Mon	Tue	Wed	Thu	Fri	Sat
1	☉	☽	♂	☿	♃	♀	♄
2	♀	♄	☉	☽	♂	☿	♃
3	☿	♃	♀	♄	☉	☽	♂
4	☽	♂	☿	♃	♀	♄	☉
5	♄	☉	☽	♂	☿	♃	♀
6	♃	♀	♄	☉	☽	♂	☿
7	♂	☿	♃	♀	♄	☉	☽
8	☉	☽	♂	☿	♃	♀	♄
9	♀	♄	☉	☽	♂	☿	♃
10	☿	♃	♀	♄	☉	☽	♂
11	☽	♂	☿	♃	♀	♄	☉
12	♄	☉	☽	♂	☿	♃	♀

Sunset Hour	Sun	Mon	Tue	Wed	Thu	Fri	Sat
1	♃	♀	♄	☉	☽	♂	☿
2	♂	☿	♃	♀	♄	☉	☽
3	☉	☽	♂	☿	♃	♀	♄
4	♀	♄	☉	☽	♂	☿	♃
5	☿	♃	♀	♄	☉	☽	♂
6	☽	♂	☿	♃	♀	♄	☉
7	♄	☉	☽	♂	☿	♃	♀
8	♃	♀	♄	☉	☽	♂	☿
9	♂	☿	♃	♀	♄	☉	☽
10	☉	☽	♂	☿	♃	♀	♄
11	♀	♄	☉	☽	♂	☿	♃
12	☿	♃	♀	♄	☉	☽	♂

Table of Rising and Setting Signs

To find your approximate Ascendant, locate your Sun sign in the left column and determine the approximate time of your birth. Line up your Sun sign with birth time to find Ascendant. Note: This table will give you the approximate Ascendant only. To obtain your exact Ascendant you must consult your natal chart.

Sun Sign	6–8 a.m.	8–10 a.m.	10 a.m.–12 p.m.	12–2 p.m.	2–4 p.m.	4–6 p.m.
Aries	Taurus	Gemini	Cancer	Leo	Virgo	Libra
Taurus	Gemini	Cancer	Leo	Virgo	Libra	Scorpio
Gemini	Cancer	Leo	Virgo	Libra	Scorpio	Sagittarius
Cancer	Leo	Virgo	Libra	Scorpio	Sagittarius	Capricorn
Leo	Virgo	Libra	Scorpio	Sagittarius	Capricorn	Aquarius
Virgo	Libra	Scorpio	Sagittarius	Capricorn	Aquarius	Pisces
Libra	Scorpio	Sagittarius	Capricorn	Aquarius	Pisces	Aries
Scorpio	Sagittarius	Capricorn	Aquarius	Pisces	Aries	Taurus
Sagittarius	Capricorn	Aquarius	Pisces	Aries	Taurus	Gemini
Capricorn	Aquarius	Pisces	Aries	Taurus	Gemini	Cancer
Aquarius	Pisces	Aries	Taurus	Gemini	Cancer	Leo
Pisces	Aries	Taurus	Gemini	Cancer	Leo	Virgo

Sun Sign	6–8 p.m.	8–10 p.m.	10 p.m.–12 a.m.	12–2 a.m.	2–4 a.m.	4–6 a.m.
Aries	Scorpio	Sagittarius	Capricorn	Aquarius	Pisces	Aries
Taurus	Sagittarius	Capricorn	Aquarius	Pisces	Aries	Taurus
Gemini	Capricorn	Aquarius	Pisces	Aries	Taurus	Gemini
Cancer	Aquarius	Pisces	Aries	Taurus	Gemini	Cancer
Leo	Pisces	Aries	Taurus	Gemini	Cancer	Leo
Virgo	Aries	Taurus	Gemini	Cancer	Leo	Virgo
Libra	Taurus	Gemini	Cancer	Leo	Virgo	Libra
Scorpio	Gemini	Cancer	Leo	Virgo	Libra	Scorpio
Sagittarius	Cancer	Leo	Virgo	Libra	Scorpio	Sagittarius
Capricorn	Leo	Virgo	Libra	Scorpio	Sagittarius	Capricorn
Aquarius	Virgo	Libra	Scorpio	Sagittarius	Capricorn	Aquarius
Pisces	Libra	Scorpio	Sagittarius	Capricorn	Aquarius	Pisces

Blank Horoscope Chart

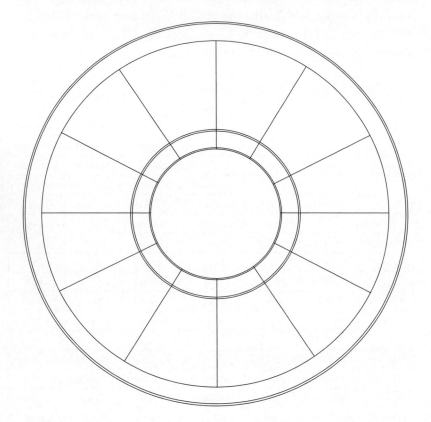

Address Book

Name

Address

City, State, Zip

Phone   Phone

Email

Name

Address

City, State, Zip

Phone   Phone

Email

Name

Address

City, State, Zip

Phone   Phone

Email

Name

Address

City, State, Zip

Phone   Phone

Email

Name

Address

City, State, Zip

Phone   Phone

Email

GET MORE AT LLEWELLYN.COM

Visit us online to browse hundreds of our books and decks, plus sign up to receive our e-newsletters and exclusive online offers.

- Free tarot readings • Spell-a-Day • Moon phases
- Recipes, spells, and tips • Blogs • Encyclopedia
- Author interviews, articles, and upcoming events

GET SOCIAL WITH LLEWELLYN

Find us on 🐦 @LlewellynBooks

www.Facebook.com/LlewellynBooks

GET BOOKS AT LLEWELLYN

LLEWELLYN ORDERING INFORMATION

 Order online: Visit our website at www.llewellyn.com to select your books and place an order on our secure server.

 Order by phone:
- Call toll free within the US at 1-877-NEW-WRLD (1-877-639-9753)
- We accept VISA, MasterCard, American Express, and Discover.
- Canadian customers must use credit cards.

✉ **Order by mail:**
Send the full price of your order (MN residents add 6.875% sales tax) in US funds plus postage and handling to: Llewellyn Worldwide, 2143 Wooddale Drive, Woodbury, MN 55125-2989

POSTAGE AND HANDLING

STANDARD (US):
(Please allow 12 business days)
$30.00 and under, add $6.00.
$30.01 and over, FREE SHIPPING.

INTERNATIONAL ORDERS,
INCLUDING CANADA:
$16.00 for one book, plus $3.00 for each additional book.

Visit us online for more shipping options.
Prices subject to change.

FREE CATALOG!

To order, call
1-877-
NEW-WRLD
ext. 8236
or visit our
website